# Gastronama

## The Indian guide to eating right

KALPISH RATNA

LOTUS COLLECTION
ROLI BOOKS

Lotus Collection



First published in 2023

The Lotus Collection
An imprint of
Roli Books Pvt. Ltd
M-75, Greater Kailash II Market, New Delhi 110 048
Phone: +91 (011) 40682000
E-mail: info@rolibooks.com
Website: www.rolibooks.com
Also at Bengaluru, Chennai & Mumbai

*Layout design:* Bhagirath Kumar
*Production:* Lavinia Rao

ISBN: 9789392130670

Typeset in Minion Pro by Roli Books Pvt. Ltd
Printed at Saurabh Printers Pvt. Ltd., India

# Gastronama

OTHER LOTUS TITLES

| | |
|---|---|
| Ajay Mansingh | *Firaq Gorakhpuri: The Poet of Pain & Ecstasy* |
| Aruna Roy | *The RTI Story: Power to the People* |
| Ashis Ray | *Laid to Rest: The Controversy of Subhas Chandra Bose's Death* |
| Dinesh C. Sharma | *Indian Innovation, Not Jugaad: 100 Ideas that Transformed India* |
| Bertil Falk | *Feroze: The Forgotten Gandhi* |
| Harinder Baweja | *A Soldier's Diary: Kargil – The Inside Story* |
| Jenny Housego | *A Woven Life* |
| Kobad Ghandy | *Fractured Freedom: A Prison Memoir A Story of Passion, Commitment and a Search for Justice and Freedom* |
| Kunal Purandare | *Ramakant Achrekar: A Biography* |
| Lakshmi Subramanian | *Singing Gandhi's India: Music and Sonic Nationalism* |
| Maj. Gen. Ian Cardozo | *Cartoos Saab: A Soldier's Story of Resilience in Adversity* |
| Maj. Gen. Ian Cardozo | *Param Vir: Our Heroes in Battle* |
| Maj. Gen. Ian Cardozo | *The Sinking of INS Khukri: What Happened in 1971* |
| Moin Mir | *Surat: Fall of a Port, Rise of a Prince, Defeat of the East India Company in the House of Commons* |
| Monisha Rajesh | *Around India in 80 Trains* |
| Munshi Faizuddin | *Bazm-i Aakhir: The Last Gathering A vivid portrait of life in the Red Fort* |
| Narinder Singh Kapany | *The Man Who Bent Light* |
| Pramod Kapoor | *1946: Last War of Independence, Royal Indian Navy Mutiny* |
| Ralph Russell | *The Famous Ghalib: The Sound of My Moving Pen* |
| Rasheed Kidwai | *The House of Scindias: A Saga of Power, Politics and Intrigue* |
| Rashmi Sadana | *Metronama: Scenes from the Delhi Metro* |
| R.V. Smith | *Delhi: Unknown Tales of a City* |
| Shrabani Basu | *Spy Princess: The Life of Noor Inayat Khan* |
| Shahrayar Khan | *Bhopal Connections: Vignettes of Royal Rule* |
| S. Hussain Zaidi | *Dongri to Dubai: Six Decades of the Mumbai Mafia* |
| Sunetra Choudhury | *Behind Bars: Prison Tales of India's Most Famous* |
| Sunil Gupta and Sunetra Choudhury | *Black Warrant: Confessions of a Tihar Jailer* |
| Tamal Bandyopadhyay | *Pandemonium: The Great Indian Banking Tragedy* |
| Vappala Balachandran | *A Life in Shadow: The Secret Story of ACN Nambiar – A Forgotten Anti-Colonial Warrior* |
| Various | *The Dark Hour: India Under Lockdowns* |
| Vir Sanghvi | *Men of Steel: India's Business Leaders in Candid Conversation* |

FORTHCOMING TITLE

| | |
|---|---|
| Devika Sethi | *Banned & Censored: Proscribed Writings from Colonial India* |

# Contents

**Part Two**



**Part Three**

## Part Four



## Part Five



## Coda

*Gastronama*?

Ah, you haven't heard the word before?

Google won't find it for you. *Gastronama* is a word I just minted because it conveys the taste of this book.

You've heard of the *Shahnama* – the Tale of Kings. Add a bit of Greek to Farsi and – you got it!

*Gastronama* is the Tale of the Stomach, yours and mine.

Imagine its pleasures, terrors, indiscretions, tantrums, adventures; its every caprice through a life of enjoyment. Surely, this is a tale that must be told with not a burp withheld?

The stomach keeps its secrets, especially when it sulks, grumbles or rebels at what we throw its way, and misery is never far away. These secrets must be discovered, and, where else but in the kitchen? This book is the *why* with the *how* explained.

# Dear Reader

Did I hear you murmur 'How quaint?' You are right. No writer for at least a century, has begun a book with *Dear Reader*.

Archaic, yes, but necessary to this book.

*Dear Reader* clears a space, where, ensconced in privacy, a conversation can begin.

This book is a conversation about the pandemic life, the one you, I, and 7.6 billion others have been living in since January 2020. We are trapped in a paradox. A pandemic threatens life, yet life has never been louder, or more insistent. It roars above dread, it shatters the silence, and it breaks down barriers to assert itself. Life always finds a way.

This book is about how life works during a pandemic.

***COVID-19 = the coronavirus SARS-CoV-2 + us***

I wrote about the coronavirus last year as the pandemic unfolded in *A Crown of Thorns**. Much has happened since

---

**A Crown of Thorns – The Coronavirus & Us* by Kalpish Ratna; Context, 264 pp.; 21 Sept 2020.

but the virus still monopolizes the limelight.

I thought I should write about life instead, of how it works within you and me.

We notice other people, we listen and respond to them. But have you considered doing the same with yourself?

This conversation is about how to do just that, about how to listen to your body. I trust you won't resent the intimacy.

So park that cup where you can reach it, settle that cushion just so, and now, dear reader, turn the page.

# Prelude

# Why?

In 2014, 39% of the global adult population was classified as overweight.

In 1975, 6.4% women and 3.2% men were overweight.

In 2014, 14.9% women and 10.8% men were overweight.

Four years before this pandemic, the prevalence of obesity was 30% in most states of India. Men and women were equally afflicted, and for the first time, a rise in obesity in rural populations was recorded. Most of these people would go on to develop diabetes mellitus.

I recall the panic I felt when I read these figures. It pushed me to write a book the following year where I explored the causes for this explosion.* I was specially distressed by the rising obesity in children and young adults. But I didn't find too many people sharing my alarm.

When SARS-CoV-2 emerged it was evident who would be the worst hit – the vulnerable population with 'co-

---

**Fat: The Body, Food & Obesity* by Dr Ishrat Syed & Dr Kalpana Swaminathan; Speaking Tiger; 10 November 2018.

morbidities'. Most people in this unfortunate group were overweight, if not frankly obese. It was a great opportunity to address these problems – but did we?

It started a worry in my head – what had happened to this population during the pandemic? Had they grown more vulnerable to COVID-19 – or indeed to any of the illnesses they are prone to? Had overweight people become obese? Had many developed florid diabetes, heart disease, hypertension? The lockdown and other 'protective' policies had made medical aid more difficult to access and more expensive. This meant a boom in self-medication under Google-*acharya* and WhatsApp prescriptions. My anxiety was based on rock-solid evidence.

This pandemic has transformed home food like never before.

*Here is the home food profile, circa 2020:*

The first month of the pandemic witnessed a buying frenzy, which intensified as isolation and lockdown became sober realities. Shops and markets were mobbed. Stores sold out within hours.

What did people buy?

Basics mainly: cereals, pulses, sugar, oil.

A fortnight into the lockdown, our attitude towards food became more relaxed. Now that we were shored up against the threat of starvation, we could afford to get curious about food.

Many of us who had never cooked before, mastered scrambled eggs.

Experts who had cooked, to date, a million meals for family, humbly took 'How to' lessons on YouTube.

Guys previously challenged by basic tableware, talked

freely of cast-iron skillets and rustled up dishes strictly inedible, but eminently Instagram-able.

Gals who had spent decades sneering at Mom's stainless steel *bartan* ordered crates of pots and pans, plates and peculiars of the same material, disguised now as gourmet cookware.

Kids went wild 'helping' in the kitchen, and looked on puzzled as their parents wept, first from pride, then soon after, from sheer helplessness.

After Mom was discovered silently banging her head against the wall, scrubbing out the kitchen became quality time.

And all of this is immortalized on social media. The only entity more viral than COVID-19 is banana bread.

Then, everything changed.

Somewhere into the fourth week of orgiastic gastronomy, we just weren't into it anymore.

Then, mangoes arrived.

Who eats anything else this season?

But that palled too.

Kids rebelled. Those that didn't, fell sick. Anything sticky, yellow and sweet, shot right up the Yuck List.

2022 is no different, is it?

International chefs mob the kitchen. Those rustic implements you were so passionate about last year have become this year's gardening tools. Your American relatives weathered the worst on sourdough alone, but you can't keep up anymore. You throw out the stinky starters, make peace with your neighbours, and spend a fortune on artisanal breads. You can't store your provisions because you are all out of jars and bottles – they're bursting with immune boosters. You've forgotten their names, but they are busy now, growing beards and supporting local insect life.

Meanwhile, work begins before you're out of bed – and darn, you're sleeping with it these days. Time zones blur. Everybody is so connected, it is a perpetual home invasion.

Your laptop is now the most overworked piece of kitchen equipment. Frankly, who has the time to *cook* anymore?

Now we're back to asking:

*'Who cares what we eat during a pandemic, as long as there is enough to eat?'**

Food matters more than anything else when you are facing a pandemic. You are facing fear, uncertainty, isolation, PLUS a dangerous disease.

How are you going to muscle up for all that, if you don't care about what you eat?

That's why this book.

---

*Food and eating are, in a sense, what theorists call a VUCA domain: volatile, uncertain, complex, and ambiguous... collectanea for 'Hello! It is all crazy out there!' But this is misleading, as our book will show. 'Well informed is well armed' is what we say.

# Warning!

## *The Chefs in Your Kitchen May Be Making You Sick!*

Cyberspace threatens culinary fatigue. The world's best chefs, not mere men and women, but culinary gods and goddesses, have taken up permanent residence with us home cooks. Remember the time when we spoke about them in hushed voices? We are on backslapping terms with them today. They breathe down our necks as we cook to remind us it takes three tablespoons of butter to scramble an egg.

We all have our favourites. In the madly promiscuous trawl through serious cyber-cooking in 2020, I found it impossible to say no. But I'm older now, and have coned down to just three. I've learnt a lot from all of them – even from the crowd I no longer keep up with. The three chefs who still take up kitchen space cook very familiar cuisines, so they persistently shadow my day. From them I learn techniques, and gape awestruck at their skills.

But were I to follow their recipes, I would soon be in trouble. Serious trouble.

I would turn out marvels for sure, for these kind men and

women generously demystify everything they do. For this alone, they have my deepest respect. They teach with a *guru*'s true humility; simplifying but never editing their knowledge.

Yes, I did turn out marvels, crisp, melting, creamy, every promise fulfilled. But – I felt weighed down in stomach. My spirits were heavy, my purse extremely light. I hadn't even tricked out ambience, and yet felt as if I had dined in a very expensive high-end restaurant. So did the others. 'We must do this again next year,' one of them remarked. And this was just and only, simple *Home food!*

My three chefs still haunt my kitchen. I love them to bits, and when all this is behind us, I plan to make frequent pilgrimages to their restaurants. But cook like them? I wouldn't dare!

Home food, cooked restaurant style, will make you sick. You are safer eating in a restaurant.

And, believe me, it is not the chef's fault. Many home cooks also perpetuate this mistake in their effort to stay traditional. They have watched the sacred mother/grandmother/aunt do it exactly this way, so it must be failsafe.

That sacred ancestor wasn't cooking for a family of three. She cooked for a very elastic 'family' that included every passerby. She threw in ingredients by the fistful or the pinch, poured in liquids with the nearest convenient jug, and swished it all around in the same skillet you still use because it was hers.

Preserve that ancestral skillet. Use it as serving ware or revere it as museum piece. Don't cook in it.

Your fist may not be the same size as your favoured chef's, nor your 'pinch' as much as your grandmother's – they would both have encouraged the use of spoons. The ancestor would have jumped with joy, poor woman, at the sight of all your kitchen aids, and your favourite chef has even more complicated gear at home. So go ahead and use your machines, you have their blessing.

Even if you do love the cuisine Paleolithic, why cook like a Neanderthal?

# The Scientist in the Kitchen

This book is about linking the science of food and cooking to the way our body works in health and disease.

Oh, science isn't your thing?

If you are a home cook you are a scientist already. Cooking combines all the sciences in its reach of enquiry, observation and inference. Botany and zoology. Physics and chemistry. And as much mathematics as I can take. What's left? Only poetry, the stuff that distinguishes an artist from a mere functionary. That's the only difficult bit. The science is, as a matter of course, evident.

So don't let the mention of science deter you. As a responsible home cook you need to know:

- What food you are cooking
- What cooking does to food
- What food does to your body
- What your body, under the influence of food, does to your health
- What that state of health does to your life

When you reason that out, believe me, your curiosity will lead you to question everything: ingredient, recipe, menu, and link it with your state of health.

We ought to follow this chain of reasoning every day, but somehow, we don't. We have reached a level of expertise (we think) where we work automatically, with near-robotic precision. That's the drawback. The moment we reach that state of being, all actions become ritualistic – their meaning long forgotten, their implications ignored – science flies out of the window and the home cook cozies up with tradition and belief. Truths, especially in food, must be questioned. If something is bad, why? If something is good, why?

Tradition and belief are the science and reasoning from an earlier time. They worked then, in an age which was yet to discover the scientific truths we now know – especially those about *how the body works in health and disease.*

Home cooks should leave the investigation of traditions and beliefs to qualified food scientists in distant laboratories who earnestly study molecules and mice. We have no time to waste. Our time in the kitchen is limited and very very functional. I know mine is.

My kitchen is my laboratory. It is where I test out those earnestly researched methods and molecules. This book contains my findings, my errors, and my conclusions.

And so, from one home cook to another, from one scientist to another, from my kitchen, to yours ...

# Part One

# Health and Disease

When you utter the word 'health', most people think of disease. They see 'health' as recovery from disease. And invariably use the horrible word 'wellness'.

We must start on a cleaner slate.

Health is our natural state of existence. It is the usual unobtrusive unconscious working of the body.

Think of it.

Even thinking needs a directive before we become conscious of the process.

Health is what we are.

Sick or 'well' is what we become.

Right now, these figures tell us we are not healthy:

- National Obesity Risk: 7 out of 10.
- Childhood Obesity Risk: 4 out of 11.
- 5% of India's population is morbidly obese.
- We rank third on the list of countries with the highest prevalence of obesity.
- We have 72.96 million cases of diabetes.

And yet, most of us aren't reporting the experience of illness. We can be unhealthy for a long time before we experience illness. This book is meant to address that long twilight zone. It is here that we home cooks can make all the difference. Our responsibility is huge. We can only meet it if we begin with the most neglected person in the family: You.

Unless you get yourself out of this twilight zone, you will push those you cook for into that disaster zone – disease – and they will join you for company. So apply everything you read in this book to yourself first.

What's happening in this twilight zone?

A shift in energy balance is leading to a shift in function – *of all body processes*. We experience this, but we don't give credence to it. A good place to start is to see how you can notice this in yourself.

# Listen to Your Body

We don't notice our body until it complains, and even then, our response is to shut it out. For example, if your leg aches you reach for an oil, a liniment, a gel, a pill. If your head aches, you reach for a pill. If you can't sleep, you reach for a pill.

Okay, stop reading and step over to your medicine cabinet. How many medicines does it contain? Most of them are for emergencies? Right. So that when the next headache comes along you don't have to call the chemist.

If you are *prepared* for sickness, you are not healthy.

As you read this, take a quick mental inventory of yourself from the top of your head to the soles of your feet. Just saying 'Hi!' to every bit of yourself starts off a conversation that reveals your state of being.

We look in the mirror and compulsively shoot selfies not to admire ourselves, but to validate our existence. Trapped in the seethe and shout of life, I need to remind myself: *Hey, I'm here too.*

As you begin a conversation with your body you will learn to respect its signals. If you are a parent, remember the early days when you suddenly became aware that your baby's cry didn't have to be shushed at once? First, you needed to understand what your baby was *saying*. Your response comforted her because you understood her need. If you had yelled, 'OH SHUT UP!' – and there are moments when every parent feels pushed to that – the baby would have decided *you* needed help, and thrown a tantrum.

In the twilight zone, your body behaves just like the baby who is trying to make a slow, but basically educable, parent understand. If you don't, it throws the tantrum that gets your attention immediately: illness.

'Illness' and 'disease' – what's the difference?

Illness is the experience of disease. And disease takes a long time to experience.

So in the spectrum of this extended twilight zone, we may experience no illness at all, no discomfort, no pain.

How then do we know we're no longer in a state of health?

We don't feel energetic. We are suddenly 'lazy'. There's none of the self-indulgence of true laziness about this feeling, but we tell ourselves otherwise. We get tough. We tell ourselves what we need is a change. Fresh air and exercise. And we have enough science to back that feeling.

So, we get fresh air and exercise. We go for a vacation and take a week to recover from it, then crawl back to work counting the minutes till bedtime.

And now that we are all working from home, we are working all the time – and this feeling is just about permanent.

I will ask you not to be so severe on yourself. If your energy is missing, there is a reason. So let us go look for it.

# Energy

Everybody knows how energy feels, but do we understand *what* it means?

Energy certainly doesn't have polarity. Negative and positive energy, so popular among the wellness cognoscenti, has no place in science.

Energy is a molecule the body uses to power every single process in every single cell. You could call it the body's currency. It can be spent or saved, but without it, the body is bankrupt.

There is a Universal Basic Income needed for survival. Some body parts, like the brain, need energy every moment. So does the heart. Without the energy required for life processes, we would, obviously, die. So, it is worth taking the time to look closer at Energy.

The molecule synonymous with energy is Adenosine Triphosphate, a molecule discovered in 1929 by Yellapragada Subba Rao, the forgotten da Vinci of twentieth century medical science. ATP, as it is familiarly called, is nature's workaholic. It powers life.

ATP is an unstable molecule that releases energy which can then be used for cellular processes. For *all* cellular processes.*

Where do we get ATP from?

The process of turning food into ATP is called *metabolism.*

Situations that demand a great deal of energy call for more efficient metabolism, and for food that can be easily metabolized.

*It is not what you eat, but how you eat it, that assures energy.*

The pandemic places a very heavy energy demand on us, even if we don't catch the bug. The times we are living through demand an optimized metabolism of the right kind of food.

*Immunity, by virtue of the enormous number of cellular processes taking place in the innumerable cells recruited to attack and vanquish the invading germ, uses up an enormous amount of ATP.

# In Sickness and Health

The body is wedded to food. In sickness and in health, survival depends on food. It is our only source of energy. Sickness and health impose different requirements on energy, and consequently, on food.

How much energy does one need under restful conditions of health?

I won't answer that with the usual number: 2, 500 – 3,000 Kcal, depending on age and gender.

In practical terms of nutrition, counting calories has no meaning, but it is a unit of measuring energy consumption. Think of it as the body's power bill.

Look at the power consumption of various organs:

- Bone, the scaffolding of the body, uses very little – 2 Kcal/kg/day.
- The overworked heart needs much more – as much as 440 Kcal/kg/day.
- The brain is the greediest. It mops up nearly a quarter of all the body's energy per day.

- Muscle, for all the work it does, demands a very modest 13 Kcal/kg/day.
- Fat – adipose tissue – demands very little too – about 4.5 Kcal/kg/day.

So, even on a lazy Sunday, you need a huge amount of energy just to stay alive.

Most of this energy has to be eaten. The body has very poor stores of instantly available energy.

To understand how the body manages its fuel, let us follow the breakfast you've just digested. The digested food must reach hungry cells. Blood is a convenient vehicle because it goes everywhere, so the digested food signs up for the ride, ready to jump off the bloodstream when its station arrives. To detrain, food must pass from the bloodstream into the hungry cells awaiting energy. The body has a clever way of doing this – there are porters waiting at the platform to carry the load. These are transporter molecules which work like the electronic key at a ticket barrier. Once the digested food is piggybacked on a transporter, it is allowed inside the cell.

The basic food molecule used as fuel for energy is *glucose*. The transporter molecule waiting to take it past the barrier must be allowed in by a hormone called *insulin*.* Without insulin, or with inefficient insulin, the transporter won't report for duty.

The year 2021 marks the centenary of the discovery of insulin, and its first therapeutic use in diabetes by Frederick

---

*This hormone is secreted by the beta cells of the pancreas in response to digestion.

Banting, Charles Best, James Collip, and John Macleod at the University of Toronto. Despite many lifetimes of research spent on this hormone since then, its ways remain mysterious.

The level of glucose outside the cell is always higher. This is because once it gets inside, glucose is quickly burnt up for energy. This concentration gradient is sufficient to permit glucose to diffuse into the cell.

But the cell demands more than just this trickle – hence the need for transporter molecules to carry enough glucose into the cell.

Many of these transporter molecules cannot act without the guidance of insulin. The most insulin-sensitive tissues are muscle, liver and fat. There are more than 30,000 receptors on the cell surface of these tissues. With insulin in action, cells guzzle glucose within seconds.

When insulin has moved glucose into cells, it is broken down in a series of steps, to release energy.

Besides permitting the entry of glucose into cells, insulin encourages the storage of energy. We have known this since 1949, but we are still working out its mechanisms. We do know insulin manages a very complex signaling network, so almost every cell process takes its cue from insulin.

Health depends on optimum insulin activity. The food we eat can then be metabolized to provide immediate energy, and the excess converted into body stores. The liver has an important role to play in this, as do our muscles.

Look at how this energy balance changes in the twilight zone between health and illness.

# In the Twilight Zone

This pandemic ambushed us in the twilight zone. Not just India, the entire planet has been in this twilight zone for a while now. It is correct to say this pandemic of SARS-CoV-2 was superimposed on a much more serious pandemic. And it is this *underlying* pandemic that cost us so many lives and so much misery. This is a pandemic of 'co-morbidities' – diabetes, hypertension, heart disease, auto-immune diseases. These have a common denominator: *Obesity*.

Till very recently (2013), obesity was not recognized as a disease. It was merely a cosmetic problem. This unleashed an unprecedented degree of craziness. A damaging metabolic disease was hijacked and mismanaged, equally, by 'wellness experts' and plastic surgeons.

We are wiser today. Obesity has nothing to do about how we look. It is about how we feel.

Tired and rundown. Out of breath. Irritable. Eating surprisingly little. Or else, bingeing. And discovering nothing really satisfies our cravings.

Surely, there must be more behind these discomforts than just a dress size outgrown?

There is.

Obesity is the outward sign of a very serious metabolic disturbance. Insulin fails to act effectively. There is plenty of it being produced, but tissues seem resistant to its action. The result is a serious energy deficit. Everything you eat, good or bad or middling, is not being efficiently converted into energy. The deprived tissues – liver, kidney, muscles, fat – adopt alternate methods of functioning which lead to damage. This in itself increases the resistance to insulin, setting off a vicious cycle. While this doesn't always make you overtly diabetic – it is a definite push in that direction.

What it does achieve is a chronic 'run-down' feeling as, no matter what you eat, energy is not available.

'Obesity' is a label none of us likes to wear. We look at the weight machine with relief. Of course, we're not overweight. Want more proof? Check the BMI – wow, just 25. That's not even overweight. So this isn't about me, right?

Ouch. Brace yourself for some really bad news. We Indians, no matter where we live, are very susceptible to the ill effects of obesity, much more than the Western population. 'Obesity' in Indians needs to be redefined. To begin with, if your BMI is over 23, you should consider yourself overweight. But there is something much more important to first understand, and then notice in yourself.

Accumulations of fat in and on the abdomen are directly linked with diabetes, high blood pressure and heart disease. Put simply, a paunch means big trouble. I may have a BMI of 22, but that wobble in my shirt puts me at risk for heart disease. The message to us Indians is plain: *get rid of that paunch.*

Which is not easy. But when we look at the factors that added up to that paunch, many are under our control.

To understand them, look at what has made all of us on the planet so suddenly and so massively obese.

India may seem less obese compared with other nations on international maps of obesity, but look at the figures for diabetes, and you can't look away:

- 77 million Indians have diabetes.
- 700,000 Indians died of the complications of diabetes in 2020.
- 2% of all deaths in India are from diabetes.

We do need to worry about obesity because:

1. It leads on to diabetes.
2. Which isn't just 'high blood sugar' but a tissue damaging disease; the tissues that are damaged include the heart and blood vessels, the brain and the retina, liver, kidneys, bone marrow.
3. Obesity, in itself is dangerous as the fat cell actively produces factors that make the body even more resistant to insulin, and encourages further obesity by converting everything we eat into fat. This more than just increasing bulge and bulk. There is deposition of fat in the liver, kidney, blood vessels, and tissue destruction because...
4. Fat cells secrete the factors of inflammation. These chemicals set off a reactive process that causes tissue damage and prevents repair.

*Inflammation* is the basis of what we call 'lifestyle diseases'. Since we have very nearly made disease our lifestyle, we need to understand inflammation. Now more than ever, because the basis of damage in COVID-19 is unbridled inflammation.

1. Inflammation is the normal bodily response to injury or infection. It is a necessary defense against invasion by germs. In health it is switched on only when these intrusions occur. It is then tightly controlled, and once its purpose is achieved, it is switched off. This sounds so much like immunity, because it *is* part of the immune response.
2. Inflammation is achieved by a spectrum of molecules which are secreted by blood and tissue cells.
3. Fat cells secrete inflammatory factors in the absence of injury or infection.

Why should this be connected with 'lifestyle?' Surely, my lifestyle is nobody's business but mine! It is so entirely your business that it is worth finding out what it entails:

1. EXCESS! This is the single most important factor in the pandemic of obesity and diabetes. My idea of excess may not match yours, but when it comes to the twilight zone in which we simmer diabetes, heart disease and a host of other illnesses, *excess is what is on our plate.* Over the last two decades, there has been a shift towards processed and packaged foods. All of them contain unconscionable amounts of sugar, fat, and additives.
2. A single high-fat, high-sugar meal can raise inflammatory factors which increase insulin resistance.
3. Our physical activity has reduced considerably. I'm not talking about gym time, which is the unnatural

imposition of unphysiological activity. I'm talking of the exercise an ordinary work-ridden life entails: walking, climbing stairs, running for the bus or train, trekking through the market for the week's produce, housework. All this has dwindled. We take the lift, drive to and from work, order provisions online. The only parts of the body that get regular exercise are our fingertips. Exercise reduces insulin resistance. The life sedentary increases it.

4. We are also breathing highly polluted air. There is increasing evidence that the fine particulates we breathe increase insulin resistance and actually contribute to obesity.
5. Late nights and lack of sleep cause insulin resistance.

Most of these 'lifestyle' choices are personal. The first, that of dietary excess, concerns us home cooks.

You've just brought home the month's provisions. Quick check – how many tinsel packets? How many Tetra Paks? How many 'refrigerate when opened' items? All of them are high-sugar and high-fat, some not so bad, some bloody awful.

And that's just the obvious.

Hidden amounts of fat and sugar lurk everywhere in packaged foods. Most of them as thickeners, emulsifiers and additives. These are usually concentrates. Instant foods, ditto.

I hasten to say these foods may not kill us, but they alter our food decisions in very dangerous ways.

The reason is that most convenience foods are high satiety foods that prevent us from eating enough of what is necessary for metabolic stability.

Oh, you read the labels very carefully?

So do I.

I've read enough to issue a blanket ban on packaged/processed foods. They are very convenient when we eat them, and very inconvenient afterwards.

Still, no matter how often we eat packaged and processed foods, India is still a nation of home cooks. We still eat 'normal Home food' – rice, roti, dal, vegetables, milk, eggs, fruit. Why should this cornucopia of 'healthy foods' make us sick?

'Nothing' is a common descriptor when patients are asked what they have recently eaten. They may have had a full meal, but the answer is still 'Nothing.' I've learnt to interpret this as 'Nothing out of the ordinary'.

So, if the ordinary puts us in the twilight zone between health and disease, we must find out why.

# How a Pandemic Works

The pandemic affects us all. It has pushed us from the twilight zone to the edge of disease.

When COVID-19 broke out, it was not unanticipated. I began tracking its progress in early January 2020. I documented my views in a book by July. I hoped my apprehensions were misplaced. Sadly, 2021 proved them right. Unfortunately, the lessons of the so called 'second wave' haven't been digested yet.

COVID-19's public image is still that of a respiratory disease. Cough, breathlessness, pneumonia. It does affect the lungs in the worst way, but its real target is the body's immune response.

The immune response is the recognition of everything that is non-self – any protein that is not part of the body. This is a very specific response, and it is carried out by a vast number of cells in the blood and in the tissues. Their job is to induce inflammation through the secretion of chemicals which will combat and destroy the invading germ.

COVID-19 caused by the virus SARS-Co V-2. It causes an

uncontrolled release of inflammatory chemicals with severe tissue destruction. The primary target is the lung, but this virus doesn't stop there. The generalized disorder in inflammation causes widespread damage which affects all vital body organs.

In people already in a heightened state of chronic inflammation, this uncontrolled immune response to COVID-19 is likely to be disastrous. The 'co-morbidities' so often cited – diabetes, high blood pressure, heart disease, auto-immune diseases, obesity – are all states of long-standing inflammation. As we saw earlier, obesity is the common denominator in producing, sustaining and enhancing inflammation.

The outcome of COVID-19 in obese people is noticeably different. They experience more serious forms of the disease, and frequently succumb to it. All over the world, obesity is now acknowledged as one of the highest risk factors in COVID-19.

The immune process is disordered in obesity. Excessive fat deposition impairs the production, integrity and function of immune cells that produce antibodies. Increased insulin resistance hampers cellular immunity. The receptor with which the virus engages to infect the cell – ACE2 – is enhanced in obese people. That means the virus has more binding sites, and thus greater cell entry. There is also the physical element. Obesity, especially abdominal obesity, pushes up the diaphragm and exerts a compressive force on the chest cavity. This prevents the complete expansion and aeration of the lungs.

As a larger population gets vaccinated, we are likely to discover even more ways in which obesity may increase vulnerability to COVID-19.

Meanwhile, as the pandemic continues, it should be world policy to curb obesity. Governments, including our own, seem to feel no such urgency. Even more tragically, neither does the medical community. Market forces continue to encourage, sustain and enhance obesity.

What's left?

Just us, home cooks. And we can do it too!

Keep reading...

# Energy Needs in a Pandemic

Any illness is an extra demand for energy. A 'simple' fever requires one and a half times the day's energy. Complicated illnesses like COVID-19, demand even more. Viral illnesses practically bankrupt the body. Caregivers, most of whom are home cooks as well, have the unenviable task of providing the energy a sick person so desperately needs.

The increased energy demand comes from the immune system. Immune cells have to respond very fast by producing the chemical factors needed. Like capitalist countries, they splurge on inefficient methods that waste a lot of fuel. The body takes innumerable shortcuts to cope with the increased energy demand, and enters a phase of 'catabolism' or breakdown.

Every cell alters its metabolism during an infection, and in the presence of inflammation, so that it can produce instant, or at any rate, very rapid, energy through alternate biochemical pathways. These changes cannot be sustained for very long, and if the energy demand stays high, the major life-sustaining organs begin to fail.

'Serious illness' is a term that means 'power failure' in the body. To take a closer look at the massive power consumption during illness, let us tour the very sick body:

Immune cells, which are activated everywhere, consume huge amounts of ATP. This must now be produced through alternate shortcuts which are inefficient. When this switch cannot be made, immune cells begin to falter. Antibody production fails. Cells can no longer kill the virus.

The *brain*, which, in health, is a perfect glutton for energy, demands even more during illness. It orders the breakdown of body tissues to provide energy. If the brain does not get this energy, the patient becomes less alert, confused, drowsy, unconscious, and eventually slips into a coma.

Unstoppable in activity, the *heart muscle* has very high rate of energy consumption in health. It contracts and relaxes more than 100,000 times a day. In health, heart muscle gets more than 60% of its energy by burning fat. Insulin action guarantees the rest of the energy comes from glucose. In diseases states, insulin activity is poor or blocked, and fat becomes the only source of energy. In conditions of poor oxygenation, when energy must still be produced, toxic levels of lactic acid buildup in heart muscle and cause heart failure.

The *kidneys* are very high consumers of energy. Most of this is spent in regulating blood pressure. In fact, the kidneys use up energy as fast as the heart does, and twice as fast as the brain. They also regulate the metabolism of all three major nutrients: carbohydrates, fats and proteins. Fat-soluble vitamins also come under their purview. The kidneys carry out an important stress response – they convert other foods into glucose for the production of instant energy. They are also concerned with the action of insulin. All this takes place unobtrusively in health. When the kidneys are challenged by infection, their energy demand goes up tremendously. They overstep the production of glucose from digested proteins. This leads to direct injury of the kidneys, and ultimately to kidney failure.

The *liver* sustains an energy balance in health, but it uses up a great deal of available energy in doing so. In the presence of infection, it alters its usual metabolic pathways. It breaks down stores to flood the circulation system with glucose for instant energy. As its demands stay unmet, liver cells accumulate fat and toxic metabolites, leading to liver failure.

Because we toured a very sick and bedridden body, we failed to see the principal target of tissue injury in any infection – the muscles. But even without suffering a major illness, we have all experienced the discomfort of the body ache that's part of a simple viral flu-like illness. This ache is caused by the release of inflammatory chemicals in the muscles. These chemicals carry messages to other organs as well, and change their rate of metabolism by increasing insulin resistance.

Severe infection results in large-scale muscle breakdown, plus the release of chemicals that damage the kidneys. Recovery from severe infections is usually accompanied by a wasted appearance, due to the loss of muscle mass.

Illness is a state of siege.

Evolution has provided us with a primitive response that has helped us survive the most unimaginable of threats. Modern life holds few of those physical threats to our humdrum everyday existence. Our inherited response, though, remains the same. It is the 'fight or flight' response which puts very cell in the body on red alert, to provide maximum energy. This is controlled by hormones called adrenaline and cortisol, produced by the adrenal glands. Together they block the actions of insulin. This floods the circulation with glucose by releasing it from all body stores, and also producing it from other molecules. While it is a grand idea to have so much of fuel at hand, it comes with the bitter cost of knocking the metabolic balance for a Mahendra Singh Dhoni sort of six. As a consequence, every organ in the body misbehaves.

Recovery and convalescence are the two most neglected phrases in modern medical practice. And it is here, my fellow home cooks, that you and I step in.

# Eating Through the Pandemic

If you've cared for a sick child, you know the anxieties of 'getting her to eat'. It is a battle of will and wit – no matter how persuasive you are, the loved one won't be coaxed. A change of hands, while you hide your tears in the kitchen, doesn't help much. The patient is labelled 'stubborn' or if in hospital, 'uncooperative'.

Illness is a very Gandhian noncooperative movement. The body craves isolation to guarantee rest, so that all available energy can be maximized for sheer survival. This is the evolutionary response to all distress. The brain signals 'No!' by way of its neural circuits and the result is a complete loss of appetite. It is hard to overcome, but the clever home cook never admits defeat.

Recovery, though, is a period when appetite can be coaxed back. This phase, which we recognize as a retreat of illness, is usually one of extreme exhaustion. The fever, or whatever the main complaint, may have left, but its residue is just as worrying. The act of eating is exhausting, and the recovering patient has no energy to spare. We address this by employing more intelligent ways of delivering food – guided by the person's preferences certainly, but also sensitive to her exhaustion. The amount she is able to eat may be very small – instead of bullying her to finish the meal, offer her very small amounts frequently. Don't go by the usual routine: breakfast, lunch, dinner are labels that no longer apply; not just in time, but also in content.

Convalescence is completely ignored in modern medical practice. Doctors do recognize its need, but patients refuse to acknowledge it. We expect instant relief, and once relieved, to bounce back with alacrity. That is a neurotic expectation. *The body will not be hurried.* Repair takes time. It has its own schedule. Sometimes we do recognize and acknowledge it. When we break a bone, for instance, we seldom quarrel with the plaster cast. As surgery becomes increasingly invisible – endoscopic – we tend to overlook the extent of injury. The tissue that needs repair is just the same as it was in the days of 'How many stitches, doctor?'

Convalescence is the invisible phase of sickness that is always out of mind for both doctor and patient. Which is why we home cooks bear the brunt of it.

What happens when we don't deliver?

The body, eager to recover, switches to the fight-or-flight mode again. It continues to experience the stress of energy deficit. It builds up insulin resistance, and enters a state of chronic inflammation. A few months later, weight gain, exhaustion, and all the signs of impending metabolic syndrome set in.

Er… what's *that*?

# Metabolic Syndrome

*Metabolic Syndrome* is the medical label for the twilight zone in which 30% of humanity existed, when this pandemic struck. The numbers for India were probably much higher, as Asians develop this condition *even when not very overweight*. A 2020 analysis came up with this staggering figure: every third Indian has Metabolic Syndrome.

I see no reason to doubt this. The evidence is in plain view.

If it is so common, why haven't we heard of this disease?

True, very few of us doctors will actually use the term as a diagnosis – probably because we are already treating its fallout.

If three of these features apply, you have metabolic syndrome:

1. Overweight: BMI >23. Especially abdominal obesity a.k.a. paunch. Maximum abdominal girth >35 inches if male; 33 inches if female.
2. High blood pressure.
3. Diabetes, or a fasting blood test showing glucose >100mg/dl, indicating Prediabetes.

4. Your blood test shows an abnormal lipid profile: High LDL, low HDL, high triglycerides.
5. An isolated low HDL, even with other indices normal.

Metabolic Syndrome leads to diabetes and heart disease.

Also, in this critical time, it can lead to serious illness in case of COVID-19 infection. One out of every three of us is already poised on the extreme edge of the twilight zone.

Why should this have happened to us? We aren't so rabidly 'Westernized', are we? Most of us still eat three meals at home. And since the pandemic, all our meals at home.

We read of Americans and Europeans going vegetarian or vegan to escape Metabolic Syndrome, and here is our *shudha shakahari* nation reeling under the very same disease!

The answer lies with us home cooks. It is caused by our manner, method and choice of foods.

We can identify and rectify mistakes only if we acknowledge them.

If we stay rooted in what we mistakenly think of as 'tradition', we are a doomed nation.

Do we deserve that destiny?

More importantly, do our children deserve that?

Indian children face starvation, undernutrition, malnutrition and obesity. These are all part of the same spectrum.

While there is little each of us can do about policy, we can ensure that our children get food that keeps them safe from Metabolic Syndrome.

Our worst enemy is the market place. It is the market place we have helped create. All Indians, irrespective of caste and creed, worship the market. It dictates our consciousness and our greed. It is only by resisting its tyranny that we can survive.

That isn't impossible for a home cook. Even for an occasional and uncertain one.

It is easier than you think. But in addition to being a whiz in the kitchen, there are other factors we need to consider *at the same time.* Not space them out, a week here a week there. All said and done, these three things need attention:

1. Food
2. Physical activity
3. Sleep

For your efforts as a home cook to pay off, factors 2 & 3 must be optimized. There is a lot to be said and understood about physical activity, so I'll deal with sleep first.

# Sleep

Our lives are paced by light. Light perception by the brain sets the body's clock. We have sleep-wake cycles that parallel night and day. The dark/light change signals the secretion of the hormone melatonin by the pineal gland. This sets the rhythm for activity within every cell in the body. Sleep is not just an alteration in consciousness of our surroundings. It is a state of rest experienced by every cell in the body.

Sleep deprivation disrupts metabolism by altering hormonal balance. This has been studied extensively in people who work shifts. They struggle to match their sleep cycles to their work demands and their glucose-insulin balance becomes very shaky. It eventually adapts, but not without a propensity to quickly go out of kilter.

The effects of missing out on sleep are far more severe. This denies the body the short break of slow metabolism that sleep provides.

Metabolism releases reactive oxygen species and free radicals which have to be cleared. Sleep achieves that.

The sleep-deprived body faces a build-up of these toxic

byproducts of metabolism. This unleashes the body's first line of defense, inflammation. Insulin resistance soon follows.

The overall effect of sleep deprivation is reduced glucose metabolism, resulting in energy deficit, increase in fat deposits, obesity and Metabolic Syndrome.

Sleep deprivation need not be long term, nor very severe, for these effects to set in.

A century ago, people slept much longer than we do today: eight to nine hours as compared to the present average of six hours.

A minimum of seven hours of restful sleep is necessary for metabolic stability.

We home cooks can contribute to a restful night with the right kind of night meal, but our responsibility goes a little further. Call out those long hours! Reduce screen time and get your rest – and this means us, not just the folk we cook so lovingly for!

# Exercise

Exercise makes us feel good. This 'high' isn't just the exhilaration of fresh air and the beauty of a bright day, though these are important elements too. The feeling of lightness – joy and optimism – is because of the shift in metabolism that physical activity brings about. As an added bonus, some 'feel good' chemicals give the brain a sense of self-worth and smugness that make us regard couch potatoes with pitying scorn.

Today most people think of exercise as going to the gym. In my opinion that's completely wrong. The gym provides you with exercise you would not usually do. Not all of us are athletes or wrestlers. We need only as much muscle development as befits our life choices. An athlete needs to train to an unusual degree of muscle efficiency. A sedentary worker needs to exercise enough to maintain normal metabolism.

How do we judge that?

You set your own limits.

A game is the best way. Or a swim, or a bicycle ride. Or a brisk walk. Or, best of all, dancing.

Daily chores around the house offer brisk exercise, but if you're the home cook, this is best left to your dear ones.

We home cooks need a lot of exercise, because no matter what else we work at, cooking is a chore that's repetitive, unavoidable, and sometimes boring. Why not put on some music, and rock between shelf and stove? Personally, I find it enhances flavours, improves textures, and adds that bit of panache which lends a whisper of gourmet to the simplest dish. I'll tell you why in a minute, just let me put on my favourite Kishore Kumar song...

Right.

Why should five minutes of muscular activity improve my cooking skills?

Two immediate reasons:

1. My brain fog lifts.
2. My movements are quicker and more nimble – witness that perfect brunoise readied for a sauté.

There is a third reason, perhaps even more important. The joy of dancing makes me adventurous, and cooking becomes fun.

Let me add – it was a grumpy, grouchy, kind of morning to start with, a not-again, same-old, same-old Monday feeling even though it is Wednesday in the middle of a hectic and unpredictable week. Ten minutes of dancing changed all that.

It is the body's brilliant biochemistry that pulled off that trick.

Movements are caused by the contractile activity of muscles. Muscles require energy (ATP) for contraction. Muscle stores of ATP are very low, so prolonged muscle activity, that's five minutes of vigorous dancing, cannot be sustained by stored energy. Muscle needs to burn fuel to produce energy. The choice of fuel depends on the intensity and duration of my dance.

For a thirty-second prance, my muscles burn glycogen and phosphocreatinine.

For a ten-minute romp, they will switch to glucose and utilize oxygen. That's what we call 'aerobics'.

Were I to go on a brisk walk for an hour, I would start burning fat as well.

From where do I source these fuels?

From stores within the muscle and the liver for glucose, and from the glucose in the circulating blood.

Fat comes from my fat stores, which are rather plentiful, and from stores within the muscle.

How well these fuels access the muscle cell depends on the action of insulin. On a long tough trek, my stores would need to be efficiently mobilized, and I would need to eat frequently to replenish the diminishing stores of fuel.

For high intensity and prolonged exercise, carbohydrates are the only fuel utilized.

A longish walk can produce a 40% improvement in glucose availability to the cell by lowering insulin resistance – but the effect is limited to a day or two. You can't exercise insulin resistance out of your system. It has to be coupled with a change in food choices as well. *In fact, insulin resistance, in itself, is an evolutionary response to food surplus.*

We see fitness freaks straining at weights, jogging out of breath and guzzling gallons of 'healthy' botanical extracts at the local park – why are they still paunchy, overweight, obese? Why do they still complain of aches and pains, diabetes, high blood pressure and worse? It's enough to turn you bitter. There seems to be no justice in these things...

Oh, but there is science. And science, really, is the only form of justice left to us, one that we can grab and hold on to, certain that it won't betray us. Science tells us physical activity is essential, but it is only *one* of the essentials to ensure health. Its effect is to make what you eat work better for you, *but you still have got to eat right to make exercise work.*

**WARNING:** *If you are diabetic, and being treated for it with medication, exercise may make you prone to a dangerous and sudden fall of blood sugar. You need to check with your doctor about timing your food intake correctly before exercise.*

# Why We Eat

Our motivation to eat is self-evident; we eat to live.

More often than not, we observe that axiom overturned.

Humanity apparently, is living just to eat, shoveling in delectables as if there's no tomorrow. Fact, not hyperbole. If we keep swallowing delectables at this rate, there will be no tomorrow – not for individuals, not for our species.

In a world where a child dies of hunger every ten seconds, where one billion people do not get one square meal a day, 1.9 billion suffer from illnesses induced by eating too many meals in a single bite.

That's right: the foods that drive obesity contain enough energy to feed a family of four. These foods aren't necessarily large in size, but they are concentrated in energy, most often from sugar and fat. Surely, we couldn't be eating them just to stay alive?

We did, two million years ago. Back then, as we wandered long distances hunting and gathering, high-fat, high-sugar foods meant the difference between survival and death. The brain recognized them as superfoods. Unfortunately, the brain still does.

We no longer perceive these foods as lifesaving. Instead, we perceive them as delectable.

In most animals, eating is driven by hunger.

In us humans today, it is driven by taste.

Appetite is what we feel in anticipation of a delicious meal. If the meal is likely to be tasteless, we may eat out of a sense of duty, but there's no joy in it.

We don't eat for nourishment, we eat for taste.

It goes without saying that for food to nourish us, it must be tasty.

Unfortunately, most people regard 'healthy' as synonymous with 'boring'. The word invariably produces a grimace. 'Tasty', on the other hand, produces a twinkle in the eye.

Taste, as we experience it on the tongue, is perceived as sweet, salt, tart, bitter, and umami. This last, umami, is more sensing the molecule glutamate, rather than the food that contains it. There also is growing evidence of our ability to taste fat.

Most of the time, taste and aroma are perceived together. We have all experienced the loss of taste that accompanies a heavy cold. During the present pandemic, loss of smell and taste took on an ominous meaning, as they became the first informers of COVID-19 infection. (*Anosmia* and *dysgeusia* became common parlance. What cachet Latin gives to plain speech!)

In evolutionary terms, this twinning of the sensations of taste and odour informs the brain of what we can expect from this meal: nourishment or threat. Bitter and sour tastes, and 'off' odours are primitive signals of dangerous foods.

Today, the brief that the brain gives taste and odour is

very different. The differentiation is between pleasure and, well, the not so pleasant. The brain registers pleasure by the release of chemicals that urge us to eat more. But the brain can't take this decision without reviewing the state of affairs within the body. What is the energy level like? How empty is your stomach? Is it really time to eat?

The answer to these questions may be completely at variance with the urging of the pleasure signal.

And guess what, pleasure always wins.

You might will yourself to refuse that delicious *gulab jamun* or that crunchy *chakli*, but the desire is definitely strong. Whereas, if the brain operated on necessity alone, the very thought of that *gulab jamun* would make you sick.

So, we are stuck with a brain that shows a strong preference for the soft life.

No, it isn't 'weak character' as some people persist in thinking. Far from it. The brain is a jury, and how it votes depends on the most persuasive opinion.

And the opinion, again, is swayed by need.

Haven't you experienced the delight of a mouthful of rice, a sip of milk, or a morsel of banana when you're hungry and tired after a long day's toil? How tasty such plain fare seems then, and a prayer of gratitude escapes us without thought. At this moment, food has answered the need of hunger, and the motive forces of hunger and pleasure are in complete synchrony. The same foods may not seem so tasty when you are more at leisure.

Taste is also heightened when we are hungry. That's surprising. We need less sugar, less salt. We pass up that twist of lemon and can definitely do with less spice. Whereas, when we are not exactly hungry, it takes more of all these substances to convey taste. So, it is not a question of simply craving a taste – our ability to perceive taste is blunted when hunger signals are dampened. It is a persistence of evolutionary wisdom: *nothing tastes good when your stomach is full, so why eat at all?*

Why, indeed.

My experience with patients with Metabolic Syndrome leads me to believe that this dampened perception of taste is the most important reason for weight gain, obesity and insulin resistance – all leading up to diabetes.

The high-energy foods we eat with such eagerness reset our expectations of taste – so *MORE!* becomes the credo. More 'taste' becomes more high-energy, sweet, crisp, fatty foods.

Experimentally, it has been proved that insulin heightens the perception of taste. This is proved also in clinical practice every day. I wait for the moment when a patient reports that she 'doesn't enjoy spicy food anymore'. I know then that her insulin resistance is backing off, and I can expect her to improve quickly.

Let us sneak into the brain and see how it makes these decisions.

As food is tasted, information is whizzed off to lower brain centers, which then relay it to the cortex which will both interpret the taste and predict its value:

Will it satisfy hunger?

Will it give me pleasure?

When we are hungry, we continue to eat till we are satisfied. This produces the same response to two different 'value' foods: both pleasant and unpleasant. We continue to eat the pleasant food eagerly. But if only the other sort is available, we still eat till we are satisfied.

The pleasure factor overrides this. The brain dampens its 'satiety' signals for foods that are valued as pleasure-giving. So, we continue to eat them *even when we are way past full.*

It begins to look as though everything depends on the brain's value system, so we must look at its work ethic.

This is the focus of intensive study, as can be imagined. *How does the brain evaluate the worth of a food?*

Studies show, rather shockingly, that the brain is a sucker for advertising. It rates foods that are attractively packaged and presented very highly, even when they are nutritionally empty. Similarly, labels contribute towards evaluating tastes and odours.

In one famous experiment, two groups of subjects were asked to smell the same odorant and required to state how appetizing it was. The odorants wore different labels. One read: Body Odour. The other: Cheddar Cheese.

You can imagine how that went down.

Labels that resonate with our value system influence our choice of foods. 'Organic', 'Sustainable', 'Ethically Produced' all press the right buttons no matter what the content. Expensive foods are rated higher. So are socially in foods.

The brain works just the way we consumers do: market happy, socially wired, and desperately keeping up with cool.

Does this mean that the evolutionary wiring of appetite and satiety that made us human is no longer sending out the right signals? Or does it mean that we aren't giving it much choice?

Although when it comes to cuisine we are spoilt for choice, I still say the second reason applies.

To examine my conviction, over the next half hour, trawl

the internet for the most popular recipes of 2021. You will come up with a variety of cuisines, sweet and savoury – but they will all have a common denominator of very high sugar and fat.

In 2020, banana bread was everywhere.

The name lies.

Banana bread, by virtue of its prevalent recipe, is a *cake.*

Banana *bread,* the genuine delectable article, is low in fat and its sugar is all from the banana.

I doubt if it would qualify as comfort food in our pandemic-stricken cyberverse.

The cyberverse seems to mirror human consciousness, even though it only represents about 1% of humanity. I'll use that for my next argument.

The pandemic is a period of intense stress for all of us – even if we have managed to escape infection so far. Most of our energy has been expended on adapting to the new circumstances – in work place, in change of work, in the lack of work, forced cohabitation within small spaces, caring for children and the elderly through times when medical aid has been difficult or impossible to obtain. Under this sort of continuing stress, a sustained 'fight or flight' state of metabolism is likely. This alters eating behaviour.

Snacking is one feature, so is food adventurism. Both favour high-fat, high-sugar foods.

Their effect is dangerous: weight gain and obesity which increases our vulnerability to the virus.

When I was writing *A Crown of Thorns* in 2020, I kept a finger on the consumer's pulse – as recorded in the quickest moving items at my local grocery outlet. After the initial panic buying of staples, packaged snacks overtook all other sales easily. These were closely followed by 'healthy' foods, mostly nuts and dry fruits.

This merely reflects the change in our eating habits over the last hundred years.

The annual sugar consumption in the year 1800 was 7 kg per person.

In 2006 it was estimated at 70 kg per person.

Even if we Indians fall (a little) short of this figure, it is still an unconscionable amount, enough to blow aside all the body's sophisticated controls. Should we be surprised at obesity, Metabolic Syndrome and diabetes?

To me, the mad scramble for drugs to treat obesity, Metabolic Syndrome and diabetes seems to miss the central issue: *the reduced sensitivity to taste.*

The tangential ways we have historically employed aren't succeeding too well in curbing our fixation on 'sweet'.

Sugar substitutes lead this list of failures. They are 'no-calorie' sweeteners. Their taste is not acceptable to some, and their effects should be unacceptable to even more, for they encourage over-eating and obesity, by buying into and increasing the 'enough' limit in the brain.

We are crowded with 'sweet receptor' tastebuds, not only on the tongue, but on the palate, the back of the throat, and even in the larynx. Surprisingly, this (last) receptor is very new to our understanding. It was only discovered in 2001. In addition to sending messages to the brain, the receptors are also in sync with the intestinal lining in the most surprising of ways. The arrival of a sweet food in the mouth triggers hormonal responses way down in the intestine. There is more to that taste than just sweetness.

Sweet food triggers the release of the Glucagon-like

peptide-1 (GLP-1) which 'informs' the nerve endings to send off signals to the brain.

Incredibly, this also has a distant and immediate effect on the neuro-endocrine cells lining the intestine – it induces the pancreas to release insulin way ahead of digestion. So, the tongue takes the first step in the maintenance of blood sugar. This understanding tells us how alert and disciplined the body's responses are – *until we push them into chaos.*

Sweet receptors are present in locations far removed from taste.

What could they be doing in the pancreas, in the intestine, in the upper airways and the lower respiratory tract?

Two explanations are likely: they function as controls for glucose metabolism, and they alter the local immune response.

The last, of particular interest during this pandemic, is that over-stimulation of the sweet receptors dampens the immune response in the upper airways, and also lower down in the respiratory tract.

Sweetness evidently has a wider agenda than mere pleasure. It has its set of punishments too: chaos, both in glucose control and immunity.

Sweetness is not all about pleasure, its effects on why we eat and how much we eat are also influenced by hunger and metabolic status. Advising the brain about this is the internet that operates at quantum speed between the intestine and the brain – *the gut-brain axis*. The coax cable here is the vagus nerve which stretches all the way from the brainstem to the abdomen. The information relayed tells the brain how much, and how effectively, glucose is available for energy.

It is now likely that the gut-brain axis has more to do with the brain's 'reward' chemicals. When it operates at optimum, sweetness is awarded brownie points only if the metabolic status demands a high energy meal. *Then*, I may reach for a square of chocolate. But if I'm obese, the gut-brain axis goes into a sulk, and I've eaten the entire bar.

Sweetness remains very important to life. Glucose is the end-product of sugar digestion, and the only fuel used by the brain for optimum functioning. Yes, the brain can switch fuels, but only with a potential for damage.

As it is so important, glucose is also sensed directly by brain cells which regulate appetite and satiety. With signals from the gut-brain axis, this informs the brain's decision about how much sugar I should eat. Just one square of chocolate, or the entire bar.

# When We Eat: Feasting/Fasting

If we the think of the country as an organism – and we should – our pattern of eating is not quite human. Not modern human, anyway. We resemble some of our evolutionary forebears. We are torn between extremes. What would we call them?

Feasting and fasting? Gluttony and deprivation? Greed and starvation?

Our bipolar culture demands both feasts and fasts, irrespective of our energy status.

We differ from other organisms that also employ cycles of feasting and fasting, according to energy status and the state of their environment. We feast and fast through social diktats which evolved in our murky past and persist in our present as the follies of 'tradition'.

The Indian festive season begins mid-monsoon and persists until the height of summer. That is ten months of gluttony! These festivities validate our existence, and we feel compelled to celebrate them.

*Pait pooja* is a wonderful phrase that says it all. Diwali,

Eid and Christmas continued lavishly through the pandemic. At what cost?

Should it not be a national impulse to have a year of austerity?

Not really.

There may be no tomorrow, so let's eat while we can.

Perhaps this pattern of feasting makes no dent among the rich and middle class, but in a country where poverty is rampant, the compulsion to feast ensures a fast for the rest of the year. It is not a personal compulsion. It is a social obligation. More homes are ruined by weddings, *poojas,* and communal dinners than are by the travails of daily existence. What then?

*'Dost thou think, because thou art virtuous, there shall be no more cakes and ale?'*

Bring them on, by all means, this Diwali, Eid and Christmas, but must there be so much of so many things?

Do we actually eat all this stuff?

We do, as we'll learn by January, by May, by mid-October.

By then this excess would have shown up as exhaustion, irritability, and clothes that no longer fit even before we concede to a paunch.

We will of course do our annual pilgrimage to the neighbourhood laboratory and 'do all our tests' and may even come away reprieved.

These cycles reduce us to a state of helplessness. The most free-thinking Indian is still a slave to festivity.

But it sits easy on the soul because we also fast.

Till of late, most fasts were religious rituals. Now, intermittent fasting is being promoted as the answer to optimum metabolism.

Is it?

When we fast, the body goes into starvation mode, and mobilizes glycogen stores to release free glucose for energy. After twenty-four hours of fasting, glycogen stores are depleted, and the body must now break down protein and fat to stay alive.

The body has its priorities: blood glucose must be maintained, at all costs, above 40 mg/dl to ensure the brain gets its fix of glucose. It must also conserve its protein, mainly muscle.

To meet these priorities, the body shifts fuels, and switches to using fatty acids. Fasting is stage managed by the hormone that opposes insulin – glucagon. Plasma levels of adrenaline and cortisol also rise, and all cellular processes switch to the 'fight or flight' mode of metabolism.

Fat stores in adipose tissue are broken down into free fatty acids and glycerol. The liver converts these into ketones and glucose. At the same time, muscle breaks protein down into amino acids which are converted into glucose for energy.

As starvation continues, the body is fuelled by ketones, not glucose.

In the absence of insulin, glucose can no longer enter muscle, so muscle burns fatty acids for energy.

Gradually, all organs switch to this fuel.

After three days of starvation, the brain too switches to burning ketones, content with very little glucose. Survival now depends on how long the depots of body fat will last.

Fasting can be dangerous. It tampers with the hormonal control of metabolism. Its benefits are spiritual – the fruits of denial. But even such benefit is suspect if fasting is followed by reverting to the original high-fat, high-sugar sustenance we call our 'daily diet'.

'Daily diet' is often a miniaturized version of fasting/feasting.

After a meal, insulin takes charge. The liver manufactures glycogen. Branched amino acids enter muscle and protein synthesis takes place. Glucose enters adipose tissue and provides glycerol for the storage of fat as triglycerides.

In the fed state, carbohydrates, proteins and fats are processed effectively within cells by the action of insulin.

In the fasting state, when we wake up, the low glucose state is corrected by the secretion of glucagon, which encourages the mobilization of glucose from stores in the liver and muscle.

Now, consider a day when you delay breakfast.

Glucagon has to keep working. In a few hours, the glycogen stored in the liver is spent, as this is minimal. The only source of energy now is by the production of glucose from amino acids. Muscle must supply this by breaking down its protein.

Skipping a meal pushes the body into the catabolic phase. Fat is released into circulation, as is glucose. Under the influence of glucagon, cortisol and adrenaline, tissues start to break down.

Feasting and fasting cycles worked early in evolution when food was hard to come by.

In our beleaguered times, food is accessible, and rich food is in excess.

Our best bet for a quiet life is to let the body follow its own rhythms and not impose schedules on it.

The feeding rhythm of the body is based on satiety

signals. Two hormones control it. Leptin blocks appetite and ghrelin encourages it.

Leptin is secreted by adipose tissue in response to the amount of fat storage. Its job is to cross the blood-brain barrier and inform the brain to optimize the body's energy status. The brain then sends out a STOP EATING signal, and we refuse that second helping. People with obesity have higher than normal levels of leptin, yet the STOP EATING signal fails to register.

Ghrelin is secreted by the stomach when the energy status is low. The brain responds with a GET A SNACK, QUICK! signal. Levels of circulating ghrelin fall after a meal. In obesity, high levels of ghrelin are maintained irrespective of energy status.

In addition, the stomach also signals its state with a hunger signal.

The stomach takes three to four hours to empty after a full meal. A high-fat, high-protein meal may stay in the stomach for six to eight hours.

In a time when high-fat meals are the norm, we often start our next meal *before* the stomach is empty. This is often interpreted as 'lack of appetite'.

Why not get smarter?

Eat, not by the clock on the wall, but by the clock in your brain.

# How We Eat

The trick to eating is enjoyment. We have lost out on enjoyment of late, haven't we? Our meals are rushed, too often eaten standing up or walking around, phone in hand. Or left at the elbow to cool, forgotten, and consumed absent-mindedly as the afternoon wears on.

None of this is intentional. We'd love to have a leisured meal – but who has the time?

The quick meal, bolted, half-chewed, has certain familiar uncomfortable fallouts: bloat, burps, a feeling of edginess that demands a nibble within the hour.

To understand this better, let's review our ENOUGH signals.

Insulin and leptin are both hormones that signal ENOUGH.

Though insulin is secreted by the pancreas in response to low blood sugar, the basal insulin circulating in a steady state is controlled by the fat deposits in adipose tissue.

Leptin is secreted by adipose tissue.

When we have large collections of fat, insulin and leptin

levels in circulation are high. So they can be read as indicators of body fat. Both hormones cross the blood-brain barrier and inform the brain that the energy bank is full. And the brain, confidently, should signal ENOUGH. But in obesity, the brain falters and hesitates.

There is a strong ENOUGH signal from an array of gastrointestinal hormones – led by cholecystokinin (CCK) – released at the first trickle of food into the small intestine. CCK and friends reduce the size of the meal.

All these ENOUGH signals can be overridden by pleasure.

When a meal is bolted down, there is no time to register pleasure. The brain gets mixed signals and the meal is over with a sense of bewilderment which translates into poor satiety. So, we go looking for a nibble of something sweet, something crisp, and something that will fit the evolutionary definition of pure pleasure.

Quite the same thing happens when we eat too often. The pacing of the signals from the gastrointestinal tract gets botched. Insulin is already acting at optimum when we begin on that fresh meal.

Eating is a sensory experience. The rest of this book is about how we home cooks can get the best out of food in the kitchen. But the sensory experience of eating is all your own. Delight your other senses before you taste. Restaurants impose 'ambience' on you. In your own home, comfort is all you need to experience the delights of a meal.

# Part Two

# Evolution, À La Carte

Two years into this pandemic, ours is a different planet. We struggle for a foothold in a changed world. Home has become workplace. Outdoor life has all but vanished. Schools are shut. Childhood is a virtual space.

We have done this survival bit before. Indians have lived through cycles of famine and epidemics in the past. We used the same ways of coping then, as those we employ today. *If you grit your teeth and hang on, it will be quickly over.*

And then what?

When this pandemic has passed, will we get back to normal?

What is 'normal'?

Is 'normal' what we were before January 2020?

COVID-19's Indian profile is a social disaster. Policy was all expedience, no science, and hence tragic in its monumental stupidities. But the truth is sterner still. Policy does not matter. Health is a personal experience. For each of us, the pandemic is defined by our experience of anxiety and suffering, and by the irreparable grief of loss.

Inevitably, the past, even the very recent past, before January 2020, seems a golden time. But, was it really Utopia?

I hate figures, but sometimes they work better than words:

- Total deaths: 5.24 lakhs
- Deaths associated with co-morbidities: over 80%

A look at these co-morbidities:

- Global burden of diabetes: 463 million
- Global burden of heart disease: 523 million
- Global burden of obesity: more than 1.9 billion adults and 39 million children

77 million have diabetes.

45% of Indians over the age of 40 die of heart disease.

The Indian burden of obesity is increasing much faster than the global trend. 30% of Indian men are projected to be overweight by 2040; of these, 10% will be obese. Twenty-seven per cent of Indian women are projected to be overweight by 2040; 14% of them will be obese. Fifteen million children are overweight, of whom 4 million are obese (urban figures only).

Since the onset of the pandemic, the Indian burden of poverty increases with every passing day.

It is obvious we were already a sick population when COVID-19 hit us. Our state of existence brought us disaster, grief, hunger, poverty.

Is that the 'normal' we aspire to?

Surely, we don't want to be found standing at that same signpost when the next pandemic ambushes us?

Oh yes, there is another one coming. And another. And another. That's because we refuse to address the factors that make these pandemics emerge. I've written about that elsewhere, but in this book, I don't want to retell that story.

Instead, I want to turn the COVID-19 story inside out.

And I can't do it without you.

The new story reads something like this: *Pandemics may come and pandemics may go, but I and mine can stay healthy through them.*

And no, it is not an over-ambitious or unrealistic expectation.

Even if we never find a drug that can cure COVID-19; even if new COVID variants keep emerging, health can still be, if not a certainty, at least a reliable possibility. And illness, when it strikes us, will not devastate or kill.

This book is not a fairy tale, but it does anticipate a happy ending. It is about the change that will permit us to live happily ever after.

We are familiar with the scientific term for such change. It is called *evolution*.

Evolution, in biological terms, has a time-frame of millions of years. A human lifetime is, at best, a century. And yet within this brief period even the humblest human being achieves evolution of thought, action, and spirit. Our achievements are equal, but their arenas vary.

If you are a home cook, as I am, our arena is the kitchen.

And our achievement?

Nothing less than evolution on a plate – a change that ensures a happily ever after.

A few definitions to begin with:
*Home cook*: Person or persons who assume all the responsibilities of feeding the family. And we all know this goes way beyond cooking.

*Home food:* Familiar food cooked at home. 'Familiar' is the operative word. It relates not just to the dish but to ingredients, recipes, cooking methods, presentation, aroma, flavour, taste, texture, and ultimately digestion – as in the phrase for the rejection of all things alien: 'I can't digest outside food.'

*Outside food:* Unfamiliar food which may be eaten at home or in a restaurant, which may be cooked by the home cook, or by a chef in a fine-dining restaurant, or in your local *khau-galli.*

Home food/Outside food is the Indian trope by which all food worth is judged.

Home food is high in virtue, weighted by considerations of love and loyalty.

Outside food is indulgence, equally weighted by considerations of love and loyalty.

It is high time Home food and Outside food dropped their baggage.

Food is not about love, loyalty, tradition or spiritual uplift.

Food is about staying alive.

And during the pandemic, it is ALL about staying alive.

The distinction of food as Home food and Outside food is important. We love Outside food, but it is Home food we rely on.

So, dear fellow home cook, this book is about Home

food. Your Home food – not mine. Your Home food may be totally different from mine, but we can use the same set of rules to bring about evolution on a plate.

We home cooks cater to people we can't afford to displease. They set the rules, we don't! They're the faddy, fussy, finicky, utterly fabulous people we love! We cook because we want them to enjoy their food, to relish and revel in its flavours, tastes and textures. But in this book, we are going to push that a bit further. This is evolution à la carte – every dish special to your loved ones can show the change.

We are going to make your delicious Home food nourishing as well.

What's that?

Home food is always nourishing?

Always has been, from time immemorial?

Then, how come it has got the nation so obese and diabetic? Why are we crippled by heart disease, liver and kidney disease, and arthritis?

Because, apart from the occasional indulgence, Home food is all we ever eat, right?

Right. But does that mean we have to get used to a new way of eating? New foods? A new cuisine? A menu of healthy tasteless stuff one has to swallow by the ton? A shelf full of pills, extracts, potions, nutraceuticals? A *diet*?

Phew – I'll take those questions all in one breath, if you don't mind.

Yes, we need a new, more intelligent way of eating. But neither new foods, nor a new cuisine, and one without a nutraceutical or potion or pill or extract in sight. Just a new and more delicious way of eating the familiar dishes we love.

Diet?

I have a long-standing quarrel with the word. Today *diet* means the exact opposite of what it meant at its 3,000-year-old Greek origin. *Then* it was used to describe routine, 'the way of life'. *Now* it describes a restricted menu.

Diet = deprivation.

It has also become synonymous with faddy, unscientific, and damaging health advice. So the answer is no. This book is not about that misused word – a diet.

Now that you have agreed to divest Home food of its baggage, are you prepared to challenge it?

Or will you point out there are only two ways of cooking Home food: your way, and the wrong way.

Of course it isn't your way at all, you're too modest to claim that. It is your mother's way, and her mother's and her mother's and so all the way back to Mitochondrial Eve.

I see the light of battle enliven your eye.

Who am I, indeed, to challenge these sacred sources?

I doubt if my grandmother would have recognized Home food, circa 2021, as her brand of cooking. Simply because home cooks have always used ingredients and techniques prevalent in their time. It may have worked in their time (or not, considering the average life expectancy of Indians 200 years ago was 40, not the 68.1 it is now).

Today, Home food uses ingredients and techniques that don't stand up to scrutiny.

A combination of market forces, lifestyle decisions and environmental factors push us into eating wrong.

But it is not too late to put things right.

As I said, this means challenging home truths about Home foods. It means changing ingredients and techniques.

# Part Three

# Welcome to My Kitchen!

Welcome to my kitchen!

I make no apology for it not being the slick modular wonder that is constantly being recommended to me. Maybe your kitchen is like that? Great!

Mine has the usual stuff. Counter. Heat source. Shelves. Fridge. Sink.

A heavy-duty blender.

My cookware is the usual: *kadhai, tawa,* skillet.

I'm a bit low on non-stick cookware, but yes, I've picked this pan for us today.

Certainly, we're going to be cooking!

Thank you for letting me into your kitchen. It isn't very different from mine.

Evolution à la carte, eh?

We can fix that easily once we get familiar with what we already have here.

You're so well stocked, there's nothing left to shop for.

Oh, is the fridge empty?

We'll get to that later.

First, there are all these dabbas, canisters, and bottles to investigate.

The funny thing is that every kitchen, no matter how over-stocked, contains just three foods. All nature does, too. Imagine, thousands, perhaps millions of ingredients, and all they amount to are three basic nutrients:

Fats
Carbohydrates
Proteins

A quick survey, and presto, everything is down to three groups!

*FATS*

Oils
Butter
*Ghee*

(There are more fats concealed in the fridge, but that's for later.)

*PROTEIN*

Pulses
*Dals*
And stuff in the fridge.

Hey – wait! Where do we fit in grain?

CARBOHYDRATES

Cereals – we have about four sorts here.
Sugar
Jaggery

Er ... shouldn't *dals* be in this group too?

No, all done and dusted here. There will be overlaps, yes, but we'll get to those later.

Why do we need to group everything like this, you ask?

Ah.

You're a stickler for quality, right? Nothing but the best?

Absolutely.

What's on your plate eventually depends on the raw material. Shouldn't you know all about it?

I think grouping your ingredients like this will leave you better informed – and not just about the ingredients.

You will discover what your cooking methods achieve, besides taste.

You will track the dish you cook through its travels in the body, and watch it transform into energy.

And once you're familiar with that, I can't wait to see how you will apply your intelligence to make the simplest dish an evolution on the plate.

## Love and the Kitchen Gorgons

Every time I enter the kitchen, I ponder the mysteries of love. This is especially true since this pandemic began. In every kitchen across the planet now, love has squatting rights. The culinary cyberspace is boggy with the stuff, especially the baking section. It is the one ingredient that makes bread softer, cakes lighter, and desserts heavenly. It works for savouries too: the feather touch *paratha,* the *mallipoo idli,* the *biryani* that perfumes your very marrow, all owe their magic to love.

Yesterday, I was told the only way to get *puranpoli* as soft as mother's love was to submerge the dough in a bowl of oil till it sucked in every drop.

Do I detect a sneer?

You're right.

Oil is a poor measure of love. It's got to be *ghee,* and dollops of it.

Take a simple household sweet: call it *sooji halwa* or *rava kesari* or *sheera,* it is the same delectable meld of sugar, semolina and *ghee.* It can be made to perfection with a modicum of ghee, but it isn't. It glistens with more than sweetness. At the touch of the ladle, it breaks into a perspiration of gold. The first scoop reveals vacuoles of liquid gold within, all studded with nuts and raisins. When you've eaten it all, you can cook a lavish dinner for three from the ooze of ghee left on your plate. That's love for you. And as a festive occasion comes but once a year, enjoy!

*But what if it is every day?*

Sure, nobody eats halwa every day.

But what if its equivalent of fat became an everyday expression of love?

If you judge based on the advertisements for *ghee*, butter, cheese and oil, it probably is.

All those sterling studies that show us the rising rate of diabetes and cardiovascular disease are simply stating the consequence of such extravagant love.

There are two puzzling conundrums in the kitchen: fat and love.

On my daily walk, I treasure silence and solitude. Most days my brain blocks off all extraneous sounds except birdsong. Occasionally, conversations not only intrude, but stay branded in memory. Like this exchange between two women:

'Today, I made pakodas.'

'Oh?' A very judgmental silence follows.

'Olive oil,' she says, almost pleadingly, and is reeled back in from the darkness with a forgiving smile.

She explains eagerly, 'I never touch anything else. Only olive oil.'

'Deep frying also?'

'Everything! Every day! Yesterday we had poori, today

*pakoda,* tomorrow *kachori.* Extra virgin only. Kids want crispy crispy all the time, and I just make sure it's olive oil. Pure and safe.'

'Very healthy. But can't use for sweet dishes, no?'

'No, we have to use *ghee* for those, so I avoid making sweets. I just buy them.'

'But who eats mithai these days?'

'Honestly. Double chocolate truffle or jalebi? Is that even a choice?'

That conversation encapsulates everything in the fat conundrum, but the love conundrum needs another story, one that you already know.

This one is a Greek myth, the one about Medusa and her sisters, Stheno and Euryale. They were called Gorgons, a growly word for something ferocious. They were beautiful girls, but one look of love from them could turn men into stone.

This is a myth we should take literally, because those sisters are perpetually kitchen-bound. They are irresistible and generous. No grudging spoonfuls for these girls, they simply ladle out love.

And smitten, we petrify.

Men, women, children, the lot of us, we turn into stone. We 'sclerose'. Our channels of life, our arteries, are silted with fat plaque in a condition we know as arteriosclerosis. And to 'sclerose' simply means to turn into stone, to petrify.

So, now you know the Gorgons in your kitchen: the unctuous sisters, oil, butter, *ghee.*

In Sanskrit, this quality of unctuousness is described as *snigdha.* It is also the word for the clinging quality of love.

There were once, about two million years ago, reasons to equate fat with love as it was the premium food for brain evolution and survival. But our brains have evolved now, and we are supposed to be sapient. Why threaten our survival with this ancient fixation on fat?

We Indians have more recent reasons for this fixation.

Tradition, our word for 'because it's good for you' harks back no further than seven or eight generations. Beyond that is Deep Time. But in this very proximal past, within a narrow bracket of two hundred years, our burden of misery was immense.

We lived from famine to famine through most of the nineteenth century and the early decades of the next. We died in the millions from epidemics. Food meant survival. The rich hoarded survival foods – fats and sugar.

A paunch became equated with worth.

Today, a paunch is practically a life sentence. It makes us vulnerable to every kind of disastrous illness, not just the worst forms of COVID-19.

If we want a future, we must have the courage to refuse the past and confront the present.

We cannot live as our ancestors did. The only thing we really know about them is that they are dead. And life as we know it is running out for all of us, unless we take responsibility for our health.

So, you see, the conundrums of fat and love are really the same. Let those three sisters squat in your kitchen, but don't let them gorgonize your love.

# Crisp![*]

Now that you've decided never to gorgonize your kitchen, let's go fry some chips.

Why? Just after we shuddered at oil, why deep fry?

It is personal. I hate the word 'banned'. It rouses the worst in me.

I would rather make an informed choice, and so, I'm sure, would you.

Do I hear you whisper 'air fryer'?

We can deep fry just as crisp, using as little oil as an air fryer – *IF we follow a few guidelines.*

Further down the line, we are also going to explore other techniques of frying – and of frying other foods.

I have, waiting for me, two raw *nendran* bananas. Peeled, they weigh 250 gm together. Their energy value is high – about 275 calories.

For frying, I've chosen rice bran oil. I weigh out 250 gm

---

*Or *croustillant*, a French word I like.

and pour it into the kadhai. This oil has a high smoke point, which makes it ideal for deep frying.

Mine is a stainless steel kadhai.

I'm using an induction stove, which has a temperature indicator.

I have a mandolin to chip with.

I use the standard technique of getting the oil to the right temperature, then chipping the banana into it using a mandolin. When the chips are half cooked, I'll salt them by sprinkling some salt water I have ready in a pan, and then let them cook to end point

The end point I'm looking for is the perfect banana chip. Crisp, golden. It must leave no trace of oil on my fingertips, nor coat my tongue with grease. Very lightly salted, just enough for the banana's innate sweetness to shine through.

The perfect temperature for deep frying is between 140–160°C. I'm about to test this out.

My first lot of chips go in with the oil at 120°C, raised immediately to 140°C – and out they come, crisp and golden.

The second lot – with the same temperature settings are slightly redder – not burnt, just one shade deeper than gold.

I let the kadhai cool down. Then, I repeat the process – again a perfect treasury of gold mohurs. For the second batch, I get canny. I set the temperature at 100°C, and come up with real beauties.

And then, just because I'm obsessive, I do the last two batches on the gas stove in a cast iron kadhai.

This time, I have to rely on my senses – my ears much more than my eyes. I listen for the right 'woody' note that signals the moment to salt. I wait till the oil stops its back chat to drain out the chips. Both batches are uniformly crisp and gold.

I let the oil cool down and measure it: 230 gm.

The chips weigh 150 gm.

They now have the added energy value of the 20 gm oil they have consumed = 180 calories.*

The frying process has removed 100 gm of water.

150 gm of chips = 275 + 180 = 455 calories.

Time now to evaluate:

1. The product is perfect in colour, taste, and texture.
2. It is dry to the feel. After 6 hours of residence in a paper-lined tin, it leaves only the faintest trace of oil.
3. Frying consumed 20 gm of oil – can this be reduced?

For chips, where a waterlogged vegetable is dehydrated and crisped, it is not possible to consume less oil. BUT, a lot more can be consumed while deep frying other products in less-than-ideal situations, such as:

a. The oil temperature is too low: food tends to absorb more oil as the exterior is not cooked quickly enough to seal off.
b. The exterior of the food is too moist.
c. The interior is so moist that it reduces the temperature of the oil.

Why then did my first lot of chips brown at the 'correct' temperature?

There's so much science crowded in that question!

---

*1 gram oil equals 9 calories.

We'll look at the science behind browning a little later in this chapter, and just address the temperature question now.

My stainless steel kadhai quickly overheated. The cast iron kadhai did not, so it was able to maintain a stable temperature. Again, my senses judged the timing better.

What if I fry potatoes, not bananas?

Should I skip the science and state the obvious?

No, I'll do both.

Frying potatoes will take up a tad more oil because potatoes are simply boggy with water, even if you dry out the chips on a towel before frying.

Bananas are stickier, I'm sure you've noticed. That ick is a lovely sealant when it hits hot oil – so banana chips absorb less oil.

Now I've put the chips away, and can take a look at the cooled oil.

It is a shade or two darker, and a little thicker than it was originally. I make a note of that, before I take up the next experiment.

## Shallow vs. Deep

Frying is frying, and when all you need is hot oil, why jump off the deep end? Why slosh oil into your kadhai when you can shallow fry in a pan?

I'm going to test out these truisms.

I'm going to make potato croquettes, the *alur chop* of my childhood.

A very simple recipe: mashed potato cuddled around a

racy sweet-sour filling with a bite to it. The potato is faintly spiced and aromatic with garlic. The shaped croquettes are dredged lightly in rice powder before crumbing.

My first croquette will be shallow fried.

I use a cast iron ladle. Into this I measure out 3 ml of oil.

When it is hot enough, in slides the croquette. It sizzles encouragingly as I rock the ladle, coating it with oil. After the third or fourth rotation, it is only faintly ochre, and the ladle looks dry. If it stays a second longer, it will char: out it comes, looking pale and puffy like an overworked techie.

Darn.

I've been too niggardly.

I'll do the next few with steady increments of oil.

10 ml gets me a fair croquette, but I'm really pleased with the 15 ml croquette. It is plump, perky, and golden. And greasy. I leave it to exhale on a bed of tissue.

The ladle has just a trace of oil left. Wiped clean, it will do fine for my next croquette.

I'm deep frying this one. I use 25 ml of oil.

The croquette dives in, sizzles, curvets, comes up for air while listening to the oil's chatter. Then does a quick pirouette and turns a burnished gold, leaving the oil dumbstruck. This is the perfect croquette. Its streamlined elegance leaves the merest trace of oil on the waiting tissue.

I measure out the oil remaining in the ladle: 23 ml.

The proof, of course, is in the eating.

Of the shallow-fried croquettes, only the one that soaked up 15 ml of oil makes the grade – almost.

The deep-fried one that used up 2 ml of oil is – sheer heaven.

We move on to the next frying technique: *grilling*.

## Grilling

You could use an oven grill or a sandwich toaster. I'm using my cast iron tawa, turning it into a grill with the simple expedient of jamming down a lid on it.

I'm making another childhood delight – beetroot cutlet.

The recipe is simple. Combine the two components of the croquette, amp up the spice, and flatten it into a cutlet. It takes a drop of oil on either side to crisp to perfection.

But it needs to be more lush. The interior could use more structure, so I borrow my recipe for Breakfast *Kabab.* (p. 246). With my fingertips, I work in a tablespoon of cooked black-eyed beans (*lobhia, karamani, payir, chowli*). For this second cutlet or kabab, I refuse any sealant beyond the first dusting of rice powder. It takes the same amount of oil – a drop on either side, and about a minute to cook on each side.

It forms a crisp brown toasty crust with an earthy flavour. There's heft to its rich interior: a deep sweetness from the beetroot, the sting of spice, and the silky umami of the beans. I like it much more than the first iteration.

There is no difference in taste between the interior of the fried chop and the grilled kabab/cutlet. Both are delectable.

Yes, there is a difference in the exterior. The deep-fried chop is crisp. The grilled cutlet is toasty.

I make two more kababs, crumbing them this time, one in an electric toaster, the other in a sandwich toaster. The result is no different from the tawa toast. While at it, I decide to bake a couple too – there's just enough potato and beetroot for two patties. I brush them with oil and pop them in silicon cups. They brown grudgingly. Nice enough, but nowhere as luscious as the deep-fried croquette.

## Crisp or Soggy? Tough or Tender?

Those are the questions that decide technique. The answers depend not only on temperature and timing, but also on the food material.

I loathe the word *crispy*. It is cute as a button, but as infantile as *potty* and shouldn't be part of adult discourse. *Crisp* is adjective enough. Onomatopoeic too.

*Crisp* is India's favourite mouthfeel. So, Indian cooks strive to achieve this texture across a variety of ingredients. A crisp texture is achieved by the formation of a crust. Depending on the food being fried, the interior can remain soft, or participate in the process, crisping the food completely.

A crust is the result of rapid heat transferring between hot oil and cold food. The surface of the food (generally a starch) rapidly loses water and dehydrates as it bobs around in oil hotter than 100°C. Starch granules first swell and then gelatinize as the temperature rises. The rate at which this happens depends on the moisture content of the food. A high moisture content slows the process and also fragments the starch, forming more 'holes' through which oil can enter the interior. As a result, the product will be soggy and squelchy with oil.

Uncooked dry food has starch in a solid phase. After it topples into oil as the temperature rises, the starch first liquefies into a gel, then boils and loses water. During this phase, the interior also heats up and dehydrates. The sign that the dehydration is complete is when the oil stops chattering. This silence is because water is no longer bubbling out into the hot oil. This is the end point of deep frying. Retaining food in hot oil any longer will not only brown the chip to charring, but will also, rather mysteriously, turn it rubbery.

Lifted out of oil at this point, the chips must be shaken or tapped to release adherent oil. Draining them on tissue paper draws out surface oil through capillary action, and you're left with dry, non-greasy chips. Don't drain fried foods on newspapers. The inks are toxic and fat soluble, and will invisibly enter the fried food.

That was the surface story. But what's been happening *within* the chip? The same changes, but much slower, as the temperature is lower.

This is more perceptible in a thicker food like potato julienned for a French fry. As the crust is forming, the temperature in the interior rises.

Potato is 90% water – and all that water within gets boiling, and steams the interior. So that's what a French fry really is – mush in a crisp shell.

The potato chip industry is one of the biggest on the planet: worth US$ 31.2 billion in 2020.

So you can imagine how desperate food scientists are to produce the perfect chip: crisp, not soggy, tender-hearted not tough interior, and with an oil content that's, well, not so bad.

A potato chip, commercially made, contains more than 30% oil. So, if you've eaten 100 gm of chips, you have also swallowed 30 gm of oil.

To me, this is a US$ 31.2 billion industry dedicated to the destruction of the human race.

Meanwhile, the home cook has long mastered the necessary skills with no investment, no fanfare, no applause. She doesn't expect any. These skills are no-brainers, and should be self-evident.

To crisp anything squishy, all you have to do is shake some flour into a bowl, beat some water into it, spice it, salt it, dunk in your squish and pop it into hot oil.

The hiss tells all.

You have a perfectly golden mound of fritters in no time – *bajji, bhajiya, pakode,* or whatever you choose to call it. It is the perfect deep fry. Crisp outside, with perfectly cooked squish within.

It is all about the batter, this time. And here's why: when you make a batter, you use flour and water. Starch molecules have already begun their journey out of the rigid state once water is introduced. When they hit hot oil, they are quick to dehydrate. They don't fragment, so there are fewer holes for hot oil to penetrate and swamp the food within before it has a chance to steam cook itself.

But there's more to the batter. Yes, it's just flour and water – *but what flour?*

Our home cooks will answer that with a volley of choices, all of them sound.

Our batters, all of them, combine starch with protein. The commonest source of protein used is chickpea flour or *besan,* which is rich in both carbohydrate and protein.

When protein meets heat it seals off at once. However, the crisping element is starch, so the batter contains either rice or refined wheat flour (*maida*). The Western version adds egg to flour, while Eastern cuisines use soya flour. All these batters have the ideal ratio of protein and starch that ensures:

1. A crisp exterior
2. Reduced entry of oil into the food

Contrary to what advertisements tell you, it is not the cooking oil but what you put into it that determines oiliness in the fried product.

A deep-fried food will be less oily if:

- Its covering contains a little protein.
- Where there is no covering, if the surface is allowed to crisp gradually. Plunging food into very hot oil results in a brown, soggy and oily product.
- When the interior isn't very moist. Otherwise, as the water boils out into the oil, it will leave large openings for the oil to sink in.

Quite a large amount of oil is absorbed as the food cools – but you can prevent that quite easily. Shaking the food in the draining basket removes clinging oil droplets. Quickly placing it in a loose swaddling of tissue will dab off surface oil. Then, as steam escapes from the cooling interior, there won't be much oil left to seep into the pores and crevices. Similarly, a 'cracked' surface will allow much more oil absorption.

Maida-covered foods, like samosa, will inevitably soak up oil, as the protein content in the covering is too low.

To tenderize the crust of a samosa, to prevent it from tasting like a pappad, the dough must contain a very high amount of fat. The standard amount is 20%. That's 20 gm of *ghee* or *vanaspati* to 100 gm of maida. Baked samosas contain more.

The pinnacle of expert deep frying is our fabulous spectrum of *vadas*. The word is generic for gobbet – rather shaming when we consider the finished product.

The ease of making a *vada* is matched by its satisfying perfections. Unlike the fritter, which can grow tedious, *vadas* are unpredictable. Each region has a local speciality, call it *vada* or *bonda*. But the most challenging of all these is the *medu vadai*. The miracle of contrasts: crisp carapace and the airy cumulus within is achieved by the smooth aerated batter consisting entirely of *urad dal* (*ulundu, Vigna mungo*), which has the interesting physical quality of viscosity.

Now that we have the perfect chip, the perfect fritter, the perfect *vada,* it is not the end of the story. The story of Crisp is a love triangle.

That first installment was crisp's coming-of-age narrative of perfect love. That's just one side of the triangle.

As you crunch your way through a hopefully small serving of chips, spare a thought for the oil in the kadhai.

Listen, now to...

# Oil's Lament

Dear Home Cook,

I'm the oil left in your kadhai after being heated to 180 degrees thrice over. It has aged me, this heating and cooling, it has changed me. I look different, smell different, feel different. Maybe I *am* different. All I know is that I'm a different oil from what's left in the bottle on your shelf. What do you have to say about that?

To begin with, I, Rice Bran Oil, had a low level of polyunsaturated fatty acids, a high level of oleic acid, and a bit of saturated fatty acids (30% linoleic acid, 44% oleic, and just a jot of linolenic acid with about 23% saturated fatty acids, if you are a stickler for minutiæ).

Those unsaturated fatty acids were oxidized and thermally degraded during heating.

I had other good stuff too. What? Tocopherols, tocotrienols, phytosterols, polyphenols and squalene, if it is chemistry you crave.

I wasn't even a bit viscous before – and now look at me!

I'm so delicately neutral, I leave no trace of body odour on your foods – but your foods have left their pong in me! I'm going to smell of onions long after those *pakodas* have left your breath.

I've gone from a faint yellow to amber. The next time you heat me so cruelly, I'll turn brown. My phospholipids turn dark, and all sort of stuff gets oxidated when I get that hot.

My label told you I had antioxidants – the oryzanol and tocopherols that were in me. I still have oryzanol, but the tocopherols are all degraded now, so don't fool yourself with that antioxidant chat anymore.

Oh, and you should know a bit about the three unsaturated fatty acids I came to you with: oleic acid, linoleic acid, and linolenic acid. Naturally, they oxidized when you heated me. Those oxidation products make me sluggish and viscous. But I'm lucky – or you are – not much of these fatty acids have turned into trans-fats. That isn't what happens with most oils.

Oh, you didn't know?

Well, if you bought chips instead of frying them yourself, they would have been fried in a PHO – a partially hydrogenated oil, which you recognize as vanaspati. These PHOs are dirty guys – as much as 50% of their fatty acids can be trans-fats, and nasty eliaidic acid leads the list.

You don't know what trans-fats are? Tsk tsk. Maybe you'll find out. Meanwhile, take my word for it. That stuff is pure poison.

We ordinary oils are much nicer. True, we don't put the crumb in your biscuit or cake they way margarine does. You can't make icing with us the way you can with gobbets of *vanaspati*. I hear there are zero trans-fats margarines.

Probably. But till that first coronary, how can you tell?

Now, we guys, we are low on trans-fats. But we don't stay that way. Other oils, I will not name them, become trans-fats *factories* when you heat them repeatedly. That's something the advertisements won't tell you. What's on the label is not what's in your kadhai and certainly not what's circulating in you.

I see you have a lot to learn about the fate of that last samosa you gobbled. Especially now, pandemic and all, you better be bothered to find out.

No need to chuck me down the drain. I can be used for low temperature stuff. Just don't *fry me,* okay?

And when there's so much to eat and so much good you can do with me, so much deliciousness I hoard – really, *must* you fry?

If you keep reading you'll discover the dark secrets of crisp, brown, and crunchy.

Till then, take care. Filter me and store me in a dark place where I can put my feet up and read the rest of this book.

Yours Truly in Turmoil,
Oil

# Translating Fats

Oils. Fats. Fatty acids. Cholesterol good or bad. Lipids. Triglycerides. Lipoproteins. Trans-fats. For heaven's sake, *WHAT* must we not watch out for?

We could go into the chemistry of each of these tags, but some other time, eh? *Not* when we are so full of chips.

I'm going to translate those chips instead. So, let's leave the cooling oil to whine in the kitchen and go someplace else where we can be as lighthearted as the morning sky. We'll answer that lament a little later.

The great thing about morning is that the world is new minted, and everything urges us to sparkle. To dance not walk, to sing not talk, to greet that horrible neighbour with cheer – heck, morning is no time for a grudge.

Reality check.

The day bares its teeth. Chores to be done, breakfast to be produced, lunch to be planned if not cooked, lunch boxes to be filled, lost things found, tears dried, quarrels quashed, tantrums endured. Add to all this your phone is convulsing with pings – a friend's having a meltdown 5,000 miles away, another's just discovered true love, a cousin's lost his job, your favourite uncle is mourning his constipation, and the in-laws call to say they're about to board a flight that will get them to your doorstep in two hours. Phew!

There! All done and dusted. Showered, dressed, the house neat as a packet of pins.

And then that eleven o'clock feeling hits you. Breakfast weighs you down like a stone. Your back's giving way. Your legs are pure jelly – the very thought of the walk to the store across the street feels like advanced mountaineering. You flop on the couch, stuff a cushion beneath your head, and briefly, very briefly, wish you were dead.

Ah. You say, 'Yes, but ...'

I hear you.

Yes, but *why blame those chips you ate yesterday?*

Let's translate those chips into our 11 a.m. blues.

It is simple.

Very simple.

Think of yourself, for a moment, as a collection of trillions of hardworking cells.

They've all got to be fed.

Sure, yes, you've had breakfast. But that's still in your stomach.

Your hungry trillions are clamouring for energy.

You experience their protest as tiredness.

Let's look at it from the cell's point of view:

Energy = available glucose

Glucose is made available by the hormone insulin.

Fat blocks the action of insulin.

As a consequence, no matter how much food you've eaten, your cells are starving.

This is what all your cells experience:

Your muscles register their protest loudly, but all your important organs, those that work unceasingly to keep you alive – heart, lungs, liver, kidney – all of them feel the same exhaustion.

The brain manages to grab what energy it can, and allows you to register your exhaustion. But it can't sustain intensive thought and you find yourself growing irritable, and making mistakes as you work.

*How did those chips contribute?*

A cardinal rule in crime investigation is *sequere pecuniam* – follow the money.

In crimes against the body this rule can be amended to *sequere adipem* – follow the fat.

Fat is as important to a healthy body as money is to a healthy life.

But the greed for fat, like the greed for money, is *radix omnium malorum* – the root of all evils.

Define greed, you challenge?

Pandemics demand precision: So, I'm going to be very specific.

Greed – *cupiditas* – in adult man or woman = anything beyond 15 ml (one tablespoon) of added fat per day.

Added fat = Fat used in cooking + fat present in purchased foods, cooked and uncooked + butter or *ghee* added at the table.

When I state this, I've been greeted with a variety of responses, all of them important. It has compelled me to classify them into three major groups. (There are outliers, splinter groups, and the occasional maverick, but I'm, for the moment, ignoring them.)

Here are the three groups, and my responses to each of them:

1. **Unbelievers:** O ye of little faith, I did not invent this standard 15 ml/day. It is the recommended intake for our population. At the end of this book, you'll find a list of the studies that contributed to this recommendation.
2. **We would if we could**: You certainly can, if you read this book.
3. **Tradition tells us different**: Ok, you tough guys, define tradition! Or let's leave that one for next time, and I get what you're telling me: *ghee is good for you.* Not according to Sushruta and Charak and Ibn-e-Sina and all the rest of those hoary sages of a past we know nothing about. We do have their texts, though, and I've read enough to know they aren't by any means recommending the wallop of fat consumed in Indian households of our time. And in their times, heart disease was uncommon.

So, what happens when we get greedy about fat?

I'm afraid it's happened already.

I don't like statistics, but they are good danger alerts sometimes.

Take a look at some figures:

**In 2019, there were 77 million diagnosed diabetics among us.** Nobody is counting the shadow undiagnosed population.

**One out of every four Indians over the age of eighteen has high blood pressure.**

- In 2000, 118 million Indians were diagnosed hypertensives.
- By 2025, that is expected to rise to 213.5 million.
- Hypertension is responsible for a staggering 10% of overall deaths in India.

**Obesity?**

30–60% of adult urban Indians are overweight or obese. Rural obesity is increasing too.

**What about blood fats aka lipid profile, dyslipidemia, or, with simple affection, 'my cholesterol'?**

79% of Indians have a disordered lipid profile, making them prone to cardiovascular diseases.

*Now, let's relate these figures to those chips.*

Serving size?

That's one of the legends all packaging carries.

Nobody *counts* chips.

Ok – that small bowl, half of it. Actually, a little more. More like 3/4$^{ths}$. That was the first helping, right?

That works out to 50 gm of chips.

That, in yesterday's exercise, consumed 6 gm of oil, 1 and 1/4$^{th}$ tsp. Not much at all, if that's the only fatty food I had. But it wasn't. My meals included 25 gm.

That's 31 gm of added fat.

*What about* ***concealed fat****?*

4 gm from an egg, 6 gm from milk, 6 gm from curds, and if you're going to be so darned particular, *every cereal, legume,*

*pulse, vegetable also has an element of fat.* What do you expect me to do about that?

Concealed fats in foods that nourish us are essential. We certainly don't need to omit them. Yes, we can limit fat concentrates like nuts and oil seeds.

But, surely, added fat can be limited.

I could have easily cooked my meals luxuriously in less than 2 teaspoons of oil. Do I hear a sound of disbelief? Try out the recipes in the last section.

And, I could have skipped the chips. I had plenty of variety without them.

One splinter group I ignored was: **'We have guests'**: If you like your guests, you should respect their health just as much as you should respect your own. Will they be mortally wounded by your lack of samosas? If so, then they aren't people worth knowing, are they?

And when you land up with a 50 gm + daily fat diet, what happens, exactly?

It's funny, but just the opposite of what you expect will happen.

50 gm = 450 calories. (1gm fat = 9 calories)

Your daily caloric intake should be around 2,000.

But this amount of fat makes you feel too full halfway through your meal, so you eat less of the foods you really need – less rice or *roti*, less protein, and way way less vegetables.

I can't say this often enough:

***Vegetarian India doesn't eat vegetables.***

So, a large part of the day's energy requirements are supplied by fatty foods. *What's wrong with that?*

Let's take a look at what happens to a swallowed fat.

Fat includes all the greasy stuff we know: oil, butter, *ghee*, and the solid oils packed into nuts and seeds.

Biochemically, dietary fats are diverse. Even the usual tags: saturated, unsaturated, polyunsaturated (PUFA), monounsaturated (MUFA), omega-3 and omega-6 are far too superficial.

For us home cooks, it pays to think of the whole shebang simply as fats.

1. The mouth recognizes fat not just by the texture of the food. It can detect the actual presence of fat. So, while my fingertips missed the trace of oil on the chip, my taste buds can recognize it, and *Ping!* goes a signal to the stomach to gear up for action *long before* I've swallowed the chip.
2. The chip, now the kind of mush you don't even want to think about, enters the stomach where an enzyme puts fat through the first phase of digestion.
3. In the upper part of the small intestine, fat is attacked by a multiplicity of enzymes that make it ready for absorption.
4. Fats are absorbed by diffusion into intestinal cells, and by hitching a ride on transporter molecules. The digested fat is insoluble in plasma, so to reach organs where it is needed, it must be packaged as lipoproteins.
5. Chylomicrons are complexes that transport digested fats from the intestine into the lymph. They shed part of their load, but retain a core of cholesterol that they deposit in the liver. The liver uses cholesterol to produce lipoproteins that can be carried into the circulation.

6. As they circulate through the body, these lipoproteins are cleverly 'unpacked' by enzymes in the walls of fine blood vessels – splitting them into components that can enter fat cells. Once within, they are reassembled and stored as fat.
7. The load of fat in the chips is recognized by the body as 'extra'. So, instead of being used for energy, it is tucked away as 'fixed deposit' inside fat cells.
8. Fat cells overloaded with fat produce chemicals that block the effects of insulin, and effectively choke the body out of 'available energy'.

That is how yesterday's chips can translate into today's mid-morning tiredness.

Well-meaning friends and family urge us: *'Do your blood tests!'*

So, we do.

And, since we're talking here about fats, let us look at that bit of the report that tells us about how we are managing our fats. You'll find it as LIPID PROFILE.

# Profiling Fats

In art, a *profile* is a side view – a line drawing that gives us an idea of the features that are concealed. In James McNeill Whistler's famous profile of his mother, the woman's personality and her punctilious life are laid bare by the mere outline of her face.

The lipid profile on a blood report does much the same. With a few numerical values, it conveys a fair conclusion about the state of health.

As you might be worried about just 'your cholesterol' – we will start by defining cholesterol.

**Cholesterol** is an essential substance manufactured by the body, necessary for growth, and for any number of cellular functions. It can be manufactured from all dietary excesses – sugar, protein, or fat.

If you have 'high cholesterol' you didn't eat it. You made it from everything you ate.

Remember those digested fat particles that were transported in the lymph as chylomicrons and then landed up in the liver to make lipoproteins?

**Lipoproteins** = Triglycerides+Cholesterol+Protein

These lipoproteins are what your blood report profiles.

VLDL – very light density lipoproteins – carry digested fat (triglyceride). At the target tissues, the enzymes in the walls of the capillaries release triglycerides, which enter cells either to be used for energy or to be stored as fat. This process converts VLDL into LDL.

LDL – low density lipoproteins – popularly hailed as 'bad cholesterol', are heavy on cholesterol, and low on triglycerides and protein.

HDL – high density lipoproteins, have more protein than cholesterol.

So, if you grade these various lipoproteins by fat content:

- Chylomicrons, in the lymph, are 99% fat.
- VLDLs, fresh from the liver, are 90% fat.
- LDL is 80% fat.
- HDL is only 50% fat.

That explains why LDL is BAD and HDL is GOOD.

But these aren't moral judgments, so what do they mean in terms of health?

LDL is engaged by a special receptor that takes it into the cell. A high amount of fat disables these receptors, and leaves more LDL in circulation, where it can get oxidized to initiate the formation of an *atheroma* or plaque in the walls of blood vessels. These plaques cause the narrowing of blood vessel channels in the disease *atherosclerosis*.

Cells are exposed to, and accumulate, cholesterol through the circulation, but they also manufacture cholesterol. Most cells cannot utilize cholesterol. HDL unburdens them by transporting this accumulation of cholesterol to the liver. It also reduces the build up of plaque. So, HDL, really, *is* the good cholesterol.

What about **Triglycerides**?
Interpreting them is a little trickier.
Let's do that after we have a piece of cake ...

# Trans-fats

Trans-fats aren't transitioning into nicer, kindlier molecules. They are just as fat as fat. The '*trans*' part has to do with a physical property that knocks the fat molecule a bit straighter. It doesn't sound significant, but the manner in which this change affects metabolism is very grave.

Some trans-fats are present in nature, so we eat them without noticing, because the amounts are negligible.

*But trans-fats are also deliberately introduced into our diet by industrial processing.*

The simple step it takes to convert any ordinary vegetable oil into its *trans* version is the introduction of hydrogen. This industrial process, *hydrogenation,* changes a liquid oil into a fat that is solid at room temperature. Its name cuts quite a swagger: Vanaspati, Lord of Vegetation.

A very malevolent one then. *Vanaspati is the ultimate revenge of the Plant Kingdom against humanity.*

We home cooks need to know all about trans-fats because there is very little regulation over them in the Indian market. So we must do all we can at a personal level to exclude them from our diet.

Why? Did I hear you ask *why*?

Are you sure you want to know?

Trans-fats cause heart attacks. Strokes. They make us quickly obese, precipitate diabetes, make us infertile. They affect the unborn baby by causing severe abnormalities. And before we're quite ready for the end of life, they push us into senility and dementia.

Still want to use *vanaspati*?

No, there is no SAFE hydrogenated fat, not in our country where every third adult is obese and every fifth is diabetic. But the target Indian consumers are not in this group.

***THE TARGET CONSUMERS OF TRANS-FATS ARE OUR CHILDREN.***

Indian children are being fed large quantities of trans-fats from the time they are toddlers. They are being trained to acquire heart attacks, strokes, diabetes, obesity, and enough reproductive problems before they are thirty.

Do we really want to endanger our children?

All bakery products contain a huge amount of trans-fats. I am not going to argue this point with you.

You won't find *vanaspati* mentioned anywhere on bakery goods. It will be called margarine, shortening, butter substitute, PHO, vegetable oil, and a hundred other euphemisms.

In an earlier chapter, we looked at exactly how much margarine it takes to make a simple butter icing on a birthday cake.

Conceded, that is an annual event. What about everyday items like biscuits?

Some oils and *vanaspatis* have acquired a **zero** trans-fats label. That means they have below 'admissible' amount of trans-fats. What is admissible?

In India, it has recently been capped at 2%. A welcome move – earlier it was 5%, which is way above the amount admissible in other countries. And we, remember, are a population prone to cardiovascular disasters at lower levels of body weight and obesity.

So, why are we still eating so much of trans-fats?

The answer, of course, is because we worship the market. We are schooled in a brand of reverence, which makes us doubt our own intelligence.

Please, dear home cook, ignore advertising, and look at facts instead.

1. Commercial foods and home cooks use *vanaspati* because it gives a crisper and fluffier fried product. This explains the *vanaspati* revolution that overtook Indian cooking in the early 1960s: *parathas* were softer, *pakodas* crisper, sweets just melted in the mouth. And as for our Kingdom of Crunch – chips, *chivda, murukku* – who would ever want to return to frying in oil? (We weren't so much into patisserie in those days. But we are, *we are,* oh so much into pastry today.)
2. Commercial foods use *vanaspati* because it gives the packaged product a longer shelf life. Home cooks have discovered this too. Foods fried in oil quickly turn rancid.

But *vanaspati* is not the only source of trans-fats. It is also produced – in all innocence – by the industrial 'refining' of oil.

'Refined' oil is extracted oil treated to 100°C to remove organic material, which interferes with flavour (or the lack of it).

And since we don't want 'the smell of oil' here, it is further deodorized by heating it to an even higher temperature.

This repeated heating converts a hefty amount of fats into their trans-state.

Now, extend that bit of intelligence to your own kitchen.

You may use the best oil in the world, but when you deep fry at 160–180°C, the oil in your kadhai begins to change. Some oils change more than others. But, all change to some degree. This change knocks the oil molecules in their spine and turns them into the *trans* configuration.

Oh, it isn't all in your kadhai either.

A good bit of it clings to the food we have just fried. And the next time you use that cooling oil to fry your next snack or treat, you will be swallowing even more.

You have read the facts.

The choice is yours.

Presently, statistics are available from North India: the average intake of *vanaspati* is 20 gm/day.

I don't doubt that figures for the South, West, and East will be any different. Although these regions have traditionally used other oils, everybody everywhere eats what's on the market.

You can buckle under market forces and peer pressure, or you can take charge of your health and of those you cherish, particularly your children.

# *Tumhaare Moonh Main Ghee Shakkar*

*Tumhaare moonh main ghee shakkar* – this phrase is an apotropaic common in our Himalayan vicinage. Predict a joyous event and this blessing of plenitude follows instantly to ensure your words come true. Even if they don't, the *ghee* and sugar wished on you is for keeps.

That's one more example of how urgently we need to lose the past. Today, *tumhaare moonh main ghee shakkar* is more of a curse than a blessing.

Let us discover why and how by baking a cake.

# A Piece of Cake

Yes, I know, cakes aren't usually made with *ghee*, but they can be, and with especially delicious outcomes. But, today, we are not using *ghee*. Let's use butter, which is 80% fat.

A very simple cake will do very well as an assertion of cake's basic qualities, but because it is raining heavily in the middle of the afternoon, and you are dropping in for tea, I'll make that a chocolate and walnut cake. No change in measurements, I assure you.

That's one of the most educative things about baking a cake – you have to measure. And when you do, you discover that weight is more reliable than volume. So here goes:

*100 gm of flour*
*75 gm of sugar*
*50 gm of butter*
*1 egg*

That's all there is to it.

Oh yes.

*Two heaped spoons of cocoa powder and a few walnuts*
*Baking powder*
*A pinch of salt*

The steps are quick and simple.

*Beat butter and sugar together.* Sift flour, cocoa, baking powder, and salt. Whisk the egg with a drop of vanilla and add it to the frothy mass of butter and sugar while gradually folding in the flour a little at a time as you go.

There!

Toss in the chopped nuts lightly coated in flour, and you're ready to bake.

The oven is ready pre-heated, but – wait a moment – you did mean *cake?* How is this viscous liquid going to become an airy tender sliceable cloud of delight?

The answer is in that classic meld of sugar-flour-butter (equally sugar-flour-*ghee* or oil). It is the universal formula for luxury. Add eggs, milk, and curds or besan, and you can transform texture endlessly.

Let us put this in the oven and see what happens to the batter.

*What is the batter all about?*

The first step, creaming butter and sugar together, traps air within the fat-sugar mixture. Adding eggs provides two important elements that are going to be vital in changing texture. Egg albumin is a protein and egg yolk is a lecithin.

Lecithin – a phospholipid, a fat-protein combination – is an emulsifier. It keeps the mixture from splitting.

I have used not *maida,* but a specially processed wheat

flour, sifted fine. It contains the precursors of an elastic substance that's presently terrorizing millions of netizens – *gluten.*

The difference between cake and bread is texture. Cake is tender, bread is chewy. It is gluten that makes that difference. Well-developed gluten will turn cake into a sweet bread.

The technique of making the batter prevents the development of gluten.

Once in the oven, as the temperature of the batter rises, two other substances assert themselves:

- the starch in the flour, and
- the protein in egg white

Starch has two sugars – amylose and amylopectin. Water and heat change the structure of these sugars into a gel. As water begins to bubble out from the gel, its mesh is retained as a scaffolding.

The egg white, which has been so uniformly dispersed in the batter as foam, begins to coagulate as it heats up and forms a delicate, but strong, reticulum.

But a cake's texture is very different from that of an omelette or a *dosai.* The omelette relies on the same property of egg. The *dosai* relies on the same property of starch. Yet, cake doesn't resemble them in the least. The difference is: air. The spongy texture of cake comes from entrapped air. The mesh of both egg and starch trap the bubbles of carbon dioxide and water vapour, and, because gluten is elastic, the cake rises.

Ah, there goes the doorbell.

As you enter, you are greeted by the aroma of baking cake. My house sings with it – but wait, the cake is still cooking. So *what is that smell?*

It is the scent of sugar spinning itself loose and reassembling itself into smaller particles. Beginning at around 160°C, this will go on to release the volatile molecules you can smell right now.

Still struggling to put a name to it?

It is fruity (*ethyl acetate*), buttery (*diacetyl*), nutty (*furan*), toasty (*maltol*) – it is *caramel*!

And there's an even deeper scent that wells up slow as story, sweet but intelligent. A voluptuous scent that stirs up memories of delights past and fills your mouth with juice. The meld of sugar and amino acids produces a gamut of molecules that make up this accord. It tells me that the cake is done.

Out of the oven, it wobbles a bit, exhaling wafts of chocolate and walnut.

I get the coffee going and it adds a nervy edge to the cake's luxurious aroma.

The first slice trembles on the plate, airy, with a soft light crumb that melts in the mouth.

With a sip of coffee – sheer heaven.

Let us look at nutritional values now:

| | |
|---|---|
| 100 gm flour | = 350 calories |
| 50 gm butter | = 450 calories |
| 75 gm sugar | = 300 calories |
| 1 egg | = 72 calories |
| 20 gm walnuts | = 130 calories |

At 1, 300 calories, that is a very modest cake and it yields eight generous servings.

Each serving gets me around 160 calories: this from two

teaspoons of flour, a teaspoon of butter, and two teaspoons of sugar! (The protein is negligible.)

That is, as I said, a very modest cake. The bare bones of it. In taste and texture, it's perfect.

But this is not a cake you'll find in a patisserie.

Why is that different?

Obviously, the patisserie cake is iced, and we'll come to that in a minute. But more importantly, the ratios of flour:sugar:fat are changed. Flour is cut back, butter (or worse) is increased, and eggs are amped up. This makes the cake softer and more pliable; in baking terms, 'tender'. From now on, it gets a bit out of hand. Terms like *gateau, genoise, torte, chiffon,* and *mousse* define ingredients and technique to the pastry chef, but they merely bewilder the rest of us into believing they are superior creations.

Flourless cakes, eggless cakes, vegan cakes, and lactose-and-gluten-free cakes are all on the ascending sugar and fat scale.

*Then* comes the icing.

Gone are the days of the cakewalla's trays of three standard pastries: pink, yellow, and green hard frosting.

Today, we just call the stuff *cream* and trust in it.

It isn't. It is not cream!

A good rule of thumb is: *the softer and fluffier the icing the higher the fat content.*

The fat, unless otherwise specified, is *vanaspati,* even though it is seldom called that. It is hydrogenated fat, which may contain anything from 20–60% trans-fats (more on that after we've eaten the cake). That icing is just *vanaspati* and icing sugar beaten until fluffy. There are very solid technical reasons for that. You can't argue with a recipe for buttercream.

And I need plenty to sandwich and frost my cake luxuriously.

If I only ice the top, I need less than half of this:

- 100 gm of *vanaspati* (butter alone flops in hot weather)
- 300 gm of sugar

(Egg whites can be used to stabilize the cream, but I'm not using them today.)

That works out to 900+1,200 = 2,100 calories being added to my 1,300-calorie cake.

This is a plain butter icing. I'm not even talking chocolate.

So a generous serving of this cake will give me nearly 400 calories as opposed to the 160 from a generously nutty plain cake – and, of course, much much more fat and sugar.

Cupcakes, even the more modestly frosted ones, deliver a minimum of 8 gm of fat per serving, and a great big whack of sugar.

Muffins skimp on icing and cut back mildly on fat.

Brownies have thrice as much fat, not to speak of sugar.

Which would you rather have – a slice of home-made cake or a frothy pastry?

Why cake?

Because urban India seems to feast on the stuff.

The hundred-yard stretch that leads from my home to the main street has six high-end patisseries. Once I turn the corner, I start counting and come up with fifteen in just one direction.

When I moved in here, thirty years ago, there was just one honest-to-goodness bakery. Ten years later, as the hills were blasted to make room for housing, the city's oldest and most renowned patisserie opened a 'birthdays only' branch.

Twenty years on, Black Forest is practically street food, and hole-in-the-wall patisseries scream 'PURE VEGETARIAN, GLUTEN-FREE CAKES IN ONE HOUR'!

ALL of childhood obesity can be blamed on birthday cakes.

Still, you have a point. Let us consider a common homemade sweet: *kesari/sheera/sooji halwa*. Some version of this is usually made in every household.

The ratio is akin to cake – but the end product is amorphous.

| | |
|---|---|
| Semolina | 100 gm |
| Sugar | 100 gm |
| Fat (ghee/oil/vanaspati) | 50 gm |

This is not quite festive enough for most home cooks, let alone chefs. The more usual ratios approximate:

| | |
|---|---|
| Semolina | 100 gm |
| Sugar | 125 gm |
| Ghee+oil | 100 gm |

That puts even a modest helping on par with birthday cake.

Festivals are annual events, and sweets are appropriate on the feast menu. But, today, they are eaten far more frequently.

If you want to give in to that compulsion – is there any

way to cut back on sugar and fat in these treats?

Certainly, there is.

But I note your sceptic look.

Will these healthier treats tick all the boxes?

1. Aroma
2. Appearance
3. Texture
4. Sweetness
5. Mouthfeel
6. Luxury
7. Decadence

Boxes 1-6 get a joyful tick, but 7 gets a big fat NO.

There is no gentle way of delivering bad news.

Birthday cake is a harbinger of obesity, diabetes, and cardiovascular diseases.

To wish your loved ones a long and healthy life, *please do not serve up a slice of death.*

# The Zzzzen of Lunch

Does lunch leave you tired?

Do you nod over your work in the hour after lunch?

Do you desperately down cups of coffee or tea just to stay awake through that afternoon meeting?

Or perhaps you aren't sleepy – just tired. Does the need to rest overcome you after lunch?

Either way, you are experiencing a reaction that may be an important indicator of your state of health.

There are many biochemical reasons for this:

1. Following a high-fat meal, levels of inflammatory chemicals increase. They increase even more after a high-fat, high-sugar meal. This group of chemicals, interleukins, especially Interleukin-1, are particularly elevated in overweight and obese people.
2. A heavy fat and sugar meal produces a surge in insulin. This 'good hormone' urges our muscle cells to draw in amino acids as well as glucose. Some amino acids enter cells very easily. Tryptophan is

one that does not. Tryptophan elbows its way into the brain where it is quickly changed into serotonin and melatonin, both sleep-inducing molecules.

3. A heavy meal tells the stomach to take it easy – and the involuntary nervous system sends off a 'Relax!' signal.
4. The rise in blood sugar after a heavy meal makes the brain release a chemical (adenosine) that makes the 'awake' pathways sag a bit. That's why coffee – specifically caffeine – which blocks this chemical, keeps you awake.

Most people seem to think all oxygenated blood is shunted to the intestines for digestion, and the brain, deprived of its oxygen fix, nods off for that 'power nap'.

This idea is wrong at every possible level.

The brain does not *ever* take a break from its need, its greed, for oxygen. Not in life, it doesn't.

And when you take a nap, you are not brain dead.

There is enough evidence to tell us that meals high in fat and quick-release sugars will make you sleepier than a balanced meal.

And, as most of us work through the day, we can't always afford a nap, can we?

# Sugars, Not So Sweet

As an exclamation of delight, 'How sweet!' is universal. We use taste as an adjective for things that have no relation at all to food, but share the same denominator of pleasure.

We have just seen how the brain converts this taste into pleasure. But what is *sweet* all about?

It is about sugar, of course.

Let's list all the sugars in your kitchen:

- Sugar
- Jaggery (*gur, vellum*)
- Brown sugar
- Demerara

Why did you stop? You haven't reached the end of the list!

- Rice in all its forms. Ditto wheat. Ditto millets. Ditto dals and pulses.
- Potatoes and sweet potatoes, certainly, but onions too!
- That enticing bowl of fruit, but also most vegetables in your fridge.

- And, of course, honey, jam, raisins, figs, dates, and other delectables.

*There is sugar everywhere in your kitchen, hiding in plain sight.*

Now that we've listed them, a very obvious fact glares back at us: *not all sugars are sweet.*

***What is a sugar?***

Good question.

There are a number of words that describe a sugar, and all of them sound very different.

All the sugars just listed are very different. Chemically, they are all carbohydrates – the same stuff the internet keeps warning us about. How often have you seen your friends shudder at the very mention of 'carbs' and every time over a chocolate brownie or a pizza oozing cheese?

FOR OUR CONVERSATION, *SUGAR* = ALL CARBOHYDRATES.

Carbohydrates are the stuff of life. Without them, we cannot produce the energy needed to sustain life. It is as simple as that. We, in India, have thrived on a largely-carbohydrate diet for millennia – but it isn't working for us now. Why not?

The reason is obvious. We are eating too much of 'instant gratification' foods, and we have adopted a lifestyle that doesn't deserve these foods.

We condemn carbohydrates at our peril.

Why not get to know them better and use them with intelligence and, yes, wisdom too.

Chemically, carbohydrates contain simple elements: carbon, oxygen, and hydrogen linked in molecules of varying size and complexity.

That's scarcely a sensible way of getting to know them.

An easier way is to ask the obvious question: *Can this be eaten raw, or does it have to be cooked?*

The carbohydrates we can eat raw are called 'simple' – and that's a chemist's word too.

In fact, we cannot understand carbohydrates without a little chemistry.

*Simple carbohydrates* have fewer linked molecules.

The chemical names of most sugars end in *-ose,* and most of us are familiar with many simple sugars.

*Glucose* has only one sugar molecule (it is a monosaccharide). Fresh fruit has enough free glucose to provide instant energy, which is why eating a fruit when you're tired revives you. Fresh fruit contains even more of another simple sugar, *fructose.*

Cane sugar, which is the usual sugar we add to foods and beverages, is *sucrose.* It is a disaccharide made up of a molecule each of glucose and fructose.

Another common sugar, which is not quite so visible, is the milk sugar, *lactose.* It is a disaccharide too, with a molecule each of glucose and galactose.

Of all these sugars, fructose is the sweetest.

Dried fruits are concentrates of glucose and fructose, especially dried figs.

Jaggery or *gur* is just cane sugar. It has the same nutritional value as white granulated sugar; as do brown or demerara sugar. All the differences lie in the processing.

This first group of sugars in the kitchen are used every

day, all the time. They are instant gratifiers and they form the bulk of the sweetening agents in home cooking.

Milk, though, is never regarded as a sweetener, and it often demands sweetening. This is because lactose is only very mildly sweet.

Commercial foods accustom us to a higher degree of sweetness. They utilize *High Fructose Corn Syrup* as a sweetener. This is manufactured from starch, usually sourced from corn, and is intensely sweet because of its high fructose content (42–55%). It is practically ubiquitous in all commercial foods, from chocolate and candy to sauces, spreads, soups, instant powders, and baked products. It is cheap, it lends itself easily to crispness, and it has a long shelf-life. It is also one of the chief causes of the present pandemic of obesity.

Fructose present in fresh fruits does not hurt us because there is so little of it. However, glutting on fruits like mangoes can set off loose stools – correctly called 'mango diarrhea'.

Honey contains both glucose and fructose, besides other substances.

These simple sugars are sweet and they offer immediate gratification, which means they are digested quickly and absorbed quickly too. These are the carbohydrates usually blamed for a 'sugar rush'.

Surprisingly, the most common sugar in our diet is none of these sweet carbohydrates. It is, quite simply, *starch.*

Gastronomy sneers at starch, and yet there would be no fine dining without it. From the Western perspective, starch can be blamed for everything poor – poor health, poor energy, poor performance, poverty. It was the stuff colonized cultures fed on.

Starch is the energy stored in plants – fruits, vegetables, tubers, stems, leaves. And we humans, dedicated herbivores, eat all these.

Starch consists of two sugars: *amylose* and *amylopectin.* Cereals usually contain these in varying ratios.

The properties of starch are defined by its physical structure.

At room temperature, it is mostly crystalline.

Heat and hydration change this into the familiar 'gel' by a process called *gelatinization.*

Starches *must* be gelatinized before they can be digested. We discovered this around 10,000 BCE when farming first began in the Fertile Crescent.* Starch began civilization as we know it.

Not all carbohydrates are digestible. In fact, we eat tons of these indigestibles. Plants get their beauty, structure and functional parts from *cellulose* and *hemicellulose.* Add to these pectins, mucilage, and plant gums. This array extends beyond the vegetables. These are components of foods we consider our staples – cereals, dals, oil seeds. If we consume so much of these without actually 'digesting' them, what's the point?

Oh, there is a very important point, one that grows in importance each day as we discover more about the science of staying alive and staying healthy.

---

*The Fertile Crescent is a demilune region in the Middle East, spanning modern-day Iraq, Syria, Lebanon, Palestine, Israel, Jordan, and Egypt, together with the northern region of Kuwait, southeastern region of Turkey and the western portion of Iran. Also called the 'Cradle of Civilization,' it was the birthplace of writing, the wheel, agriculture, and the use of irrigation.

# The Good, The Bad, The Very Very Ugly

Now here's a shocking fact: carbohydrates not only provide energy, but they also *prevent* obesity and diabetes.

You've believed just the opposite, right?

That high carbohydrate diets lead to obesity and diabetes?

Both statements are correct, and please read on to discover why.

This paradox is easily explained if we consider the end product of all carbohydrate digestion.

Whether you've eaten cake or *khichdi*, it is, finally, glucose. This is the energy fuel the cell will utilize, and it is transported in the blood, where it can be detected by a simple test.

The common perception of diabetes is 'high blood sugar'. This is not entirely correct as we'll see later, but, for the moment, let us work with it.

The glucose detected on a blood sugar test comes from many sources – but mainly from digested food.

The hormone *insulin* quickly permits glucose to enter

into cells where it is used for energy. When insulin is deficient or inefficient, glucose cannot be whisked away quickly enough into cells. It stays on in the circulation to register as 'high blood sugar'.

Certain carbohydrates are digested and absorbed so quickly that they cannot be moved into cells efficiently enough. They result in what is colloquially called a 'sugar rush'.

Insulin tries its best to keep up with the sugar overload, and its enthusiasm may result in a fall in blood sugar.

Either way, these quick-fix carbohydrates destabilize the blood sugar and set the stage for disordered metabolism.

These carbohydrates are labelled as '*high glycaemic*' foods. Without thinking, you can push all very sweet stuff into this category.

The carbohydrates that are not sweet, those that need cooking, those which appear rather rough and coarse – these are not as quick to break down into glucose. Their release of absorbed glucose into the bloodstream is paced just right for insulin to work efficiently. These are '*low glycaemic*' foods.

This *high/low glycaemic* label is somewhat misleading.

It may lead you to believe, as most people do, that you should run scared of high glycaemic foods – banana and potato, to give you common examples. This is entirely untrue.

This labelling is an artifice.

The Glycaemic Index of any food can be altered by the method of cooking, by its accompanying elements, by storage time, and any number of other variables. At least one of these is within our control as home cooks. Our endeavour is to serve a meal that has an 'acceptable glycaemic value'. Let me translate that phrase: there is no number attached to it. *It merely means there is no abrupt glucose overload.*

Cooking processes change the structure and arrangement of molecules – through temperature, pH, and association with accompanying foods and spices.

And then, there is always common sense – or discretion.

One helping will do no harm, but four might.

Boiling or steaming potato, for instance, lowers its glycaemic index. This is because of a special starch it contains (*resistant starch*). As it cools after boiling, starch becomes impermeable to the action of digestive enzymes, so a good wallop of that potato passes down to the large intestine undigested. And, as we'll soon discover, that's no bad thing at all.

Carbohydrate blends – the classic *dal* and rice, for instance – also lower the glycaemic index. So, it is time to start thinking of a ***low glycaemic meal*** rather than low glycaemic foods, because you, dear home cook, can make certain of that.

Now that we're agreed that there's some good in bad, let us get to the bad bit in the good.

The good guys in the glycaemic picture are the rough stuff generally recognized as *fibre*. I resent the word as it robs the food of juice – and high fibre foods can be lush with succulence. Unfortunately, the word fibre has managed to educate the mind to award anything dingy, coarse, mushy or leathery, and pretty nigh inedible with this mark of virtue. Of course, it is presented with a dollop of cream and a bright scatter of berries! But, lurking beneath, is the same scaly stuff.

Dietary fibre, as I remarked earlier, is not necessarily bran (*bhoosa*).

Incidentally, vegetarians can skip bran altogether, *if we eat our vegetables the right way* (true, dedicated carnivores can use shovelfuls of bran). Our delectably juicy and succulent vegetables are fibre rich. That does make them sound hairy, so why not use the right word: cellulose and its twin hemicellulose. Plus, a pushy bunch of cousins too – *lignin, pectin, gum,* and *mucilage.*

The simplest definition of dietary fibre is: *edible but indigestible plant stuff.*

The virtues of fibre are manifold, so much so that we are giving it a whole chapter later on. But right now, let us address the specific question: *What could possibly be bad about it?*

Well, in a protein-deficient diet, it can reduce the absorption of protein and other nutrients if it is not processed properly.

Once again, the key to nutrition is not so much *what you cook* as *how you cook it.*

Which leaves the ugly, really disgustingly ugly, carbohydrates. They cause every possible ill that ails us: dental caries, obesity, diabetes, cardiovascular disasters, and counting.

These are the sugars used in the food industry. They aren't different sugars from what you have in your kitchen, just immensely more in quantity, and more intensely sweet. Here, too, it isn't the sugar itself, but the food it is presented in that should take the blame. Canned and bottled beverages, sauces, soups, spreads – stuff you wouldn't categorize as exactly sweet – all contain ugly amounts of sugar that make them very high glycaemic foods.

And let's not forget the icing on the cake. Do watch a YouTube video about the making of the cutest cupcakes, and you'll see what I mean.

# Fibre!

Fibre isn't always fibrous. The fibre we eat – or should eat – is luscious, juicy, delectable. So, fibre, here, is just a convenient catch-all, and if you want to know just how convenient, let me list some dietary fibres:

- polysaccharides – cellulose, β-glucan, hemicelluloses, gums, mucilage, pectin, insulin, resistant starch
- fructo-oligosaccharides, oligofructose, polydextrose, galacto-oligosaccharides, raffinose and stachyose, chitosan.

You want more? There was a time when all this was just called *roughage.*

So let's stick with fibre, shall we?

Fibre is defined by a physical attribute: it is *indigestible.* It cannot be broken down by body enzymes. Therefore, it is not absorbed.

So, how can it possibly maintain nutrition?

Chemically, fibre is a mixture of polysaccharides. They

are differentiated by another physical characteristic – their solubility in water.

Cellulose, hemicellulose, and lignin are insoluble.

Pectin, gums, and mucilage are soluble.

Soluble fibre is again categorized as viscous (mostly sticky) and non-viscous. These physical properties are of great importance to our health.

- *Viscous soluble fibre reduces the risk of heart disease.*
- *Fats bound to viscous soluble fibre are not absorbed.*

Different sorts of fibre achieve this through various mechanisms, principally in synergy with the principal secretion of the liver: bile.

Further, absorbed fats cannot be metabolized quickly or effectively when the meal contains enough fibre. This is because fibre down-regulates the genes that direct the metabolism of fats.

Perhaps the most widely advertised benefit of fibre has to do with its therapeutic effect on weight gain, obesity, and diabetes. You'll find this happy cant on oatmeal packets, and it is no idle boast.

Soluble and viscous – think 'quick cooking and sticky' – just about sums up your morning bowl of oats.

Breakfast cereals are a Rs 1,400 crore market in India. Why hasn't such enthusiastic chomping on oats relieved us of diabetes and heart disease?

Those claims on the packet are by no means false. However, fibre can't work in isolation. This is one more instance of the central thought of this book:

**It is not *what* you eat, but *how* you eat it that makes the**

**difference between health and disease.**

What's so magical about fibre?

Not a single thing.

It simply works sequentially during every step of digestion.

Think of digestion as a staircase – fibre is the escalator. It moves you from step to step by cutting down the effort of climbing.

Constipated?

All you need is more fibre, and all sorts of husks, gums, and sawdust are recommended for ease.

*They are NOT needed.*

In order to produce your morning contribution to manure, you don't have to eat food that resembles it.

Yes, all you need is fibre, but the kind you enjoy – in fruit, vegetables, and grains of all sorts – will do perfectly well.

All fibre, you see, *retains water*. That's all the magic that's needed for the food's transit down the intestine to be swift and easy.

So, if you glut on fibre and don't drink enough water, it will form a hard mass that will make your constipation worse.

But there's even more – eat less fibre and you'll find yourself getting hungry very quickly after what you imagined was a large meal. Fibre keeps the food longer in the stomach so that it can be churned better into the state needed for complete digestion. This means the stomach doesn't scream 'HUNGRY!' an hour after lunch. Consequently, you eat less.

It gets better: fibre cuts down the absorption of fats, so less of the heart-searing stuff in circulation, and your blood report smiles up at you.

All good stuff, but it has its downside – all this delay and prevarication can get in the way of minerals and vitamins being absorbed.

And all this while, no matter how it affects other nutrients, fibre stays undigested and unabsorbed, gaining bulk as it inches its way out of the small intestine into that big drainpipe, the large intestine.

This large intestine, the colon, is where fibre gets really interesting.

Obviously, the large intestine which is full of undigested matter is also full of microbes. These microbes act on undigested carbohydrates and begin a process called *fermentation.*

Fibre is, remember, for all its fancy airs, a good old-fashioned carbohydrate. So, the bulky fibre now gets churned up by bacterial action into releasing an important category of molecules called Short Chain Fatty Acids (SCFAs). These are easily absorbed into the circulation and they regulate the synthesis of cholesterol. As a result, *less fat is deposited in body tissues.*

There is one more important job fibre accomplishes before it quits the body. It makes certain the inner lining of the intestine stays tough and well supplied with mucus. This important barrier keeps toxins from getting into the circulation.

And as a result of multitasking its way so effectively, fibre achieves what we need most in these times – immunity.

# The Microbiome

The large intestine has more than $10^{14}$ bacteria* from over 10,000 species. And guess what these 'germs' are doing there.

No, they aren't about to plunge us into disease and disaster. Just the opposite. The large intestinal *flora* – I like using that pretty word rather than the condemnatory *germ* – actually make up a vital body organ: *the gut microbiome.*

Although situated in the most despised part of the digestive tract, the microbiome's activities reach far beyond digestion. Incredibly, it controls the functioning of all body organs from the brain downwards. We are only just beginning to understand the complexity of how the microbiome maintains us in a state of health.

In fact, it is correct to say that when the microbiome is disrupted, disturbed or altered, we are sick.

Conversely, every illness is reflected in *dysbiosis* – alteration of the microbiome.

---

*Hundred trillion; 100,000,000,000,000; ten to the power of fourteen.

How is this particularly relevant to us now?

First, because we might as well wake up to the truth that tomorrow's therapies will be based on the genetic, chemical, and neurological information we are gleaning from the microbiome today.

Second – or perhaps this should have come first – we can and do have a say in maintaining a healthy microbiome, largely through what we eat.

This makes us home cooks directly responsible for the microbiome.

This makes us responsible for health.

This reminds us that health is the state of existence. It is as basic as that.

So, it is worthwhile knowing everything there is to be known about the microbiome. And as that isn't very much, I will stick with just the immediate realities.

The very immediate:

*What do we know about the microbiome in this pandemic?*

*Did it get sick?*

*Did it make us sick?*

The answers are easy if we look at what COVID-19 does to the body: *it alters the immune response to let inflammation run rogue*. And the intestine, all 16 feet of it, is the largest immunological organ in our body. It has even more immune cells than the bone marrow. The microbiome controls this humungous, unwieldy, population of immune cells.

Studies have shown that alterations in the microbiome are directly linked with the severity of disease and the related rise in inflammatory markers. Moreover, these alterations persist in cases of 'Long COVID' where patients have continued to experience disquieting symptoms long after they were 'COVID negative'.

That should tell us how vital a healthy microbiome is when we are living through a pandemic.

Turn that observation inside out, and what stares back at us? The possibility that we may manage to duck this dreaded infection if we maintain a healthy microbiome.

This book shows you how to get to this.

The microbiome is maintained not just by what we eat, but how we eat. As you read further into the book, you will discover how every intelligent kitchen move adds up to a healthy microbiome.

Still skeptical?

Then, here is a second helping of science:

- The gut is considered to be the 'second brain' because of its complicated network of nerves. Signals across this network control intestinal movements, the secretion of enzymes, digestion, and absorption of food.
- Alterations in the microbiome are strongly linked with obesity, diabetes, and all diseases of inflammation.

Isn't it time we did something about this?

# A Mouthful of Rice

How do we digest sugars?

Even when we don't taste their sweetness, all sugars begin their breakdown the moment the mouth coats them with saliva.

We are conditioned, by some unknown prejudice, to flinch at the very thought of saliva. Yet, without this delightful fluid, life wouldn't be worth living. We would taste nothing. The softest food would abrade tongue and palate. The strongest teeth would be daunted by the coarse sawdust they mill out. And the throat would clamp in protest at being asked to swallow.

Starvation would suddenly seem madly attractive.

Add to these miseries bad breath, bleeding gums and ulcers, not to mention many other dreadful infections, and you are literally dry mouthed with dread – with the disquiet of falling short of saliva.

Besides dissolving, lubricating, and disinfecting the mouth, saliva also begins the digestion of carbohydrates. It contains *amylase,* an enzyme that cracks the long chains of starch molecules to break them up into smaller carbohydrates, *dextrin* and *maltose.* Take your time savouring a mouthful of cooked but unflavoured rice. After a few chews your mouth is flooded with a delicate lingering sweetness. That is maltose you're tasting as the amylase in your saliva gently begins digesting starch.

Swallowed, that mouthful is in for a long sojourn in the stomach. You would expect digestion to progress further – but it doesn't. Even though the starch is liberally coated with amylase when it arrives, the stomach's acidic environment puts the enzyme out of action. But something very important does happen – the stomach's muscular movements turn that mouthful of chewed rice into a creamy smooth emulsion, quite like a gourmet French sauce. When this stuff, called *chyme,* enters the small intestine, it sets off a powerful signal to the pancreas to produce a second brand of amylase. This *pancreatic amylase* breaks down all the remaining starch. Now, the cells of the intestinal lining get into the act by secreting enzymes that break these simple sugars into glucose. These 'brush border enzymes' are *sucrase, lactase, maltase,* and *isomaltase.*

*Sucrase* breaks down the cane sugar sucrose into glucose and fructose.

*Lactase* breaks the milk sugar lactose into glucose and galactose.

*Maltase* breaks maltose into two glucose molecules.

Glucose is now ready to be absorbed. It must be actively transported across the cell border into intestinal cells. This requires another enzyme present in the brush border of the intestine: sodium-glucose linked transporter (SGLT-1), which draws glucose into the intestinal cell.

But this cell is just a transit lounge.

Glucose now has to bend a rule. It has to move from a place of high concentration (inside the cell) to the outside, which is still hungering for sugar. So, it boards a glucose transporter (GLUT) molecule on the cell membrane, exits the cell, and enters the mesh of fine blood vessels – the capillaries. It can now circulate freely, but to enter cells that require it for energy, it needs the help of insulin.

What of those carbohydrates that remain undigested?

Oh yes, those resistant starches and, of course, fibre have now passed into the large intestine. They are now seized by the microbes in the large intestine and fermented into those health-giving SCFAs.

Now that we have digested and transformed that mouthful of rice into glucose in our blood, isn't it time we looked at what 'blood glucose' is all about?

# Sugar – Controlled and Unleashed

'My sugar's gone up.'

On a blood report, a sugar value that's 'higher than normal' appears underlined or in bold red figures.

*But what does it mean?*

Does it mean you have a disease? The disease called *Diabetes mellitus,* or, to use the ancient Indian term, *Madhumeha?*

Both translate as *honeyed flow,* a pretty euphemism for sweet urine. *Ziabetes shakri* is the oldest term in Unani medicine.

Us moderns, we are a tad more fastidious. We generally call it Diabetes type 1 or 2. Every Indian language calls it Sugar Disease – *shakar ki bimari, shakkarai noi.*

Yes, diabetes, as I am going to call Diabetes Type 2 in this book, does present with high blood sugar, but – Surprise! Surprise! – your blood sugar may be high even *without* diabetes. High blood sugar is a sure sign that you are headed the diabetes way.

The other word that's usually used concurrent with

mentions of 'sugar gone up' is 'control'. As in: 'My sugar is not controlled' or 'I must control my sugar'.

Equally frequent is the admonition: 'Don't eat sweets or you'll get diabetes!'

All these statements are both correct and incorrect. They convey the idea of sugar as a beast that must be kept on a short leash or it will go totally berserk. That's the correct bit.

The incorrect bit is that *shakkar ki bimari* is that red/underlined number on the blood report.

These days, people seldom visit a doctor. They are off to the nearest laboratory and return triumphant with a bulging file, every crevice of the body imaged, every shimmer of biochemistry analyzed. A quick glance – no bold, underlined, or red figures – and wow, you're cured! It is the most magical way to perfect health. When a doctor tells you otherwise, the first statement is always a defensive, 'But all my reports are normal!'

Let us look at the normal blood sugar value, because this book is about how *not to get sick.*

The cut-off value for diabetes is 126 mg/ml.

However, you may have a cautionary underlining if the value is above 100.

The 'normal' level is between 75 and 85.

We tracked that mouthful of rice to the point where it reached the blood stream, remember? Let us finish that story.

But a quick look first at the characters you'll be meeting:

- GLUCOSE: The protagonist, no matter what the carbohydrate you ate. (Yes, it could be fructose or galactose too, but we'll overlook them for the moment.)

- ENERGY: What glucose must ultimately deliver to each cell. Each molecule of glucose yields 2 molecules of ATP.
- INSULIN: The hormone that helps glucose enter cells to be available as energy.
- GLUCAGON: The hormone that *prevents* glucose from entering the cell.
- PANCREAS: The organ that makes both insulin and glucagon.
- ADRENALINE: The stress hormone that *blocks* insulin.
- CORTISOL: Another stress hormone that *blocks* insulin.
- ADRENAL GLANDS: Situated above the kidneys, they produce both cortisol and adrenaline.
- LIVER: The big benevolent organ that works overtime to maintain blood sugar. It is the peacemaker between quarreling hormones and our dietary indiscretions.
- MUSCLES: YES! Muscles manage our blood sugar in unexpected ways.
- OTHER ENDOCRINE GLANDS: The pituitary and the thyroid glands have a big say too.

Let's not forget the humble transporters that ferry glucose: SGLT and the GLUT family.

Most of the carbohydrate in our meal was, like that mouthful of rice, broken down into glucose. The first stop on its journey out of the intestine is the liver. The liver makes an important decision based on whether we have been feasting or fasting.

If we've pigged out, that's too much of glucose to be floating around – like walking around with your entire bank balance in your wallet.

The liver turns part of this excess into a short-term safe deposit. This is glycogen, a molecule that can be changed quickly back to glucose, if you decide to skip a meal.

The liver's manufacture of glycogen is regulated by the balance between insulin and glucagon.

Fasting?

Oops! You need more sugar, so glucagon takes over and insulin steps back.

The liver can also make glucose from the end products of fat and protein digestion.

Feasting and fasting conditions are mimicked in a dampened way throughout the day before and after meals.

The brain signals hunger and appetite when blood sugar is low. If you don't notice and keep on working, the strain of hunger turns on stress hormones that encourage glucagon and your blood sugar rises.

After a glut on birthday cake, insulin rushes to rescue. It stops your blood sugar from hitting the ceiling.

This yo-yo is being bounced all day, every day. It takes an incredible amount of work to keep your sugar 'normal'.

Once the liver has liberated enough glucose to fit your needs, this 'perfect glucose' is carried into the circulation.

The next step is supply. Glucose must enter the cell with the help of a transporter molecule – a member of the GLUT family. There are 5 of these. GLUT 4 is completely controlled by insulin and glucagon. As this is the transporter for entry into muscles (both voluntary muscle and heart muscle), to the brain, and to the fat deposits (adipose tissue), you can see how vital it is to stay on insulin's good side. With insulin's help, these tissues that make up the bulk of the body get their hit of glucose on time. Glucagon blocks this. So very simply, without insulin, cells are starved of glucose, and, therefore, of energy.

This is what happens in diabetes.

There are two types of diabetes:

Diabetes Type 1, which affects children and very young people. In this disease, insulin production in the pancreas is poor.

Diabetes Type 2, which is an acquired disease. Twenty years ago, it was called Adult Onset Diabetes. We can't call it that any longer. Even school children are now targets of this terrible disease. One of the purposes of this book is to keep you and yours safe from Diabetes Type 2.

## Insulin Resistance

If you are on the other side, the bad side of insulin, you have *Insulin Resistance* – there is plenty of insulin in circulation, but it is unable to do its job. In fact, the situation is paradoxical, because *BOTH* circulating glucose and circulating insulin levels are high.

The consequence?

High blood sugar, increasing fat deposition, high circulating fats, high circulating inflammatory chemicals, high uric acid, inflamed blood vessels, and disordered clotting.

This translates into obesity, high blood pressure, cardiovascular diseases, and poor or, much worse, disordered immunity.

And what causes Insulin Resistance?

Increased deposition of fat, especially in the abdomen where you can see it as a paunch. This is only the tip of the iceberg, really, for the abdominal viscera is anyway packed with fat.

Genetic factors may also contribute to insulin resistance, but even these are up-ticked by obesity.

A very dangerous fallout of obesity, worse than even cardiovascular disease, is NAFLD – Non-Alcoholic Fatty Liver Disease – which can lead to fatal complications.

Insulin resistance inevitably ends in Diabetes Type 2 within ten to fifteen years unless obesity is corrected.

Metabolic Syndrome develops much before that.

You can stave off insulin resistance simply by switching to more intelligent food preparation and consumption.

Isn't it time we put some of the thoughts in this book into action?

# A Protean Story

Proteins, school textbooks tell us, are the body's building blocks. Neat, if a trifle simplistic. The question is – *What do proteins build?* Walk past a gym and the first poster will answer that. Next to a carton of whey is a muscle-bound man or woman glaring smugly as us geeks slouch past.

Muscle, yes, is pure protein, but so is the rest of the body. Proteins are everywhere: from blueprint to packaging, every idea in the body is protein.

And most of this comes to us from our diet.

So, consider a quick look in the mirror – from your topmost curl to your toenail – and contemplate this. The protein needed to renew, refurbish, and *restore* you to this state tomorrow morning comes from what you eat today.

That is not overstated.

The body is in a constant state of dissolution. We are crumbling as we stand and, unnoticed, we are being reinvented. Of course, the polite word for this is *turn-over.* Cells are broken down at a rate that turns over 250 gm of protein – and renewal takes up just as much.

Strangely enough, that isn't all the protein that's being reworked through the day.

Enzymes and hormones are being manufactured, immune factors are being organized, and life-sustaining organs are being strengthened and regulated. All this is achieved by the clever network of signaling molecules – all of which are proteins.

And, if you happen to be a child or a teenager or a pregnant mother, your protein demands race way past mine.

Yet, we don't need to eat all of it.

The body manages its protein in a magical manner we're only just beginning to understand.

*How much protein do we need to eat?*

About one gm per kilo of expected body weight for your height.

So if you are 5' 6" and weigh 70 kg, you need 70 gm of protein a day – when in good health, and doing a fairly sedentary job. If you are a sportsperson, or if you are ill, you need much more.

*How much protein does the average Indian vegetarian diet provide?*

A bare 30-40 gm a day. We get by because we eat so much of other stuff – a HUGE amount of fat and a fair amount of carbohydrates. The huge isn't a weight measure, it is just excess. We get by, as I said, because the body *manufactures* proteins.

Before we look at the proteins we swallow and digest, here is a strange fact: *proteins control digestion.* Of course, digestive enzymes are proteins themselves, but the proteins we eat control appetite, satiety and the speed and efficiency of digestion – which just about puts them in charge of everything else we eat.

Chemically speaking, all proteins contain one remarkable element: nitrogen. This distinguishes them from fats and carbohydrates.

Proteins are large molecules and they are *intricately folded*. It is the folding that makes a protein functional. Folding decides the nature of the protein. A change in the conformation alters the function or renders it inefficient. Folding is determined by the constituent elements of the protein – the *amino acids*. It would be more correct to say that the body's building blocks are amino acids. So the proteins we eat must have the amino acids we need to synthesize the proteins that make us work.

Of the 22 amino acids involved in body processes, 9 cannot be produced by the body and *must be eaten*. These are *Essential Amino Acids* – phenylalanine, valine, tryptophan, threonine, isoleucine, methionine, histidine, leucine, and lysine.

It follows that we must source these from the animal and plant producers that are part of our diet.

That's what we do when we talk of 'proteins in the diet' – we are hunting and gathering amino acids, which the body can utilize in the synthesis of proteins.

Amino acids are also the end products of protein digestion – but they have to be of the right sort. Proteins that provide the whole gamut are called 'complete proteins'. If they lack the full complement of amino acids, they are dubbed 'incomplete'.

Here is a thought that gives me the same feeling the sky does on cloudless nights, when I feel the insignificance of all human knowledge in the face of the unknown. Ancient cu evolving independently, cracked the trick of ensuring a complement of amino acids in their diets by clever food combinations.

In 8,000 BCE, how on earth did they *know*?

Amino acids are linked together to form proteins by peptide linkages.

The characteristics of a protein depend on the amino acids it contains, and their pattern of arrangement.

The body has 100,000 known proteins – and they are all synthesized from 20 of the known 22 amino acids:

1. Alanine
2. Arginine
3. Asparagine
4. Aspartic Acid
5. Cysteine
6. Glutamic Acid
7. Glutamine
8. Glycine
9. *Histidine*
10. *Isoleucine*
11. *Leucine*
12. *Lysine*
13. *Methionine*
14. *Phenylalanine*
15. Proline
16. Serine
17. *Threonine*
18. *Tryptophan*
19. Tyrosine
20. *Valine*

(Selenocysteine and Pyrrolysine are not used in human protein synthesis.)

Of these, we need to eat phenylalanine, valine, tryptophan, threonine, isoleucine, methionine, histidine, leucine, and lysine (italicized in the list above).

The rest, we make. But we may need foods that contain some of them under conditions where the demand is high – as in pregnancy or in childhood – when the ability to make them is yet to mature.

So, it is not really practical to think of some amino acids as 'essential' – we need them all. And since we source them through long complicated protein molecules, let's get hunting and gathering.*

Hunters have it easy. *Most animal proteins are complete proteins* – meat, fish, milk, eggs.

Muscle from meat or fish is the most commonly utilized, though organ meats are also popular.

But, as this book is about vegetarian cooking, we shall stop at this mention.

Milk is the most commonly consumed animal protein. 100 ml of milk (any milk, including human) has between 3.1 and 3.5 gm of protein.

Eggs contain 6 gm or 13% protein. Egg white is the gold standard for all protein. However, it contains a factor that can interfere with digestive enzymes. This is destroyed by heat – so avoid raw whites.

Gatherers have it much tougher. *Plant proteins are mostly incomplete*. But, as different plant proteins have different amino acids, they overlap when several are eaten together, so the full complement of amino acids is achieved. This has been part of traditional eating patterns in all cultures.

A classic example is rice and dal, or roti and dal.

Rice and wheat are poor in lysine, but rich in sulfur-containing amino acids. *Dals* are rich in lysine but poor in

---

*There are internationally accepted scores for proteins based on amino acid availability. The Digestible Indispensable Amino Acid Score (DIAAS) has been in use since 2013. But this score is of little practical value to the home cook.

sulfur-containing amino acids. Enjoy them together, and – wow! Add a serving of curds, and you can thumb your nose at meat and fish – well, almost.

*Vegetarians, therefore, need to eat many different sorts of plant proteins.*

There are other indispensable amino acids that we cannot afford to fall short of, especially in times of siege.

*Leucine* starts off the building of great pecs, which is why that poster boy at the gym grins over a glass of whey.

*Arginine* is responsible for a number of complicated and interlinked functions that keep our blood vessels and kidneys healthy.

*Glutamine* fuels cells that multiply fast and have short lifespans – think lining membranes, immune cells. It also helps the body synthesize the other indispensable amino acids.

*Glycine* weaves collagen, that wondrous soft tissue scaffolding that gives the body structure, shape, beauty, and insulation against the rough and tumble of an ordinary sedentary life.

Because of their importance, we do need to include them in the diet – and, in a vegetarian diet, include plant proteins that contain them.

The main sources for plant protein are:

*Cereals*: They contain anything between 8–12% protein. They are usually low in lysine, and tryptophan.

Protein in cereals are of two kinds: storage proteins (albumin, globulin, prolamin, glutelin), and enzymes, which are actively used in metabolism. These metabolically active proteins have a fair amount of lysine and arginine. Storage proteins have more glutamic acid and proline.

*Pulses*: These are the seeds of leguminous plants. They contain 17–30% protein, most of which are albumins and globulins. They also contain harmful chemicals that interfere with protein digestion. We overcome this hazard in our methods of preparing them for cooking.

*Soy*: The Far East thrives on soy protein, which is the most complete plant protein known. Soy seeds have 30–40% protein.

*Oil seeds* like sunflower and groundnut also have fair amounts of protein.

Both animal and plant proteins are so important that we have given them separate chapters. So after that brief introduction, let us look at what makes protein the trickiest, most elusive, part of the vegetarian meal.

The first, and most obvious, hurdle is digestion. The protein source we harvest, usually the seed, has many substances that interfere with protein digestion. These factors are bio-active, which means they contribute to or interfere with many vital body reactions. When we eat composite food, we have to be certain of two things:

1. That the protein can be digested
2. That the accompanying chemicals are either removed or deactivated.

And yet, it is these other bio-actives in plant proteins that make them so valuable: they improve sugar control, lower blood fats, reduce inflammatory chemicals, and safeguard the liver and kidneys.

A peculiar feature of proteins is that they can quickly be identified as 'ALIEN' – and the body swiftly mounts the *rejection response* we recognize as an *allergy*. When eaten, proteins may become 'substances of interest' to the immune system. It is often difficult to identify the particular molecule that elicits this response – the best we can get to is the food source. Food allergies are common and can range from mild to life-threatening. So, if a rash or any sort of discomfort is noticed after trying out a food, simply avoid it in future. The planet teems with edibles – missing out on a handful is no deprivation.

Again, the small amounts of 'allergens' present in home-cooked proteins may not elicit an allergy. But when these are consumed as 'processed protein' concentrates, they challenge the body. This is one more reason why 'protein foods' out of a tin, a packet, or a bottle are best avoided. The other, more cogent, reason is obvious – the body may not be able to deal with such unphysiological concentrations of protein.

*How does the body deal with the protein on your plate?*

A tangy dish of *chhole* has chickpeas as the star of the show. After you're done smacking your lips over its piquancy, you've chewed the soft beans to a creamy mush and swallowed it.

Unlike carbohydrates and fats, proteins argue with the gastrointestinal tract, and finally dictate digestion by signaling through the nerves and local chemicals to enhance or oppose enzyme action.

Proteins are attacked by pepsin secreted by the stomach

lining and are broken into peptides. While this is happening, a signal of fullness passes to the brain. The brain interprets this as a 'full meal'.

Stomach emptying slows down, and the food stays longer in the stomach. It is too early into the meal, surely, to decide this!

This happens because the presence of peptides is a trigger for the secretion of the chemical *Cholecystokinin (CCK)*. Produced from the cells lining the upper small intestine, CCK acts as a pacemaker for digestion. It delays stomach emptying and conveys the sensation of fullness. It convinces you to refuse that second helping, and stimulates the secretion of the pancreatic enzymes trypsin and chymotrypsin. These are enzymes that break peptides into smaller fragments. Enzymes secreted by the brush-borders of intestinal cells finally crack up small peptides into their constituent amino acids. Anti-trypsin factors present in the ingested proteins interfere in this final step.

Although all proteins are digested into amino acids, all amino acids are not absorbed in the same manner or with the same efficiency. This makes it difficult to predict how much of the protein is ultimately absorbed. Add to this the immediate utilization of amino acids by intestinal cells – they're simply greedy for the stuff.

About 30% of the amino acids absorbed are utilized almost immediately as they pass through intestinal cells. The remnants enter the blood stream and are whizzed off to the liver.

Most of the amino acids are retained as such, but the liver breaks down a fraction, converts the released nitrogen into urea, which is later filtered out by the kidneys. The bulk of amino acids (except branched-chain amino acids)* is put to use by the liver in the manufacture of proteins. Some amino acids can be transformed into others.

Amino acids are transported in the blood to target tissues. Muscle is one of the main utilizers. Muscle converts branched-chain amino acids into alanine and glutamine. The kidneys grab the glutamine and convert it into urea – necessary to maintain acid-base balance in the body.

Undigested protein works its way into the large intestine where the microbiome feasts on it. Fermentation produces unpleasant pops of flatulence. That's an embarrassing end to the protein story.

What if we started over and began the story anew?

Once upon a time, some 15,000 years ago, after a really bad night in the cave, our ancestors spilled out pell-mell at dawn and swore a solemn oath over a pot of water. Then they lit the fire and went forth to gather beans.

We still follow that ritual, and you can read all about it in the next chapter.

---

*The branched-chain amino acids [BCAAs] are a group of three essential amino acids: leucine, isoleucine and valine.

# Protein in the Kitchen

All that talk about protein, how does it make any kind of sense in the kitchen? I'm headed there to find out.

Frankly, this morning, my kitchen is a mess, and my knees wobble a bit as I scan the landscape.

Ambition must be made of sterner stuff. Shakespeare used *should*, not *must*. With me, it's just *could*.

This morning, ambition runs deep, right from breakfast through lunch, past coffee, to dinner. I have guests!

The kitchen counter is dotted with preps for the ordeal ahead.

What's protein got to do with that?

Everything!

I sip my morning tumbler of coffee as I take a survey, and feel the prickle of challenge. Coffee wouldn't be coffee without the kindliness of milk – and who thinks of *that* as protein particles in an emulsion with sugar and fat? (Oh, you thought that was custard? It is, but some *other* mammal made this batch.)

My guests are special. One is diabetic, another lactose

intolerant, a third gluten intolerant. Three eat eggs, the others don't, can't, or won't. How on earth am I to provide enough protein through four meals for all of them?

Prepping on the counter are three bowls. One has a mixture of soaked pulses. The next a mixture of *dal* and rice steeped in cold water. The third has dough ballooning – it has a twin in the fridge. The usual suspect, a crock of *dahi*, has been setting overnight. Time to banish it into the fridge.

All these bowls contain protein, but by the time it is on the table they will all look, smell, and feel different.

Meanwhile, breakfast.

Bread first.

I pick up the bowl with ballooned dough, punch it, divide it into little rolls and get the oven ready. Before the rolls go in, I brush them with milk.

One of my guests wants very crisp toast. I have a loaf ready to slice, but would she like French toast instead? Oh yes, she would.

Egg orders: one omelette, and er … whites only. So, soufflé? Done, I say, doing my best not to sound grim.

The eggs are cracked and waiting – they all look alike now. Clear whites. Cute cuddly yolks.

Now, watch.

I separate the whites carefully for the soufflé.

The rest get whisked.

There.

That's two sorts of protein.

The whites are pure protein, (mostly) albumin.

Whisked egg has two kinds of protein: albumin and liporotein (read protein + fat). And when we use them together, they have to work together, so see how we can manage that.

We have to turn a mixture of two runny, very dissimilar liquids into something smooth.

I want a soft fluffy omelette, so I cook it on very low heat. It begins to set at around 60°C, but is still very jiggly, so I cover it for a minute, and lightly scramble its centre before I begin to roll.

Voilà!

The perfect omelette, a fluffy pale gold roll, not a streak of brown in it. The centre is creamy and layered.

My guest is surprised as I place the omelette before her.

'Oh, you've made it already? But I didn't smell anything!'

Exactly.

However, by now the house is singing with quite another aroma.

Everybody crowds the empty table, suddenly hungry.

But they must wait awhile.

I get the French toast going. Two slices of bread soaked in a mixture of egg and milk – I've added a sliver, the merest nail paring, of a vanilla bean. A brush of butter on the pan, and in slides the soggy bread. Flip. No sugar, but a glide of marmalade.

That brings them all into the kitchen, so while the toast is browning, I liberate the bread. The rolls tumble out, exhaling little puffs of warm scent, their crisp tops a burnished gold.

'You forgot me,' reproaches the gluten-sensitive guest.

Not at all.

For him, I have whipped up the soaked *dal* and rice with racy spices, aromatic herbs, and a cupful of grated vegetables, ready to be patted and crisped on the sizzling tawa.

There are cries for coffee, and now there's an entirely different scent floating around, curiously symphonic with the savoury notes of the cooking *adai.*

All these different scents – French toast, freshly baked bread, freshly brewed coffee, and a crisping *adai* – come from different foods.

The finished dishes will all taste very different. Yet, all the scents come from the same transformation of protein.

*How do proteins transform?*

The changes in egg are the easiest to follow. Egg contains more than forty different proteins – in the raw state, they are tightly folded and coiled molecules. Heat unwinds them into straight chains that soon link up to form a mesh we observe as a coagulum. As the temperature increases this coagulum stiffens, going from gel to tough rubber.

Can anything be more tragic than an overcooked egg?

This uncoiling of protein is called *denaturation* – and it can be brought about not only by heat, but by mechanical means as well.

Oops!

Those egg whites remind me that one person is still waiting on their soufflé.

As I whip them into a cloud, they are half way to forming a lattice. If I keep on, the lattice will stiffen, and I will be left with a dry stringy mass.

This is a savoury soufflé, and I like to texture it with grated gourd and a chiffonade of herbs tossed in flour. The merest touch of grated cheese, and into the oven it goes for some protein magic.

And here it comes, a perfect cumulonimbus that sinks about a centimeter – but no more – on the counter. Its foamy structure is consistent through: no puddle or clumps. This is the miracle of denatured protein in yet another form.

The rolls contain an entirely different sort of protein. Wheat proteins *glutenin* and *gliadin* change with the addition of water and mechanical stress, when kneaded, into the more elastic gluten. When leavened with yeast, carbon dioxide is produced as a result of fermentation, and the elastic mesh of gluten traps this to form a light aerated structure.

The soft spongy roll is very different in texture from a *paratha*, but the transformation of protein is the same.

The house still smells wonderful though the breakfast has been cleared away and the dishes done – what is that aroma?

French toast. Fresh bread. Coffee. *Adai*. How can they all be so different and yet have the same bouquet?

The answer lies in another magical protein transformation: the *Maillard Reaction*, named after Camille Maillard who described it in 1923. To you and me, it is the crunch in the toast, the crust on the roll, the aroma of freshly ground coffee, the crisp succulence of *adai*.

When protein and carbohydrate cook together at high temperatures, amino acids react with sugar.

This chemical change can be seen as a change of colour. 'Golden brown' is the universal descriptive. It can be felt as a change of texture from soft to crisp. And it can be smelt by the *Roasty roasty caramely* scents that make up the many volatiles released.

Animal proteins, like meat and egg, release volatiles largely from sulfur-containing amino acids.

Cereals and pulses release the byproducts of the amino acid, proline.

If allowed to continue, the Maillard Reaction can quickly get unpleasant. Witness the 'smell of egg' from a browning omelette. Push it still further and a nasty bunch of chemicals shake themselves free. These are beyond just stinky – they are downright hazardous.

Even at its best, the Maillard Reaction can interfere with the important vitamins and trace elements. So crisping foods tastes just great, but everything doesn't have to be crisp. A silky soft homemade *dosai* is surely more delicious than that restaurant-style stiff crisp *masala dosai,* dripping ghee.

My guests are off to explore the neighbourhood. They'll be back hungry as hunters, in time for lunch. And what proteins await them?

The pulses that have been steeped in water overnight are now ready to be cooked. Steeping them in water has hydrated the tough seed coat and allowed water to soften the seed. It has also removed a bunch of toxins which, though very interesting in themselves, will interfere with the proteins I want my guests to absorb.

Pressure cooking pulses in plenty of water denatures the protein, and gels the carbohydrate. The result is soft and tender beans eager to absorb the rich *masala* for the hearty stew I'm preparing.

The crock of curd gives me pause.

I decide to stick with a simple raita for the side, and hold back the bulk for the luxurious *dahi-vada* I've planned for dinner.

Instead, in honour of my lactose-deficient guest, I need a further source of protein. What better than a delicious *khaman dhokla*?

My guests have insisted on bringing dessert, and I can't wait to see what.

More protein! All the goodness of *besan* on display at the halwai's is here. *Laddoo, Mysore pak, Mohan thal, Pateesa* [I separate the *Pateesa* from the gluten-sensitive guy who swears there's no *maida* in *soan papdi,* but of course there's nothing but maida in it.)

Here too, textures and techniques are different. The Maillard Reaction is cleverly nuanced in *Mysore pak,* with its gradation from pale yellow to gold. The *laddoo* is ancient molecular gastronomy at its best, and *Mohan thal* is voluptuous in luxury. Yet, they are all made of the same stuff that makes onion *pakodas. Protein is protean.*

Replete with lunch, my guests will probably pass up on the luxurious sweet bread I've planned in lieu of cake – it is rich in fruit and nuts, low on fat and sugar, and relies for its luscious softness on yet another attribute of protein. This time it is the yolk of egg, which emulsifies the slowly fermenting dough.

By the time the bread is baked, its aroma of cinnamon and chocolate has drawn everyone to the table. The guy with the gluten allergy looks tragic till I place a dish of macaroons before him. Yet another protein transformation: albumin froth baked crisp. What did you think I saved the egg whites for?

There's still dinner ahead, but we talk the sun down and spin tales by starlight. Everyone declares, a little too emphatically, they don't want any dinner.

Well, nothing complicated, anyway. Something simple they might just about manage.

Something simple is exactly what they'll get. So simple that it is made with no effort at all, but is surely the acme of all protein wonders.

Imagine a hard little seed transformed into both foam and emulsion – and you have the recipe for the batter awaiting an oil bath at 160°C – just a quick dip and up it bobs buoyant as a balloon. It leaves barely a faint trace of oil on the waiting tissue. The exterior is perfect red gold and crisp. The inside is fluffy, perfectly cooked and soft. I always think it is a crime to plunge the perfect *medu vada* into curds.

The lactose deficient guy who's helping me thinks so too. I get him to watch the hearty *rasam* simmering on the hob while I prepare the pool of whisked-to-velvet dahi these vadas will be swimming in – all but the batch saved for the sous-chef who gets a rasam vada.

There's another protein trick here.

I taste the curd to be certain it has a milky blandness. A touch of tart will prevent the *vadas* from making an effective détente with the sauce. Acidity will nudge the denaturation just a little further into toughness, and these fluffy delights will turn into sodden knots.

Just before serving, a swirl with sweet sour chutney and a scatter of pomegranate arils that won't have enough time to push the *vadas* into a sulk.

And so the day ends on a note of satiety – and nobody misses ice-cream.

Doesn't that get you thinking why, with such an abundance of protein sources, vegetarian India should is still protein-deficient?

And what does it mean to be protein-deficient?

# *Kwashiorkor* in Kashi, *Marasmus* in Madurai

My title is more than apt alliteration, it is an artful aid to alert us to a problem. Is there *kwashiorkor* in Kashi? And *marasmus* in Madurai?

If those words seem strange to you, let me restate the question: *Are children malnourished in Kashi and Madurai?* In Sanchi and Guwahati? In Nashik and Baroda? In any or all of the cherished shrines of Indian culture? Are they?

There are malnourished children in every hallowed enclave of Indian culture.

Culture is an environment that permits growth. That is the biological definition.

Malnutrition does not permit growth.

The core tenet of Indian thought is *vatsalya*: nurture.

One out of every three children who die, dies of hunger.

Yes, we may lack the eyes to detect *malnutrition,* but why do we no longer recognize hunger?

We feed dogs, cows, birds – as indeed, we must – but why do we deprive our own children?

We are intensely inimical to children. Three years ago, the death of little Santoshi from starvation shook the nation – for perhaps a day. It should have diverted all our energies into preventing another such death. Of course, at the policy level it made no dent. Politics is not about children, and politicians have never known hunger. But I don't see any change in public attitude either. This pandemic has taken more lives from hunger and deprivation than disease. But these facts glide past unnoticed by everyone except the hungry and the deprived.

***Kwashiorkor***: the word comes from Ga, the language of Ghana. It succinctly paints the plight of Indian children: the disease of the deposed child, the disease the older child gets when the new baby arrives. It applies to all deprived Indian children as all of them are deposed – from policy, from public consciousness, and from the Constitution, which guarantees them the right to food, shelter, and education.

***Marasmus*** is Greek for 'withering'. Its Indian equivalent exists in every language as an apt descriptive of the state of being: *sookh gaya, kaanju pochu*. When the body is dried up like an ancient twig, the bones stick out and sunken eyes stare out of hollows, that's *marasmus*.

You have seen children with both *kwashiorkor* and *marasmus*, even if you don't recognize the descriptors. As a resident in pediatric surgery forty years ago, I saw many more such children in my city than I do today. Equally true is that a short train ride into the nearest suburb will show me that terribly malnourished children still abound.

No shrine, no mandir, no masjid, no church or gurudwara has any meaning in a country with hungry children because the only true object of reverence is a child. Anybody's child, not just your own. All adults are responsible for all children.

No, my rant is not out of place in this book. I cannot talk about food without a reminder about the various states of hunger for which we have many polite words/acronyms that disguise the visceral condition: severe acute malnutrition (SAM), protein energy/calorie malnutrition (PCM), deficiency.

It is easier to understand what we see without such labels.

Indian children below five years of age are seriously undernourished:

- 42.5% are underweight,
- 48% are stunted (or not tall enough), and
- A horrific 19% are 'wasted', which means skeletal in appearance.

Two out of three child deaths in India are caused by malnutrition.

Growth places a high demand for protein – and our children don't even get the starter dose to stay alive.

The main cause is – poverty.

Milk sells at Rs 60 a litre, eggs at Rs 6 a piece, *dals* at Rs 100–150 a kilo. The Public Distribution System (PDS) doesn't guarantee outreach.

The average meal of an Indian child is poor to begin with. Add to this dietary restrictions, taboos, and prejudices. What chance does a child have of even obtaining one square meal a day?

While signs like poor growth, stunting and wasting are evident, what remains concealed is the immense internal damage to life sustaining organs – liver, kidneys, bone marrow. The worst hit is taken by immunity.

How much protein does a child need?

At least the amount contained in two glasses of milk + one egg + two servings of *dal* and rice.

And no, you cannot fob them off with nutritional *laddoos* and strange powdered drinks – that's just for the sociology papers. Those promos don't work. Children need to eat what their parents give them, but can their parents afford what their children need?

Seventy-five-year-old independent India is in a state of famine. This isn't a famine of grain. This is a famine of the spirit, an aridity of the soul.

# Milk

Milk drives vegetarian India, despite the fact that more than 66% of us adults are lactose intolerant. Milk is the stuff of myth and legend and an enduring symbol of plenty – but in the real now, how much of it do we drink?

Start with a question: *Who needs milk?*

Considering we're robbing the calf of its birthright, we should at least ensure that our children drink milk.

Do they?

No, I'm not talking of the 'my kids can't stand milk' faction, a very minuscule fraction of India's 1.3 billion.

As per the 2011 census, India, with a population of 121.1 crore:

- Has 16.45 crore children in the age group 0–6 years, and
- 37.24 crore in the age group 0–14 years.

These constitute 13.59% and 30.76% of the total population, respectively.

Out of every 1,000 children, fifty die before they can enter school.

And the main cause of such terrible mortality is malnutrition.

How many of these little ones could have been saved by just a cup of milk a day?

At least twenty-five.

A cup of milk is 100 ml.

It costs anything between Rs 5 and Rs 10.

Most homes in India do buy milk – worth perhaps Rs 20. It is usually used up in tea.

The shocking truth is that milk is no longer viewed as a necessary food for children.

Would all our children be getting enough milk if it sold at half the price? Probably, but not definitely.

In 2020, India consumed the most cow milk worldwide, using over 81 million metric tons.

How much of this was drunk by protein-deprived children?

Very little.

Where did it all go then?

It went into obesity, diabetes, and heart disease. It made people who got COVID-19 very sick.

And yet, milk is one of nature's most perfect foods.

Why then did it go so wrong for us?

Milk is the provision for growth that evolution gave us. Liquid, sweet, easily digestible, milk is a complete food, with a protein content of 3.1–3.4%.

100 ml of milk gives you:

- 3.2 gm of protein

- 4 gm of carbohydrate, and
- Anything between 3 and 6 gm of fat.

Translated further:

- A glass of milk (200 ml) contains 6.4 gm of protein, which is as much protein as an egg has
- 8 gm of carbohydrate, which is, roughly, two teaspoons of sugar
- 3 tablespoons of butter if it is buffalo milk
- Half a tablespoon of butter if it is cow milk
- The rest of it, for the purposes of this discussion, is water.

Nothing wrong so far, but let's face it, few adults drink 200 ml of milk a day. What we do have a lot of is *dairy concentrates.*

*Dahi* instead of buttermilk
*Paneer*
Cheese
Yoghurt – Greek or otherwise
Cream
Ice-cream
Butter
*Ghee*
*Mithai* and pastries
Chocolate
And, there is concealed dairy in most restaurant food.

This is a paradox. We need milk protein, certainly we do. But we don't need concentrates. The truth is most of our country's milk is diverted to the food industry to make the foods on that list. And never you mind what the label says, milk concentrates are bad for this nation. We are obese and diabetic, remember?

So, let us stick with plain old milk and see what we discover.

Milk has two groups of proteins: caseins and whey.

Squeeze a few drops of lemon juice into a cup of milk and watch these proteins emerge. Clots are casein. The clear fluid is whey.

We employ this trick all the time in the kitchen, don't we?

Milk is 'coagulated' by introducing bacteria (yesterday's dahi) to make curds and buttermilk. This is fermentation, a gradual process that yields a smooth emulsion of curd.

If you want instant gratification, lemon will also split milk and give you *paneer* or *chenna.*

Casein is in the curd, which is tough or soft depending on how denatured the protein has become.

The smoothness and softness of curd depends also on the fat content.

Milk proteins are among the most digestible proteins known. Cow and buffalo milks are the commonly consumed milks in India, but we do have populations that traditionally thrive on milk from other species. Goat and sheep milk, camel and yak milk, all have their consumers.

The two proteins – clumpy curd and clear whey – are very different in their biochemical nature, not just in appearance.

A practical way of understanding how they work is to think of curd as slow and whey as quick. Curd is digested slowly, providing a slow and sustained release of amino acids. Whey is an instant gratifier – quick to be digested and quick to offload amino acids.

The amino acids are also different. After drinking a glass of whey your neighbourhood hunk has a rush of leucine and isoleucine – amino acids the liver simply shrugs off untouched, leaving them to be soaked up eagerly by muscle. After a chunk of paneer, there is a slow leak of proline into the circulation. That's really slow – six hours after you've eaten it, caseins are still at the peptide stage of breakdown. But almost all of casein is eventually broken down into amino acids.

Whey proteins soon quit the stomach because gastric enzymes can't do much for them. But they are quickly digested in the small intestine.

But milk protein is far more complex than just these two broad distinctions. For instance, much of milk protein is already in the first stage of digestion in your cup because of the action of other chemicals milk contains. So, milk is partially pre-digested protein as it teems with peptides.

And that was milk *before* we boiled it.

When milk is boiled, a few changes take place: whey proteins become more digestible and casein proteins less so.

When milk is pasteurized, it is heated to 72°C for 15 seconds or 63°C for 30 minutes – not hot enough to alter milk proteins. In high pasteurization, milk is heated to above 80°C, and at this temperature, whey proteins aggregate more tightly with casein.

UHT or ultra-heat treatment, used very effectively to sterilize milk, heats it to 130°C for a few seconds, and this denatures whey protein.

Much of the milk we consume, especially milk sold in Tetra Paks, is 'homogenized'. In this process, the fat globules are broken down into smaller droplets. The interface between fat droplets and protein molecules makes protein-breaking enzymes more effectual.

To set curds, I use a starter culture of microbes – a few drops of yesterday's curds. That starter has a complex mixture of bacteria – among them *Bifidobacterium bifidum* and *Lactobacterium acidophilus.*

This traditional method of fermenting milk used across cultures is about 12,000 years old.

Almost 150 years ago, Louis Pasteur 'discovered' that the process uses lactic acid bacteria – yeast, moulds, or combinations of these. All of them are natural 'starters'. But what changes do they start off?

Lactic acid bacteria are the most common starters. They break down the sugar lactose in milk for energy and release lactic acid. The acid denatures milk protein into a dense coagulum. This is the delectable gel of well-set *dahi.*

The same reaction is used in the formation of cheese and other fermented milk products.

Yoghurt is much the same, except that the milk has been heat treated and a specific inoculum of bacteria is introduced under tightly controlled conditions.

Even without the Krishna myth, curds make up the very ethos of vegetarian India as a metaphor for plenitude and satisfaction. More commonly consumed is the humbler buttermilk, which is thirst-quencher and food all in one. As an accompaniment to rice, *roti,* and millet, buttermilk sustains India. And how nourishing is *that*?

The most amazing fact about curd is its ability to satiate – this is not the same as a feeling of gastric distention or 'oh, my stomach is really full'. It is, rather, the 'enough' signal from the brain that ends the meal. This has more to do with the physicality of curd and buttermilk than the chemistry –

the nature of the protein coagulum signals gastrointestinal hormones to slow down digestion. The stomach stops flexing its muscles, digestive enzymes take it easy, and general peace prevails.

Milk spoils easily. Curdling is the effect of fermentation, but there are other sorts of spoilage that we often encounter.

Milk can change texture and become slimy. This is caused by bacteria that can grow at low temperatures – so keeping milk in the fridge for over Twenty-four hours can be hazardous. Fats can turn rancid, making the milk smelly. The bacteria that cause this can be dangerous, and cause explosive diarrheas. Milk that produces bubbles is contaminated too.

There is only one way to deal with spoilt milk.

*Throw it out.*

Reheating the milk will not help, as many bacterial toxins are heat stable. Breaking it down further to make paneer will only transfer the dangerous bacteria into the solid mass of coagulum where they will thrive even better. So, *don't even try.*

Babies digest milk. Most healthy adults don't.

In India, over 66% of the adult population is lactose intolerant. This is because babies are born with a high amount of the enzyme required to digest the milk sugar lactose.

Lactose + Lactase = Glucose + Galactose.

As babies are weaned off breast milk, less lactase is produced, so all the lactose is not effectively digested, and passes unchanged into the large intestine.

In adults, this situation is more marked. The amount of lactose digested may be still more reduced, with more undigested lactose. The large intestine reacts to this rather badly: with flatulence, diarrhea, and, sometimes, more severe discomforts. This is often the undiagnosed cause of a host of tummy troubles. Nearly 70% of the world's adults are lactose intolerant.

Milk concentrates appear in all luxury foods – the problem is that these are no longer luxuries. We eat them every day. We eat them *in addition* to the dairy we already consume as home food. This burdens us with, alas, not high protein, but very high fat, and contributes to an overall increase in calories we can do without. If I'm overweight, I cope with this excess by depositing more fat in my arteries and by becoming frankly diabetic.

Milk is an essential part of the vegetarian diet, so let's keep it to milk, buttermilk, curds – and save the milk concentrates for the occasional treat.

# Eggs

We Indians have a prejudice against eggs. We regard them as 'non-vegetarian'.

Eggs are as non-vegetarian as milk.

Milk deprives a calf.

The eggs on the market are unfertilized – no chick will emerge from them, no life is threatened or deprived.

Eggs are more vegetarian than milk. In a country with severe protein malnutrition, to despise eggs is to refuse life itself.

*Do not transfer your prejudice to your children.* Don't deprive them of this unbeatable, totally perfect, protein.

***Eat eggs!***

The egg is meant to nourish the chick – and when there is no chick being formed inside, the egg retains all its nutrients unspent, waiting for a hungry human to crack the shell. Inside is the rich food meant for brain and muscle growth. Indeed, for every form of development.

Scaled down to size, the hen provides much more

nutrition than a human mother does to her growing fetus. A great deal of neuromuscular development in humans takes place only after birth, in the first year of life. In birds, almost all development must be complete when the egg hatches.

Imagine, we have all this practically for free, delicious and bursting with infinite culinary possibility.

And whatever your quarrel with eggs, you must admit the packaging is irresistible. Show me a jewel, a perfume bottle, a sculpture as elegant, as tough, and as sensuously tactile as an egg.

Fabergé? Barbara Epworth? All the perfumes of sweet Araby?

Pah – imitation stuff.

Go buy yourself an egg. It is much more rewarding.

What's inside an egg?

Two incredible compartments of nutrients.

The *yolk* has suffered much abuse over the past few decades, and has been condemned for its cholesterol content. Yes, it has a whopping 275 mg of cholesterol, but that doesn't hurt us. *Cholesterol is manufactured by the liver from the caloric excess in our diet* – from the excess carbohydrates and fats we gulp down in every meal. *That hurts us.* That certainly damages every blood vessel in the body.

Dietary cholesterol, on the other hand, contributes to less than 30% of the total cholesterol in the body.

Recent findings tell us that the response to increased cholesterol in the diet is completely unpredictable. Most such studies are flawed as they don't take dietary excess of sugar and fat into account.

The consensus, as of 2020, is that yolks shouldn't be

incriminated – and it is quite safe to enjoy your egg yolk.

It certainly is – two eggs a day are fine IF you're otherwise eating sensibly. Since most of us are not, it is better to err on the side of caution and stick with one whole egg a day till that paunch is no longer wobbly.

Why not avoid it altogether?

*Because it is the most perfect food on the planet.*

It contains: 2.7 gm of unsaturated fats, 1.5 gm of saturated fat, and a practically irreplaceable molecule – choline. This is an essential nutrient for the liver and muscle to function at optimum. Besides, it has a wallop of vitamin A, folate, and a bunch of trace elements.

The lovely yellow of yolk comes from xanthophyll pigments, zeaxanthine (orange red) and lutein (yellow). Indeed, yolks may span the entire spectrum of yellow from pale lemon to deep orange, and will be equally nutritive. The proteins in yolk are in the form of minuscule granules dispersed in a clear yellow fluid – we'll return to this thought when we cook an egg.

Egg white has no fat in it. It is a gel full of protein. It is the gold standard for all proteins.

A teaspoonful of egg white has half a gram of pure protein.

No other vegetarian food packs as much pure protein.

Though albumin is the most talked about, egg white has 150 different proteins. Ovalbumin is a rich source for all the amino acids we need.

The viscosity of egg white comes from another protein, *ovomucin*. Egg white contains four compounds that retard protein digestion. They are deactivated by heat, so a cooked egg is more digestible than a raw one.

Eggs contain only trace amounts of carbohydrates, but they are bursting with vitamins, minerals, and antioxidants.

Egg allergies are mainly to the white. Like all protein, egg albumin can be recognized as 'non self' by the body, to produce an allergic reaction.

Eggs often produce a grimace – a bad sensory experience is instantly recalled. This can range from texture and taste to the most objectionable property – smell. There are two sorts of odours that turn people off eggs – and both can be avoided.

The first, the most common, is what's usually described as 'the smell of cooking egg'. Well, it isn't. It is the smell of a *charring* egg. In common with all proteins, a bunch of odorants are released when denaturation continues to a high temperature. The Maillard Reaction topples over into charring, and this releases in its final stage, compounds called melanoidins and AGEs,* which have these unpleasant 'off' odours. This can be avoided by cooking eggs at lower temperatures, and for a shorter period of time.

The second objectionable odour is that of hydrogen sulfide – not the nauseating odour of frank hydrogen sulfide from a rotten egg – but a faint whiff suggestive of it even in fresh eggs, especially if hardboiled. Sometimes, this is worsened by the appearance of a green or blue ring between yellow and white. Don't worry, the egg isn't 'bad', the green ring is not poisonous. Egg white has sulfur-containing

---

*Advanced glycation endproducts (AGEs) are harmful compounds that are formed when protein or fat combine with sugar. This process is called glycation.

amino acids. As the egg heats up, the protein denatures and hydrogen sulfide is liberated from these sulfur groups. Yolk is rich in iron, and as the hydrogen sulfide meets the iron in the yolk, ferrous sulfide is deposited at the junction. That's all it is, that sinister green ring, but why not avoid it by boiling the egg briefly and then sliding it into cold water? That will stop both the pong and the ring.

# Dal

Civilization is built upon dal.

Dal cultivation began 12,000 years ago in the Fertile Crescent. In the next millennium, Asia and Europe became legume consumers. American cultures were founded on the 'Three Sisters' – maize, beans, and gourds. Europe erased its own legume culture through amnesia, and that of the Americas through genocide. Africa and Asia have retained theirs.

Over the past two decades, the West has renewed its interest in plant protein. Their bean of interest is soy. This bean has never been cultivated in India until very recently, and has no place in our traditional cuisines. When I talk plant protein, I'm talking dals and pulses. So what's the difference between them?

## Naming

Dals and pulses are *legumes*:* seeds of plants from the family

*From the Latin *legumen*, from *legare* meaning 'to pick' (because the fruit may be picked by hand).

*Leguminosae* (also called *Fabaceae*). They are grouped together because of the unique tripartite relationship between plant-fungi-bacteria. This partnership results in 'nitrogen fixing': *the plant stores a high amount of protein in its seeds and recycles nitrogen into the soil.* Legumes assure soil viability, and so have been used for crop rotation all over the world for at least 5,000 years.

There are more than 19,000 species of legumes. I'll stick to those familiar to the Indian kitchen.

Western nomenclature is thoroughly confusing, and I'll use the familiar Indian names.

**Pulses** are *whole legume seeds,* still wearing their tough overcoat as protection against hostile elements (us).

**Dals** are *pulses manipulated to make them quick-cooking*: the overcoat is slipped off, and the seed usually split in two. The hulled and split *dal* has the same nutrients as its original pulse. However, its nutritional effects can be quite different.

## Structure, Purpose, Effects

A pulse is an egg on pause. Its job is to maintain a store of nutrients safe for the embryo till conditions are right for germination. It must resist every attempt to raid its stores. It does its job, first, by packaging itself in a very tight, very indigestible, coat – the *testa* or seed-coat. This gives it a good chance of passing through the digestive tract of a predator (us) undamaged, its stored nutrition undiminished and unchanged. But should the clever predator decide to strip off the protective coat by hulling, the pulse simply splits its sides and laughs at our credulity. The dal – for that's what we've made it, cannot germinate, but its storage proteins vengefully retain their next safeguard: chemicals that prevent the stored protein from being destroyed by enzymatic digestion.

The very purpose of the legume seed is to *prevent digestion.*

Clearly, as the top predators of legumes, we must succeed where lesser herbivores have failed. If we have to pick dals and pulses as sources of protein, we must make them more digestible.

Not only does the hard seed resist digestion, it also has a number of toxic chemicals that will make the predator sick enough to avoid a second helping. Our ancestors must have learnt this the really hard way *before* they invented ways to rob pulses of these toxins.

## Nutritive Content

Pulses contain carbohydrates and proteins, and some of them so much of fat that they are actually oil seeds.

The protein content of pulses is usually listed as the percentage of dry weight: most pulses have between 10–20% protein.

This is a very poor method of assessment. A more correct one would be to know how much of this contained protein can be digested. Unfortunately, all we can make is a rough guess. Most of the proteins are globulins, which are low in sulfur containing amino acids: cysteine and cystine, methionine and tryptophan.

## Striking a Happy Balance

Legumes contain incomplete proteins. This has been

countered historically by all cultures through intelligent food combinations with cereals.

Rice and *dal* is our magic combination, and so too is *dal* and *roti*.

A vibrant spectrum of *khichdis* exploit this combination to the maximum. Corn and beans are Mexico's staple.

The Far East combines tofu with rice.

In Africa, besides rice and beans, sorghum and cowpeas (what we call *chowli*) and Bambara groundnut (*Vigna subterranea*) and maize.

These are just a few we know of.

Traditional menus are fast fading, and so, sadly, are their intelligent combinations.

Pulses are rich in carbohydrates too. Their complex starches are digested very slowly, so they release sugar very gradually. This makes them 'low glycæmic' sugars.

In addition, many of these starch molecules are termed 'resistant starch'. These are indigestible and will be fermented in the large intestine – all to the good. But some of the end products of the digestion of pulses are molecules like raffinose and stachyose, which, when fermented, produce discomfort and flatulence.

## Anti-nutritive Content

Pulses teem with molecules that interfere with the digestion of protein by deactivating intestinal enzymes.

Tannins block the availability of the amino acid proline. This is stymied by saliva, which contains just enough proline to bind with tannins and make them ineffective. But if a pulse is very rich in tannins, this may not be effective enough.

Phytic acid is another hurdle that hinders protein digestibility. In legumes, phytic acid is found closely bound with proteins. It blocks the digestion of proteins in the stomach.

The indigestible sugars, mentioned earlier, can cause much abdominal discomfort – bloating, cramps, diarrhea, and flatulence.

Lectins are molecules that directly injure intestinal cells and produce severe reactions that range from allergies to indigestion and diarrhea.

Legumes that are actually oil seeds (soy and groundnut) contain enzymes that oxidize fat to produce a rancid smell.

## Know Your Dals and Pulses

I have, on my kitchen shelf, a rainbow array of pulses. Before we get cooking, let us find out if their difference is more than coat deep. It must be – *how else can we account for the difference in flavour*?

The earthy warmth of *chowli* is very different from the sweet blandness of *channa,* which is very different from the mealy softness of *rajma,* which is miles away from the richness of *urad,* which has nothing to do with the clingy, cloying puerility of *moong,* which is again very different from the perky, pungent flavour of peas – yellow, green, or black.

*Chowli, lobhia, karamani, payir,* cow pea (*Vigna unguiculata*)

This rich pulse flourishes even in semi-arid conditions, so it is part of most traditional cuisines. It is high in protein, low in fat, and has a slow-digesting starch. Its high folate content makes it one of the most necessary ingredients.

*Rajma*, kidney bean, common bean (*Phaseolus vulgaris*)

It is high in protein, contains unsaturated fats and resistant starch. It tops the legumes in its content of bioactive molecules (phenols), which counter inflammation. *Rajma* contains lectins, which may have hazardous effects if the bean is eaten raw or undercooked.

*Urad*, Bengal or black gram, *ulundu* (*Vigna mungo*)

While the 'white' *urad dal* is widely consumed, the whole pulse is less popular. Its seed coat is thick with minerals and trace elements – enough to give it a star rating.

*Mung*, green gram, *moong, pachai payir, pessalu* (*Vigna radiata*)

*Moong* is regarded as something of a wonder food in Indian systems of medicine. It could well be. It is rich in molecules that mop up free radicals, which makes it valuable when you are convalescing.

Traditional cuisines have been using *moong* as comfort food since 4,000 BCE.

*Channa* (*desi* and Kabuli), chickpea, *muzhu kadalai* (*Cicer aretinum*)

Perhaps the most celebrated pulse in Indian restaurant cuisine, it is less flashily used across the country in hearty stews. It is rich in every possible nutrient. It includes a hefty content of indigestible sugars, which are fermented to our great embarrassment. This is the 'gassy' pulse!

*Mattar*, pea, *vatana, pattani* (*Pisum sativum*)

Its many dried varieties, and all of them delicious, are rich in protein and resistant starch. This common pulse is uncommon in its quality of digestible sugar. In addition, the seed coat is rich in minerals and bio-actives, which stabilize many metabolic processes.

*Matki, moth* (*Vigna aconitifolia*)

Very popular in Maharashtra, it has the advantage of being low in anti-nutritional factors, which makes its proteins more accessible to digestion.

All these pulses de-hulled and split, make up our more familiar *dals* that also answer to the same name. Two *dals* aren't eaten very often as whole pulses, but form the bulk of domestic consumption: *masoor* and *arhar* or *thuvar dals*.

*Masoor*, red/pink lentil, *masoor dal* (*Lens culinaris*)

This pulse is bursting with protein, low in fibre and fat. Most of the minerals are in its seed coat. So, if you're clever with your cooking methods, this pulse is superior to its *dal*.

*Thuvar, arhar*, pigeon pea (*Cajanus cajan*)

Its delicious 'honeyed' flavour makes it very popular in spicy cuisines for its ability to absorb and retain aromatics. It has molecules that retard the rate of starch digestion, making it release sugars gradually. Like other pulses it is low in sulfur-containing amino acids – this makes it an ideal companion to rice and *roti*.

## Digestion

The digestion of pulses begins in the mouth. To experience it, here is a bowl of well-cooked whole *moong* – unsalted and un-spiced. Water is the only additive.

Let's taste.

As the tongue travels its textures, moong tastes very different from the tasteless mush one imagined. After the initial sweetness, a silky deliciousness fills the mouth, neither salt nor sweet, neither sour nor bitter. This is umami, the taste brought about by molecules in concert (glutamic acid and disodium inosin 5′-monophosphate (IMP or E631) and disodium 5'-guanylate monophosphate (GMP or E627).

Umami is a perception of these molecules, which informs the stomach to prepare a welcome for *moong*. The stomach, which is full of acid, is raring to go with a burst of pepsin by the time the *moong* arrives. Pepsin cracks up the long protein chains into smaller dipeptides and peptides, ready for the next stage of digestion in the small intestine. Here, enzymes from both the pancreas and the intestinal lining work on these peptides to release amino acids.

The story now gets complicated.

That mouthful of *moong* has molecules that block the activity of these enzymes and prevent the absorption of amino acids. And yet, I assure you, this mouthful of *moong* is going to deliver the protein punch expected of it.

How can I be so sure?

## Soaking

This is the *Aha!* moment when I uncover the bowls on the kitchen counter.

The first has mixed pulses steeped in cold water. They have been soaking for the past 10 hours. Besides hydrating the seeds to soften them, water has dissolved out many anti-nutritional molecules. When these pulses are drained and washed before cooking, they will have lost tannins, lectins, phytates, and saponins – well, at least some of them. And, more noticeably, they will also have lost some of the non-digestible sugars that make them 'gassy'.

## Cooking

I am transferring the pulses to a steel bowl filled with cold water and placing them in the pressure cooker. They will now cook at a high temperature for at least twenty minutes. Yes, I need them to cook for that long for all the expected changes to take place:

- Carbohydrates will gelatinize
- Proteins will denature, making the work of the digestive enzymes easier
- Heat will also destroy the molecules the seed uses to defend itself against predators – the chemicals that block enzymes to leave protein undigested.

But cooking also releases vitamins, minerals, and many peptides and amino acids into the cooking water, which is really a very precious commodity, and must be carefully retained.

When the pulses are cooked, many of the beans burst their coats. Miraculously, the hard, indigestible, perhaps even poisonous, seed has been transformed into a creamy mouthful of easily digestible protein that is unlikely to leave you feeling bloated or 'gassy'.

## Milling

*Besan* is the most commonly milled flour, though *channa* is also milled with its husks intact in the Bihari staple of *sattu*.

Many pulses and *dals* are powdered for 'special effects' in traditional cuisine – and some of these are spectacular. They can be milled very fine for delicious sweets and pastries; a little more coarsely for our inexhaustible range of crisps – *pappad, murukku, bhajia* – each with a regional flavour that makes it unique. Even more coarse powders are used as spice powders and chutneys.

No matter what the particle size, milling adds to the deactivation of anti-nutrients, and makes the protein in the pulse easily available for digestion by enzymes, which are no longer challenged by antagonistic molecules.

## Roasting

Roasted pulses, usually *channa,* are India's most cherished street snack. Spiced delectably, or just salted, or with no additive at all, a cornucopia of roasted *channa* enlivens the most dejected pedestrian. Marinated in fiery spices and roasted crisp, as *channa zor garam, varapayar, porikallu,* the mixture of germinated pulses provides a zesty shot of protein with every mouthful.

Roasting inactivates many of the anti-nutritional elements, but germination does even more.

## Germinating

The next bowl on the counter has mixed sprouts.

All pulses can be germinated under favourable conditions of moisture and temperature.

Steep them, drain them, leave them in a warm place with just enough moisture not to dry out, and tender shoots will show themselves within 24 hours.

Like all embryos, sprouts need enormous amounts of energy. The hard protein and the complex sugars must now become more accessible to deliver it.

Naturally, then, the molecules that kept the proteins tightly coiled and sugars in unwieldy chains, must now step back to permit the seed's own enzymes to work.

This change occurs within 24 hours of incubation, and gains in strength as the enzymes break up protein chains.

Think of sprouts as baby food. They contain predigested carbohydrates and proteins and so have a higher amount of simple sugars and amino acids than the parent seed.

As the seed continues to sprout, molecules that we regard as harmful gradually quit. A new range of bio-active compounds appear. These are strong anti-oxidants.

Fats are also broken down into compounds that are biologically important SCFAs.

## Fermenting

The last bowl contains *idli* batter. This is a mixture of rice and *urad dal* soaked together and then ground to a paste.

I left the bowl on the counter overnight. This has invited a host of bacteria (the *Lactobacillus* microbiome) to flourish and begin the process of fermentation. These microbes digest the *urad dal* first by breaking down the phytates around the protein. As this takes place without oxygen, lactic acid is produced and carbon dioxide is liberated. Acidity further stimulates the *dal*'s inherent enzymes (proteases) to break down protein. It also increases the availability of vitamins, minerals and SCFAs. In short, fermentation converts a hard recalcitrant protein into a generous and yielding source of amino acids.

Because of its combination with rice, *urad*'s amino acids are completed by sulfur-containing amino acids.

All pulses can be fermented, but some of them sour quickly and luckily for us, smell so bad that we can avoid getting poisoned!

Yes, *proteins are full of hazards,* most of which we have learned to counter by our clever cooking methods.

But despite our culinary skills, pulses and *dals* sometimes pose challenges very difficult to overcome. The 'hard to cook' pulse is one of them. No matter that you've bent over backwards to follow all the rules, after half an hour cooking time those pulses still eyeball you with a stony glare.

Relax.

Throw them out.

They are beyond rescue with asafoetida or papaya or soda or salt.

Stony they are and stony they will stay. This is a problem between the farmer and the retailer. The storage of pulses and *dals* can alter conditions within the seed and make it impermeable to protein breakdown.

G-6PD* deficiency is a rare genetic condition that makes the red blood cells breakdown easily. One of the triggers is the broad or fava bean (*Vicia faba*). With the possible exception

---

*Glucose 6-phosphate dehydrogenase.

of broad beans, other legumes seem to cause little harm.

The Parsi community has a high incidence of this disorder.

Neolathyrism is a neurological disease that results in lower limb paralysis. In the 1960s it was related to the long-standing consumption of *kesari dal* (*Lathyrus sativus*) – *kesari* or *keerai* in local Hindi and Bhojpuri. Its cultivation was banned, and it disappeared from markets.

But rural populations continue to consume *kesari dal.* The incidence of paralysis, though, is not noticeable. This has prompted many states to withdraw the ban on the specious argument that people should not be deprived of a cheap protein source. In my opinion, *kesari dal* is a protein source that will prove very expensive indeed if there is even one case of the dreaded illness linked with it.

As *kesari dal* very closely resembles *masoor dal,* people can easily be misled into buying it.

Pulses and *dals* nourish and civilize us – *if we are civilized in the way we consume them.* If we use science with intelligence, a pot of this delicious protein is our best ticket to health.

# Cereals

A cereal is not a jigsaw puzzle in a cardboard box. It is the seed of an edible grass that has been cultivated out of its grassiness and has become a powerhouse of energy.

Rice, wheat, millets are all ancient foods. They no longer resemble their ancestors, but then, do we?

The sudden food consciousness of an obese and diabetic world has made cereals suspect. We look at rice and think diabetes. As for wheat, we could be gluten intolerant. Millets that have sustained the poor for millennia are now being loaded with fat and tarted up as fine dining. And the nation glides on a slither of oats.

Whatever happened to yesterday's staples: rice, rice flakes, puffed rice, rice flour. Wheat, *atta, daliya* or *lapsi,* pasta.

We are still eating all of that too. With a shudder, perhaps, or with guilt because we are really hooked to our traditional way of eating.

Take a pause, please. I have questions: *What's wrong with rice and wheat?* We have been eating them for millennia – are they really making us diabetic and gluten-sensitive?

By the way, we are also intolerant of FODMAPs* present in all *dals* and most vegetables. The very sight of an egg imperils our immortal souls. We couldn't possibly endure meat and fish, we are *shuddha shakahari*. What's left? Cannibalism might be our only ticket to survival. And that should be easy. Cannibalism of the spirit is a national tradition, so why not roast your neighbour for dinner tonight? Just make sure you use pure ghee.

Food fadism is a symptom of surfeit. Add greed to that, and we will find ourselves besieged not just by obesity and diabetes, but by ills we haven't yet discovered.

So please, please, look at cereals with respect. They still nourish the world. Don't blame your ills on them. Take some responsibility for how you cook and serve them, and watch their 'ill effects' vanish.

India, like all tropical cultures, does not have a high-fat, high-protein dietary base. We couldn't metabolize the Western diet even if we tried – veering towards it has already landed us in trouble.

Rice, wheat, and millets have sustained us since 10,000 BCE – isn't it time we returned the favour and made their cultivation and their cultivators more secure?

---

*Acronym from *fermentable oligosaccharides, disaccharides, monosaccharides, and polyols.*

One of a group of compounds thought to contribute to the symptoms of irritable bowel syndrome and similar gastrointestinal disorders. The term is used mainly with reference to a diet that is low in these compounds (which are mainly carbohydrates): foods high in FODMAPs include barley, yoghurt, apples, apricots, pears, and cauliflower. Sufferers of bloating and other digestive complaints can gain relief from their symptoms by following a low FODMAP diet.

## Rice

Rice *does not* cause diabetes.

Nor is it true that eating only brown, red, or black rice will keep you safe from diabetes.

We might need to do that if we ate nothing but rice and only rice and always rice – but how many of us do?

So, dear home cook, if you've just set the pressure cooker with ordinary white *kolam* or *basmati,* relax. You aren't pushing the family into disaster.

You are also serving enough pulses and *dals,* enough vegetables, and a dollop of dairy, to provide what rice cannot. And under their tutelage, those perfectly fluffed tender grains steaming on your plate will curb their enthusiasm to flood you with glucose. Once more, it is not *what you eat,* but *how you eat* that makes all the difference.

So, before we get talking about rice, let us find out what the bad press is all about.

'White' rice is the rice everybody usually eats, the grain (or seed) stripped not just of its husk, but also of two further elements: the aleurone layer and the embryo. It has lost fibre, vitamin B, a jot of protein, and all its fat. What's left? Carbohydrate, protein, and a dusting of trace elements.

If you want to talk chemistry, most of the interesting chemicals in rice are confined to the bran, the husk, the *bhoosa* that humans don't eat.

Bran is rich in fat (20%), mostly linoleic, oleic, and palmitic acids, since you asked.

Of course, bran is all fibre – undigestible polysaccharides. It is bursting with vitamins and minerals – but what's the use? We home cooks can use rice bran oil, but that closes our deal with *bhoosa*. On to the real stuff.

The rice usually eaten in India is prized for aroma and texture. It is milled – dehusked and polished. It has very little fibre (0.5–1%). The soluble dietary fibre is made up of arabinoxylans and β-d-glucan. Insoluble dietary fibre is made up of cellulose, hemicellulose.

The carbohydrate is starch, almost all of it highly and immediately digestible. This has made rice our staple nutrient. It has the ability to deliver a hefty and immediate burst of energy. Indian rural diets generally have a mound of rice with only a ladle of *dal* or buttermilk for accompaniment. This sterling quality of rice works against us when we turn sedentary, and load our diet with concentrated sugars and fats. The actual culprits are these recent add-ons, but rice gets all the blame.

*What about protein?*

Rice protein is superior to other cereal proteins because it is rich in lysine. As further commendation, lysine is less irritant to the intestinal lining, and could act as a strong anti-inflammatory.

One of the traditional uses of *rice kanji* is to stop loose stools: this has been dismissed as nothing more than the stickiness of starch, which absorbs liquid to form a mass. But there is much more to this quality of rice than that, and much of it may have to do with the quality of rice protein. The main protein, 65%, is glutelin; 15% albumins-globulins and 20% prolamins make up the rest of the protein in milled polished rice.

Yes, those fractions do matter to us home cooks. Glutelin is alkali soluble – the restaurant trick of adding a pinch of soda to the cooking water washes out a good bit of glutelin. Albumin and globulins are water soluble, so we do lose a lot if rice is washed vigorously before cooking. Adding salt to cooking water removes some more. With all these limitations, a meal serving of white rice (50 gm) will still provide as much protein as the white of 1 egg.

Brown rice has some added benefits: fibre, bioactive phenols, a bunch of B vitamins and all the minerals you need.

*Why do we still eat white rice?*

Taste. Texture. Short cooking time.

Brown rice quickly goes 'off' in a few hours. If your senses are intact, you'll detect a sour, rather nasty undertow. This is because fat in the retained layers oxidizes and turns rancid.

What about the rice of many colours – red, black, purple? What are their magical qualities?

The colour – shiny mulberry black, delicious violet, delicate old rose – is a joy in itself. It is anthocyanin. This pigment is an anti-oxidant and a free radical scavenger, which means they limit tissue damage – always a happy thought. Other health claims are numerous and very vociferous – but have little scientific basis.

Yes, brightly coloured rices are great molecules with tremendous potential, but we still need evidence that they pull off their magic when swallowed.

By and large, the Western insistence on whole grains and anthocyanins is justified by their high-fat and high-protein diet, which encourages and sustains constipation. On a vegetarian diet, which is largely carbohydrate-based, we don't need this insistence – *provided we eat enough vegetables.*

White rice is dehusked and polished in the mill. This is

a fairly recent innovation, no older than a century. Before industrialization, rice was hand-pounded.

Rice is a labour-intensive grain, and through millennia, this labour has been carried out by women. Paddy transplanting and field labour apart, the post-harvest work is enormous.

Traditional treatments of rice are parboiling, flaking, puffing, and milling to form flour – every part of the subcontinent is familiar with these.

Parboiling rice puts paddy through three steps: soaking, steaming, drying. Soaking, which traditionally is overnight at room temperature, dissolves the minerals in the husk and drives them into the endosperm.

When this soaked grain is steamed at 100°C, starch gelatinizes partially. This process achieves enrichment with minerals and retention of some amount of vitamin B.

Parboiling increases cooking time. It also reduces shelf life as it makes the grain prone to insect infestation.

Aflatoxins, from *Aspergillus* fungi, which contaminate fatty rice bran, are not always completely removed by parboiling, but washing and cooking in excess water gets rid of their traces.

Nutritionally, parboiling converts much of the starch into low glycaemic resistant starch.

Flaking – the formation of *aval/poha/chira* and puffing are older than memory, and the stuff of folklore, poetry, and legend. And why shouldn't this be? It is surely the acme of culinary imagination – to transform a hard grain with a very long cooking time and short viability into an instant snack with a long shelf life. Its energy content is concentrated weight for weight as it is dehydrated – and oh, it is so quickly hydrated to make – well, just about anything! Home cooks are never without this culinary shortcut to instant energy.

Rice flour is the basis of snacks and desserts in the south and the east. At one end of the spectrum are soft, spongy delectables in fudgy, caramel-y, or creamy sauce – think *peethe,* think *modak,* think *payasam.* The other end is the snap crackle and swagger brigade of crisps, *murukku, pappad, vadagam,* and a hundred varieties of each. Rice flour does it all. You can, of course, shrug it all off as 'just starch'. Or, you can get hooked on it.

India's 'trail mix' is *chivda, chidva or mixture.* Call it what you will, it is irresistible: rice flakes or puffed rice, nuts, raisins, *channa,* a sprinkling of various kinds of sev, and all the *masala* your soul desires. It is often the energy equivalent of a full meal.

Cooking rice is an art that must be fine-tuned to the type of rice and the dish it is meant for. It must also be in tune with the accompanying dish, principally the protein.

There are two usual ways:

- The first, the traditional, where rice is cooked in excess water, and the water is drained off.
- The second, in the pressure cooker or rice cooker, where the water is measured in and absorbed completely by the rice.

Getting rid of excess water gets rid of any residual toxins, but also of minerals and vitamins that have leached out. Pressure cooking destroys aflatoxins with the high temperature and pressure, and the leached out minerals and vitamins are absorbed back in again. It is also quicker and infinitely less messy.

All plant-based foods were, not so long ago, active forms of life. We predators deny them this history. To us, they are simply produce. But plants are responsible for the upkeep of the soil, which they detoxify to an amazing degree by absorbing contaminants, which we predators, quadruped and biped, then consume.

Arsenic is one of these contaminants. Rice absorbs and concentrates the arsenic present in ground water. Inorganic arsenic is found in the outer bran layer of the grain. Brown rice retains much of this arsenic. White rice still may have enough to be significant. Vigorous washing removes most of the surface arsenic. Parboiling removes all of it. Cooking in excess water and draining off the excess is the surest way.

While all samples of rice grown anywhere may contain some amount of arsenic, it is of importance to know if cooked rice still retains this toxin.

In India, where ground water is industrially contaminated, market surveillance is poor, and there is no way of knowing where rice is sourced from. It is imperative that apex bodies should enforce standard procedures of labelling rice.

Can an obese diabetic nation continue to thrive on white rice?

Yes! Just make certain there are delicious helpings of pulses and vegetables next to that steaming mound of fluffy rice.

## Wheat

Wheat almost equals rice in popularity as a staple food. Almost – as wheat, or as wholehearted whole wheat flour. But in its avatar as that refined weak-kneed white stuff, *maida*, it is way more popular than rice.

*Maida* is probably the sole reason why we are obese and diabetic. But rice, unfairly, gets all the blame.

Take a stroll down your local Khau Galli this evening, and you'll find that *maida* is the star at almost every outlet. The high-end patisserie, the humble sandwich stall, the gargantuan *samosa kadhai,* and the momo steamer, all of them bank on *maida*. The reason is evident: crumb or crust, *maida* is both crisp and tender. But, it takes a lot of fat to keep it so.

*What is* maida?

It is wheat flour milled to a very fine particle size and 'refined' by filtering out all the bran. This results in a flour that has less gluten than *atta*. There are various grades of *maida,* which a baker recognizes, but the home cook encounters only the industrial soft white flour sold as superfine *maida*.

The trouble with *maida* is not the absence of bran. It is the presence of toxic bleaching agents that are used to render the flour a dazzling white. Among these is alloxan, a laboratory drug used in experimental diabetes studies to induce diabetes. Alloxan destroys the insulin-producing cells of the pancreas. It is highly toxic. It is no use selling the line that the amount of alloxan in *maida* is too small to be significant. That's simply inviting trouble.

China was the latest nation to ban bleached flour in 2011. European countries banned it long ago. USA still markets it.

*Maida* came to us from America in the 1950s. My parents called it 'American flour' well into the 1960s. But Americans do have the option of buying safe unbleached flour. We don't.

For Indians, just now, facing the pandemic while teetering on the edge of diabetes, *maida* is a killer. And we eat it all the time.

*Why bleach flour?*

A few years ago, I asked a number of leading flour manufacturers this question. Their answer was: 'India likes purity. Flour must be pure white for it to sell.'

Says who?

Yes, we do need *maida* for a number of treats that won't, can't, or haven't yet worked with plain old atta. Treats, not every day food.

We still eat a huge amount of maida in convenience foods – bread and biscuits. That's an awful lot of bleaching agents and additives and, well, alloxan.

So, you eat only brown bread?

Artisanal bread form a high-end boulangerie?

Sorry guys, a big fraction of that brown loaf is still maida.

If you are preparing to eat your way past pandemics, dear home cook, just say no to *maida*. At least, until there is a ban on bleached flour.

Wheat is usually eaten as *atta*, the whole grain flour.

But the grain is also sold broken – to various grades of fineness: from coarse gravel like *daliya*, to finer *lapsi kansar*, to sandy semolina/*rava*/*sooji*. And, of course, generously gifted to us from Italy, pasta. ('Noodles' unless specified otherwise, are a maida product.)

In addition to these familiar foods, wheat extract is cooked as a traditional food for toddlers. (The canny *halwai* also uses it for luxurious *halwas*.)

For practical purposes, cooking with whole wheat flour – *atta* – or one of the processed products in the last paragraph – is the same as cooking with the whole wheat grain. 100 gm of *atta* provides a hefty dose of energy: 70 gm+ of carbohydrates,

10 gm of protein, 2 gm or less of fat.

*Maida* – unbleached, sold in other countries as white flour, all purpose flour, or cake flour – is made from the endosperm of the grain, and so has more starch and a lower protein content.

Wheat protein is poor in lysine – particularly the proteins found in white flour.

The carbohydrate is 80% starch; the rest consists of indigestible and fermentable sugars, among which fructans form an important group.

Resistant starches from the grain also contribute to fermentable sugars. In addition, free sugar, as sucrose, can be detected in the sweet taste of the flour.

'Phytochemicals' is a convenient label for the crowd of molecules in plant foods that don't nourish, but nonetheless act on body processes. Most of these are contained in the bran and aleurone layer. So while *atta* is bursting with phytochemicals, *maida* misses out on the entire lot.

I often think of *atta* and *maida* as a tough pair of jeans and delicate silk *saree*. Can't do without those jeans to ride rough shod through life, but who can resist the glamour of silk?

## Millets

Our ancestors thrived on millets. Home cooks from the Indus Valley and Kutch – the Sindhu-Saraswati gang – weren't hot on washing up, and their pots and pans have vestiges of the last meal before the party broke up. Their forbears, earlier settlers in the upper Indus Valley from 3,000–2,800 BCE, relied more on large grained cereals – wheat and barley for the most part. Rice hadn't shown up yet.

But after 2,000 BCE when aridity began to set in, and the civilization shifted south to Kutch and its borders, millets became the staple. These small grained cereals didn't require as much moisture, and even when the rivers dried up, one could hope for a small harvest of millet from occasional rains.

The millets they ate are still staples in rural India. They are truly, survival foods. Sorghum, pearl millet, finger millet, foxtail millet, common millet, little millet, barnyard millet, and kodo millet.

These English names are confusing, so I'll stick with those in common use:

*Jowar*: sorghum, *juar, cholam*
*Bajra*: pearl millet, *kambu, sahjjalu*
*Ragi*: finger millet, *kelvaragu, nachni, mandua, nagli*
*Tenai*: foxtail millet, *kangni, navane, thina, kang*
*Kutki*: little millet, *samai, sava, gajro, kangani*
*Kodon*: kodo millet, *varagu, kodra*
*Barre*: proso millet, *panivaragu, vari, cheena*
*Sanwa*: barnyard millet, *oodalu, kuthiravaali, shamul*

Millets are not 'instant energy' cereals like rice or wheat. The interaction between their protein and carbohydrate content slows down digestion, and provides a slow and sustained release of energy. In addition, they work towards maintaining a healthy microbiome, thereby lowering insulin resistance.

Millets have been the chosen food of the poor for their ability to satisfy hunger for a long period of time. They were travel foods of choice in the past for much the same reason.

Reintroducing them into modern cuisine has been done energetically of late. The more muscle, the less brain. The new roles thrust on millets don't often sit easy on neither palate nor stomach. It makes little sense to foist them on high-fat snacks like bakery items or fried snacks.

A biscuit made of ragi is still a biscuit. Its biscuit-ness relies on crunch and crunch is a function of fat.

Why not take another look at traditional forms of serving up millets?

The most common is porridge – combinations of flours, usually millets, that are cooked to a gel and served as is, with flavoursome gravy or chutney, or with buttermilk or milk. They are crowd pleasers too – delicious and quick to cook and eat. The best breakfast in the world.

They are also cooked dry as *roti* or *bhakhri*. They can also be combined with wheat flour to make excellent multigrain flours for anything that takes your fancy!

## 'Healthy' Grains

A word about the 'healthy grains' that have us all in a buying frenzy, foisting onto the family strange grey-brown clumps of unfamiliar matter guaranteed to quell the pandemic and provide immortality. Even more wonderfully, their sudden appearance in health stores seems to have declared everything else we eat as unhealthy. What are these – they can't be that new as they're usually labelled 'ancient grains'.

The wheat panic has the West in its grip and its rumbles can be felt here too. 'Gluten sensitive' is quite the thing – a diagnosis usually made after a quick Google search. At a time when anxiety and panic is almost constant, so are digestive troubles. Food labels readily cater to anxieties, and every recipe on the net now has its 'gluten free' equivalent.

*What is gluten?*

It is a group of proteins in the wheat endosperm, and made up of two major proteins, *glutenin* and *gliadin*. Together, when hydrated, they produce the familiar elasticity of wheat dough.

Gluten can trigger an immune reaction in the intestinal lining – *as can any protein*. In its severe from, gluten can set off a condition called *Celiac Disease*. This is a special disease entity, quite different from the usual 'gluten sensitivity', which has a different label: *Non-Celiac Gluten Sensitivity*. Before you claim this label for yourself, please consult your doctor.* As wheat is such an important and ubiquitous source of energy, this is not a diagnosis that should be made loosely as in: 'I think I have it.' Let your doctor decide.

'Ancient grains' hit the market in the wake of worry about gluten sensitivity, which is blamed on new cultivars of wheat.

To begin with, what's so ancient about these grains?

Einkorn and emmer have a Middle Eastern pedigree dating back to 10,000 BCE. *Durum wheat*, used in the making of semolina and pasta, is similar to these, and they have the same species name, *Triticum turgidum*. Modern wheat, relatively modern since it is just about 3,000 years old, is a hybrid of emmer and wild goat grass, *Triticum tauschii*. The plant has adapted to domestication by growing a husk that can be easily separated by winnowing, as compared to the

*All cereals contain proteins, which are called prolamins, because they are rich in two amino acids – proline and glutamine. They have different names in different cereals: hordein in barley, secalin in rye, zein in maize. (The prolamin of rice is a very small fraction, and it is indigestible.) Gliadin is a prolamin. Glutenins are a more complex group. 'Gluten related disorders' cover all sorts of tummy troubles after consuming wheat.

older hulled variety. The old hulled variety persists today as *spelt*. These three, *einkorn, emmer* and *spelt* are regarded as ancient wheats.

Are these ancient wheats better in any way?

Are they less likely to induce gluten sensitivity?

Studies crowd the internet, none of them convincing.

But dinky little packets of these ancients do jostle for space in grocery stores.

Other unfamiliar cereals too are becoming visible: *buckwheat, teff, quinoa* – the last, of course, has great press as the wonder food of the Aztecs. They are probably all good as occasional diversions, but please don't let them displace our wonderful range of Indian cereals as yet.

Why not give our spectrum of millets a try?

## Baking

The lockdown brought about the Great Baking Revolution. We baked only some, but we *ate* baked all the time.

Baking is, supposedly, the use of dry heat to cook your food.

How is it different from cooking on a tawa on your gas stove? That's dry heat too, isn't it?

Absolutely, if you stick with definitions.

Ah, but you've spotted the difference – tawa crisp is stiff, turning tough. Oven baked is *tender*. The tenderness comes from *fat*.

Baking is the smartest way of concealing fat in the food. This is especially true when it relates to crisp stuff, like biscuits.

Our nation is fuelled by biscuits.

The market is worth US$ 5–5.5 billion. Plain biscuits

make up 25%. Cream biscuits and cookies account for 35–40% of that amount. The rest is taken up by cookies.

The difference between a cookie and a biscuit may seem culinary nitpicking, but ask the ten-year-old consumer. She'll tell you in excruciating detail how much crumblier, juicier, chewier, simply more delicious a cookie is compared to a rough hard dry biscuit.

Two factors make the difference: shorter baking time, and – you guessed it – more fat and more sugar. There is simply more biscuit in a cookie.

A sweet biscuit/cookie ticks all the boxes for the brain's pleasure factors: texture, taste, and content. Feeding a child biscuits entrains a higher setting of sugar and fat for pleasure perception. It is the first step to insulin resistance. A biscuit or two won't make any such difference, but a whole packet will – a packet is usually six biscuits, and is the most common filler in a child's lunch box for the short break.

Just wake up to it. There is no way you can make biscuits a healthy habit for your child. They can't substitute for food. Like cake, biscuits are dessert.

We do consider cake to be a treat. Biscuits, though, are eaten all the time, anywhere, everywhere. And for us adults, it's disastrous.

Parle-G was the highest selling biscuit on the planet in 2011, and the organization claims that 16,383,600 Parle-G rolls are eaten every hour.

During the pandemic, biscuit manufacturers registered this increased demand with jubilation. It seems right to assume that the more you work from home, the more biscuits you eat.

And strange as it sounds, industrial baked products are

less harmful than those at your neighbourhood bakery, be it that hole-in-the wall honest-to-goodness bun and biscuit affair or the high-end patisserie with a lone macron poised like a jewel on a silk-draped pedestal as display. The reason is that the fat and sugar content is so much more uncontrolled, even if it isn't margarine but olive oil, not bone-bleached white poison, but genuine unrefined Demerara dark.

The bottom line on baked goods is: *the lighter, the crisper, the crumblier it is, the more fat it contains.* And I am talking bun and biscuit, not croissant or cake.

# Spices

Spice is a metaphor for India. We were, once, the very soul of everything aromatic and perfumed on the planet. Our spices changed the course of world history. We either grew them, or they swept through our ports. Pepper, cardamom, mace, nutmeg, cloves, cinnamon, cumin, and coriander – their names, like musical notes, sang our story.

It is a bitter irony that today, when we say *spicy*, we mean just the one spice that isn't even remotely Indian.

We call the irritant heat of chilli *spicy*. The only spice we seem to acknowledge is this ubiquitous, paralyzing, vesicant, taste-destructive chilli. It is no spice at all. It is just a slap of insult on the trusting tongue.

Have you not found it strange that most Indian languages should use the same word for chillies and pepper? The only qualifier is the colour. Green distinguishes one type of chilli from the black sort – *hari mirch, pacchai milagai*. The puzzle is easily solved. We have only known chilli for 500 years. The Nuahatl word *chilli* (which should be pronounced 'cheeli') sank comfortably into Indian English. Unlike pepper, this new plant grew like a weed. Hot stuff, and practically free, what's not to like? Pepper it was – just of a different hue.

The original pepper that shaped our destiny in so many ways is all but forgotten, its wit erased by chilli's malice.

I'm omitting chilli from this conversation – reasons later. The very mention of it is inflammatory, so let me drain a glass of cold water before I open the spice box.

Ah, your spices too are stored like mine in a dark cool place? And do you too feel that frisson of mystery as you uncap those bottles?

Here we are, then.

Cinnamon, curls of scented bark.

A current of clove, shrill as a sliver of ice.

Warm nutmeg, sweet mace.

Cardamom, luxurious and generous, secret within tiny pods, and its earthier cousin, muscled with instinct alone.

Dry as old wood, hard as stone – why are spices so heady with romance? Why do they make us dream?

But it is a brisk week day and to hell with romance. The morning's been brutal. I need a good lunch to tame the rest of the day, and I reach for reality. Intelligent cumin, humorous coriander, sharp-tongued pepper, tart tamarind, and, because I need everything to fall in place with *Main Hoon Na* assurance, a sprig of curry leaf.

Those were purposeful adjectives. I plan on getting these spices to perform those roles by treating each in a particular way.

I will bruise the cumin very lightly with mortar and pestle. I will roast the *dhaniya* till the aroma changes from cloying floral to hearty chuckle – a shade hotter and it will turn into pure satire. Pepper will lose its rebuke and sparkle with wit in the dull company of coconut. As it gossips with jaggery and ginger, tamarind has the merest hint of scandal. A quick sear of aniseed, and those vegetables begin to smile.

Another day, the very same spices will sing a different *raga*.

Cumin may strike a grave note, coriander turn girlish, tamarind sting, pepper bite, *saunf* giggle.

It all depends on the menu.

The company these spices keep (with or without water), the temperature, and the particle size change their flavour profiles. And who knows that better than the traditional Indian home cook with her arsenal of *masalas*?

Wet pastes, powders coarse and fine, *masala* blends control the narrative. The actual food passes unnoticed, overshadowed by the *masala* and its aggressive seasonings. All very delicious, until you take pause to ask – what's missing?

The food, of course!

Flavour and aroma are just grand illusions – but so grand that we assure ourselves that without them food will be bland and uninteresting.

I urge you to try a small experiment.

When you are hungry, fill one *katori* with rice cooked without salt, and another with *dal* (any) also cooked without salt. Also, keep ready a hot *roti*.

Now try a few grains of rice. Hold them in your mouth. Chew. What did you smell and taste?

Repeat with the *dal* and the *roti* (separately).

Now that you have discovered the concealed flavour of these foods, do you still want to conceal them?

Why not use spices to make the food shine through?

Use a pinch of *masala* instead of a teaspoonful.

Begin with turmeric. A generous pinch will do the job without swamping all other aromas.

Ditto asafoetida (*hing*).

Ditto *garam masala.*

These are belligerent flavours that bully the rest into silence.

Curry leaves do the same, if more winsomely. All fresh herbs quickly step back, unlike the dry concentrates that tend to hover.

Time now to challenge those rules cut in stone, with a quick True/False Q&A:

1. Before you powder whole spices or use them to flavour the dish, they must be roasted till pedestrians out on the street look longingly up at your window.

   **FALSE**: All they need is mild heat to take away the surface moisture. If you roast or fry them as much as usual, the dish will be only faintly aromatic – most of the volatiles having long escaped.

2. Water is fatal to spice. It dilutes flavours.

   **FALSE.** In *pulaos* and *biryanis,* rice completely absorbs the bouquet of spices, as we well know. Steam suffuses aromatic oils through the mass of the cooking food. You can test this out by steaming vegetables with a few grains (three or four, no more) of *zeera*. You'll be able to enjoy the *zeera* flavour in every mouthful, even though you've used very little.

3. *Masalas* must be fried till they sweat out oil. A successful gravy must have an oil slick of glistening red – that is the vehicle for aroma and taste.

**FALSE.** The oil slick only shows that the *masala* has been fried out of its mind. As for flavours, most of them have long volatilized and you need to add a ton more to taste anything beyond caramelized onions, charred garlic, and tomato concentrate. And as for the actual food – where did it go?

4. Tempering: the *tadka*. Also called *poriccha kottal, chhonk, vaghar,* and *baghaar,* this needs all the oil and *ghee* you can give it.

**FALSE.** This is the very soul of Indian cuisine, and before you plunge the kitchen knife into my renegade heart, I love the *tadka,* the *poriccha kottal,* the *vaghar,* the *chhonk,* the *baghaar* as much as you do!

It can either start off the dish or finish it, take your pick. It can contain one spice or five, it can have a sprinkling of *dal* or not, it can have bay leaves or curry leaves. It can have the buzz of asafoetida or the backchat of mustard. You can use *ghee* or the oil that speaks to your soul. All this, dear fellow home cook I grant you –

BUT ...

Consider, I pray, the purpose of the *tadka.*

It is meant to temper; to suffuse the flavour of the spice through the food, to subtly alter its taste.

The food has to capture the volatiles released at a high temperature – the food is also at a high temperature, so there's steam everywhere. Steam is a wonderful solvent – it beats oil any day, every day. So, the amount of oil you need for the *tadka* is very little – just enough to contain your spices. When it begins to sizzle, add it to the food and slam on a lid. Those flavours will be captured avidly by the food. One gentle stir is all you need. Keep it covered for a few minutes. Go on, try it with one-fifth if not one-tenth the oil or *ghee* you usually use!

5. Spices are good for you. They are full of magic molecules that raise immunity, quell heart disease and diabetes, and make certain you'll never grow a cancer.
   **TRUE.** *But only if you're feeding them to a bunch of lab rats.* You, I take it, are feeding your family.

   Yes, spices contain wonder molecules. But if you cook with them in the concentrations required to produce these effects, they would be probably intolerable and certainly toxic.

   So, let the aroma and flavour of spices enhance the joys of the foods that nourish and sustain you – *but don't let them interfere with it.*

# Vegetables

Vegetarian India does *not* eat vegetables. Not enough, anyway. It took me very long to realize this and, when I did, the reasons were hiding in plain sight. So let's get to your fridge and see what you have by way of vegetables...

Oh, you're all out of them?

To the market, then!

This is the part most home cooks love: a leisurely trawl through the market, stopping by their favourite carts and stalls, chatting up the philosophers of the agora – realists all, they would put any ancient Greek to shame with their logic. Yes, there's business to be done, but intent on Socratic dialogue, the transaction is a mere irritant.

The market is still an impressionistic blur of colour, shape, and texture. It attains focus as I offload my purchases into the kitchen sink. A brisk wash, and refreshed, the vegetables crowd the counter with brilliant colour.

Take a moment to feast your eyes on them, for they won't last long. Tender green, sunshine yellow, royal purple, shiny scarlet, flagrant orange, and hot pink, they will soon be disguised with body paint to a uniform yellow brown.

Touch them now. Feel their softness, their crisp juiciness, their firm stalks and turgid leaves, revel in their line and form. These too will disappear anon, reduced to a craven mush.

These joyous, vibrant vegetables will arrive at the dining table either kicking about morose in red, yellow, grey, or brown sludge, or else sit about dejectedly in greasy clumps, trailing a yellow slick.

This is what usually happens to our vegetables.

Unless, of course, you already know ...

### How NOT to Murder Your Vegetables

All manner of crimes are committed against vegetables in kitchens across the country every day. The cruelties perpetrated on these unresisting victims are usually heavily disguised, and so pass unnoticed. So hardened and inured are we to this form of domestic violence, that we react with outrage at the very suggestion that there might be a different way of dealing with vegetables.

I will pose just one question:

*What does the home cook want from her vegetables?*

The answer is evident: tenderness.

So why not show a little reciprocity?

To serve a vegetable cooked to perfection takes a little tenderness, a little skill, a lot of attention and intelligence, the occasional touch of spice, and practically no oil. It also takes very little time.

You might want to try it out.

Let's get the vegetables on the counter sorted by colour:

Green, yellow or red, and brown.

That's also a neat classification for cooking method and utensil.

| | | |
|---|---|---|
| Green | : | quick cooking |
| Yellow or red | : | medium |
| Brown | : | takes forever |

Green stuff is cooked in a skillet. Yellow or red takes a pan. Brown goes into the cooker.

Self-evident, eh?

Not really. It is, in fact, wide open to question.

The objective of cooking a vegetable is to make it edible. Chewy must turn tender. Tough must grow succulent. Bland must absorb enough flavour to turn tasty.

And, it should be easily digested.

Ouch.

That sounds like putting the vegetable in question through an Ivy League education. It cannot, apparently, *be*. It must *become*.

And in that process of becoming, it must surrender the qualities that make it a vegetable. It must lose appearance, colour, and texture to acquire flavours and tastes far removed from its own.

Is this necessary?

It is the usual, the traditional, the right thing to do, you retort. It has always been done this way! How can we digest vegetables otherwise?

The vegetable, any vegetable, has a certain structure. The structure is a functional design: it helps the plant thrive.

The plant cell structure is vital to understanding the

cooking process. Plant cells have tough walls that are composed of proteins and complex carbohydrates, celluloses, hemicelluloses, and pectins.

But that's just the packaging. What's inside?

The difference between plant and animal cells is based on sunlight.

Plant cells are empowered to manufacture food from sunlight.

We animals lack this, and so must depend on plants for survival.

Even the most dedicated carnivore can't survive without plants.

When a plant is harvested, it loses its capacity to manufacture food. However, for a while, it continues its activity of respiration till water loss puts a stop to it. That's the difference between fresh and wilting vegetables. The crispness, juiciness, and turgor of vegetables and fruits depends on their water content, and the integrity of their cell walls in preserving this.

Vendors soak their vegetables in water to 'refresh' them, quite successfully too, as vegetables soak up some water to replace losses within their cells.

Plants store their energy as starch – as amylose (20%); as amylopectin (80%). This is stored as granules. The structure of the starch determines the texture of the cooked vegetable, particularly in energy-rich roots and tubers.

Plant cells are glued together with a mixture of hemicellulose and pectins. As a plant stops growing, this cement is transformed into the more rigid lignin. This is what we test for when we snap a French bean or okra to test for freshness – what we are testing for is youth. The older bean and okra lacks snap because the cement between plant cells has begun to change into the stiffer molecule.

Our digestive enzymes deal easily with amylose, but not with cellulose, which passes on, undigested, into the large intestine.

Cellulose is insoluble in water.

The other two complex carbohydrates in plant cells are soluble – hemicellulose and pectin. They form a clear gel when hydrated. (In making jam, this is the change you watch for as the cooking mixture of fruit and sugar 'gels'.)

Hemicellulose and pectins too are indigestible.

So, the bulk of the vegetables we eat is indigestible. And it is this quality that makes them so necessary to good health.

Make no mistake, vegetables and fruits are our only defense against this and other pandemics. Isn't it important, then, to cook them right?

The insoluble cellulose makes for stool 'bulk' and soaks up all the toxins and nasty molecules in the large intestine. It is the prize ticket out of constipation.

Soluble hemicelluloses and pectins maintain the microbiome in a state of health by fermentation.

*The true purpose of eating plant food is to provide our bodies with the right sort of indigestible starch, so that our energy balance can be maintained through the action of insulin.*

So, you see, the purpose of cooking vegetables is not to make them digestible, but to make their stored starches and other bioactive molecules accessible to us. Cooking softens plant cell walls and loosens the cement between them. We achieve this through heat, water, and a change of pH.

If the cement preferentially breaks down, the cooked

vegetable turns mushy. Let us follow the stages of making the standard tomato-onion base for a gravy:

1. Chopped onions are sautéed in a little oil. At a temperature around 60ºC, the onions will begin to sweat out water. This changes the texture from crisp to soft, the colour from white or mauve to a translucent pink.
2. In the next few minutes, as the temperature rises, cell walls disintegrate, and starch granules within the cells leak out into the cooking fluid. If you taste the juice now, you'll find it sweet.
3. As temperatures reach 160ºC and above, the cement between cells, hemicellulose and pectins, begins to dissolve, the cells separate, and the onions lose structure.
4. If you've added tomatoes *before* this step is reached, the onions will remain chewy. This is because the acid of tomato prevents the dissolution of the cement. Hemicellulose and pectins won't dissolve in acidic cooking liquid.
5. Also, at this stage, be sure to sprinkle water on the onions, so that they don't 'catch' and burn. If they do, please remember, it is not because you've added too little oil/*ghee*/butter as chefs will disapprovingly remark. They have their thought, I have mine. Sprinkle a little water and slam on that lid – a minute more, and the onions are ready to meet tomatoes.
6. Tomatoes have less cement between their cell walls, so they buckle quicker to form a mush.
7. Once you have a mush of onions and tomatoes, their sugars have leaked out. The colours begin to

brown as the Maillard Reaction takes place, and aromatic flavour chemicals are released. Inhale the toasty caramelly aroma you've been waiting for, as you take in the first hints of brown in the cooking mush. If you stop the cooking now, you will retain these flavours without destroying the other nutritive components we'll soon talk about – and I can't stress how important this is, particularly as 90% of chefs will recommend otherwise.

8. If you continue cooking, the Maillard Reaction will proceed to its end stage to form harmful compounds (AGEs* and acrylamide) and destroy all the nutritive elements.

The 'perfect' tomato-onion gravy is a nutritional disaster because of over-cooking. Why not give it a break and stop cooking a few minutes earlier?

*Why do we use tomatoes in the gravy at all?*

Tomatoes, like chilli and potatoes, are recent entrants to Indian cuisine. You won't find them in traditional recipes for festivals, for instance, not if you cook by the book. You won't find them in early Mughal cookbooks either, though you will find them in Avadhi cuisine.

We used something else then, didn't we?

We still do.

The fruit which visiting Arabs enjoyed so much they christened it the date of India, *tamar-al-hind,* now anglicized

---

*Advanced Glycation End Products [AGEs] are harmful compounds that are formed when protein or fat combine with sugar. This process is called glycation.

as *tamarind.* Other 'sours' in use before the Portuguese arrived were green mango (fresh or dried), lemons and citron, and particularly along the Western Coast, *kokum.**

We used these acids for more than taste.

Acids, as we noticed while making that gravy, stop the structural disintegration of vegetables. So, if you add any of these acids, even a squishy vegetable will sit up and take notice. Conversely, if you add acids *before* the vegetable has softened, it will stop cooking and stay raw.

I'm sure you have experienced this with brinjals and okra. Both are deceptively soft vegetables with minimal cooking time. But, occasionally, the okra keeps its feral bite, and the brinjal maintains a phlegmatic stolidity and will refuse to absorb flavours. Blame it on the acid.

Now that we have checked out how vegetable structure changes with temperature, what would be the best way to cook those colourful groups, and not turn them into grey mush?

*How does it matter if it is grey mush?*

Let me answer that with another question: Would you eat grey mush? Would your family?

Unless the recipe demands it, we need to cook vegetables so that we retain structure, texture, colour – *if we are to retain nutrition.*

90% of home cooks follow this schema for a simple sauté:

1. *Tadka* of chosen spice in oil/*ghee* (about one tbsp if cooking for 3).

---

*Kokum, *Garcinia indica,* is a story in itself. But that's an entire, and another, book!

2. Add 1 tsp of haldi (the weakhearted add only 1/2).
3. Add ginger-garlic paste and stir it around till the neighbours holler.
4. Now, add the cut vegetable (just the one sort), and keep on stirring.
5. Add salt and a multiplicity of *masala* powders, or none at all.
6. Add more oil so that it doesn't 'catch'.
7. Throw in a chiffonade of coriander, and serve.

Er ... serve *what*?

Limp and forlorn chunks and pieces glistening a dispirited yellow?

Could this, once, have been a handful of perky French beans? A jolly young cabbage? A moon slice of pumpkin? A cauliflower? All of these?

Tsk, tsk.

If you're in the happy 10% that doesn't follow these steps, congratulations. You can skip the next paragraph.

If, however, that is *your* way, and you ask with pugnacity, not curiosity, 'What's wrong with that?' I could tell you point for point – or suggest something that you can check out for yourself.

Let's do that sauté over again.

And, you know what? Let's break that golden rule and cook very different vegetables together: yellow pumpkin, green *parval*, snowy cauliflower, purple brinjal, white *doodhi*, perky okra, and solemn potato.

They are different in texture and content, and, therefore, have different cooking times.

We can cheat, to start with, by using a boiled potato.

Then, separate the okra and brinjal from the rest. Cauliflower, pumpkin, *doodhi,* and *parval* aren't exactly the same in water content and texture. So, let's cheat again to equalize their cooking times.

The cauliflower is divided into smaller florets, matched with the pumpkin cubes in size. *Parval* and *doodhi* are left unpeeled. All these go into a steel bowl, set in the pressure cooker, and steamed for one or two whistles, no more – that's two minutes.

When I open the cooker, the vegetables still look solid and colourful. They are only partially cooked. I slip them into the fridge to stop the cooking process.

Meanwhile, I have the pan ready for the sauté. A non-stick pan is never necessary if you cook with attention, but we'll use one today.

A few drops of oil to prime the pan.

And we'll use whole spices. So, let's settle for a classic *panch phoran**: *saunf, ajwain, kalonji, zeera,* and *methi* – a few grains of each, enough to fill a teaspoon. And, because I can seldom resist it, a bay leaf.

I slide in a teaspoon of oil (because *you* are cooking with me – else, I would only use half).

In with bay leaf and the spices.

Meanwhile, I've crushed a pod of garlic and a half-inch paw of ginger. In goes that too.

Also, I have sliced the brinjal and the okra – into the pan, a shake, the merest spritz of water, lower the heat, and cover.

---

*Literally, 'five spices' – fennel, brown mustard, nigella, cumin, and fenugreek.

The steamed vegetables are out of the fridge. This is the moment to peel the *parval* and *doodhi*. They emerge still crisp enough to cube. I dust them with a faint drift of turmeric and some *dhaniya* powder and salt.

Oops, I forgot that steamed potato, diced and waiting, on the counter.

I uncover the pan, and a fragrant steam wells out – the aroma is irresistible.

I test the okra and brinjal – they are tender, cooked to perfection in that minute of steam. The okra is bright green, the brinjal's purple has paled a shade, but is still a bright mauve.

I add the seasoned vegetables. Shake the pan. Cover.

A minute later, the sauté winks brightly up at me. Done!

Time now to tick boxes:

1. Colour : maintained
2. Structure : unspoilt
3. Texture : tender, not mushy; firm, not tough
4. Aroma : heady and appetizing
5. Mouthfeel : juicy, not oily
6. Taste : each vegetable has retained its distinctive taste while absorbing the flavours of the spices as accord
7. Utensils to be washed : 2 + stirrer
8. Total time : prepping vegetables: 5 min  
   cooker time: 3 min  
   in the pan: 5 min  
   washing up: 3 min

Really, what's not to like?

Yes, I agree, that was heavy on spice.

Let's use a different technique for a fresh, almost floral bouquet of green vegetables.

I have shredded a tender cabbage, broken a cauliflower into small florets, shelled a handful of peas, and sliced some beans.

We are going to blanch them.

A large saucepan of water is heating up. When it comes to a rolling boil, I drop in the vegetables.

They stay in the boiling water for a minute, no more.

Then, I drain them and plunge them into a waiting bowl of ice-cold water.

A minute there, and out they come, brisk and bright.

Go on! Taste it!

Of course, they aren't cooked yet, but can you taste that juice?

Ready for seasoning now.

I'm going to divide the vegetables into two lots at this point. Lot 1, I sprinkle salt and a few grains of sugar. Lot 2 is unseasoned.

I'm going to use the same tempering for both lots.

I have picked the classic: pinch of asafoetida, mustard seeds, a few grains of *urad dal*, and curry leaves. A drop of coconut oil + a few drops of any oil to rub the pan.

Lot 1: The tempering is ready when the mustard pops and the urad turns a lovely brown. In go the seasoned vegetables, pan shaken, heat reduced. A spritz of water, cover for a few seconds, then uncover and give it a minute.

Lot 2: I follow the same technique, but leave the lid on till the vegetables are cooked.

Let's compare the two lots.

The difference is striking at first look. Lot 1 looks bright. Lot 2 is dull in comparison. The beans and peas are no longer a striking green.

Can you guess why this happened?

We have only just started the conversation about vegetables. Because each one has a story to tell, I'll have to leave those stories for a longer book. But do remember that the quickest method of cooking vegetables is the best – and the reason is…

# Every Vegetable is a Pharmacy

*... and we are shopping over the counter without a prescription*

A little while ago, I made the outrageous claim that the only way we can fight this and other pandemics is with vegetables and fruits. It is a perfectly legitimate claim, but cannot be made with the 'this is good for you, so eat a ton of this' brand of wisdom.

Instead, we can alert ourselves to the best ways of preserving nutrients by cooking vegetables the right way.

What are these nutrients?

We can scarcely hope to garner enough carbohydrates, fats, or proteins from vegetables. For that, we plunder the hoard of energy in seeds meant to nourish the growing embryo.

What's left? Vitamins and minerals?

Yes, indeed, but also a growing library of magic molecules that we are just beginning to understand. They may indeed be the medicines of tomorrow, but they can be our nutrition now, to keep us from needing them as medicine in the future.

I expect we will be seeing all diseases from a different

perspective a few years from now. We will be looking at them from *our* point of view, not the germ's. COVID-19 has shown us that this paradigm shift is inevitable. It will no longer be about trapping the germ that causes a disease. It will be about equipping the body to respond intelligently to the threat of disease. Drugs and vaccines may take us past hiccups, but for the sustained response, health can only depend on our own body chemicals. And many of these will be manufactured from the vegetables and fruits we eat.

*Phytochemicals are chemicals in fruits, vegetables, grains, and other plant foods that may provide desirable health benefits beyond basic nutrition to reduce the risk of major chronic diseases.*

That's the tell-all definition of what we are looking for in vegetables.

A common denominator for all diseases is 'oxidative damage'. This refers to tissue injury caused by the accumulation of 'free radicals'. All cell processes liberate them in health, but they are quickly cleared away. In a diseased state, they persist or extend their sphere of damage. So, any chemical with the 'antioxidant' label tells you it contributes to tissue integrity and repair.

We need antioxidants to stay healthy, to organize accurate and effective immunity, and to achieve repair.

The antioxidant label is used widely.

So widely that it labels everything from hair gel to nail paint. Offices stock tons of the stuff as green tea. Cosmetic labels assure us that every wrinkle and spot will be instantly erased with its particular brand of antioxidant.

Antioxidants are today's bestselling version of yesterday's snake oil.

Perhaps I had better restate that.

Snake oil, the genuine article, has a market – but it doesn't sell as well as antioxidants.

This is terrible news for science.

Pop-ability is always a clear and present danger, as in: 'garlic is "good for you" so swallow a bulb a day, to hell with what it does to your platelet'.

This can have disastrous results as toxicity for most antioxidants has been documented quite commonly.

Equally dangerous is the dismissive cynicism such advertising rightly prompts. *How in heaven's name can antioxidants nourish your hair?*

Cynicism is a blindfold we don willingly and forget to slip off.

Meanwhile, what can home cooks do?

We are in luck. All we have to do is get the right fruits and vegetables, cook them right, and eat them sensibly as food – not as tonics or vitamin pills or aphrodisiacs or rejuvenators.

There are no superfoods, but there are super home cooks, you and… er… me.

So here's a list of interesting phytochemicals, and where we can source them:

*Carotenoids* : Present in yellow and orange vegetables, but also in leafy greens. They protect the inner lining of the digestive and urinary tracts, and provide vitamin A.

Look for them in carrots, tomatoes, pumpkins, spinach, kale, and the cabbage family.

*Phytosterols* : Present in most vegetables, fruits, and grains, they protect against cancerous change.

*Limonoids* : Present in citrus fruits, they act on liver enzymes that detoxify.

*Polyphenols* : (Flavinoids, isoflavonoids, anthocyanidins) Present in all fruits, vegetables, and cereals. They act on the processes of inflammation and blood clotting.

*Glucosinolates* : Present in all members of the cabbage family, they are responsible for maintaining the integrity and renewal of cells lining the gastrointestinal tract.

*Fibre* : It works in a roundabout way to maintain healthy metabolism and reduce insulin resistance.
All vegetables, fruits, and whole grains are mostly fibre.

*Phytoestrogens* : Present in legumes and berries, whole grains and grapes, they are cardio-protective.

*Terpenoids* : Present in mushrooms. Blocks inflammation and allergic response.

*Saponins* : Present in oats, and in the leaves and flowers of most vegetables.

## Tomatoes

The tomato is rich in vitamin C and the carotenoid lycopene. Its flavour comes from chemicals present in the skin – which also has sugar and amino acids – so if you must skin your tomato, add the skins pureed to a paste if you want a strong tomato flavour. The jelly of tomato has its succulent acids –

citric and malic – invaluable for the tart note. Please don't junk the jelly because it is messy. Tomatoes ripened on the vine (*gauti* tomatoes claim to be such) are rich in aroma. This comes from a group of molecules called *furaneol*. It concentrates as it cooks, so whenever you want a distinct tomato flavour, as in a *rasam*, pick *gauti* tomatoes.

When tomato is used in most Indian cuisines as a base, it must lose its '*kaccha*' flavour – that's the scent of *tomatine*. If you have grown tomatoes, it is the scent you inhale as you water the plant on a hot day – the leaves are generous with that delicious scent.

Tomatoes, which taste perfect on the day you bought them, often turn bland after three days in the fridge. Try taking them out of the fridge a couple of hours ahead of cooking them. Flavour-producing enzymes, which have been hibernating in the chill, will soon cut capers again.

## Capsicum

*Simla mirch, Kodai milagai, Capsicum annum* was cultivated from the original hot chilli with some of the *capsaicin* educated out of it – though some varieties can still sear.

The beautiful colours – green, red, yellow, purple, brown – are from the pigments they contain: purple anthocyanins, red carotenoids, and, of course, green chlorophyll.

The green and yellow varieties are rich in lutein, a carotenoid that is specially protective to the retina.

Red capsicum lacks this and packs, instead, a precursor of vitamin A, beta-carotene.

All kinds of capsicum, as indeed all kinds of chilli, are simply bursting with vitamin C.

## Onions

Ah, onions!

If you have tears, prepare to shed them now, for nothing is worth crying over as much as an onion.

You know the charming legend we were fed as kids – never mind that.

The stuff that makes us cry is something quite complicated. There is sulfur at its heart, but the onion's heartbeat is interesting. The bulb absorbs sulfur from the soil and stores it as *S-alk(en)yl-L-cysteine-S-oxide,* a compound floating free, but inactive within its cells. However, there is a trigger enzyme, *allinase,* neatly contained in a capsule within each cell. When the bulb is injured – by cutting, crushing, or grinding – the pulverized cells liberate this trigger enzyme, and, in no time at all, sulfur compounds, sulfenic acids, and thiosulfinates frisk about, lashing their tails. They are volatile and unstable as they bubble up in the home cook's head space, to irritate sensitive cells lining the eyes and nose. In protest, we weep. The 'lachrymatory factor' as the principal *Thiopropanal-S-oxide* is called, breaks up into irritants: hydrogen sulfide, sulfur dioxide, and sulfuric acid.

Did you say you'll pass on onions?

Don't!

Chill them in the fridge for a couple of hours before slicing, and stay unmoved.

The beauty of onion's sulfur compounds is their reactivity – they keep evolving into new molecules and new aromas.

The flavour profile is constantly changing too, and every cook exploits this to the maximum.

For a searing spoonful of raw ammoniacal crunch, a very fine and small chop, a mirepoix.

Membraneous slivers for a topping.

Restaurants serve up tough crescents cut hours ago, yet juicy at first bite.

Once heat enters the picture, everything changes.

The onion is a quick-change artist. Within minutes it can go from sharp to subtle, from sweet to bitter, from ammoniacal to milky, depending on whether it is roasting on an open flame, roasting in an oven, sautéing or frying in oil, butter, or *ghee*, being steamed, blanched, or boiled. We use this bouquet of aromas magnificently in our traditional recipes.

The onion works overtime for us, but what do we do to the onion?

It is a serious question because there is sulfur in that onion for our benefit.

Onions are rich in those magic molecules we listed earlier, but their organo-sulfur compounds in particular have strong anti-inflammatory and anti-microbial effects.

Their flavonoids, *quercetin* and *kaempferol,* make onions very capable antioxidants.

How do we best conserve their precious chemicals?

Unfortunately, the highest concentration of flavonoids is found in the outer layers of the onion, just beneath the dry peel, and this so often discarded while cooking.

So, do stop stripping the onion when you reach the first succulent layer, to conserve as much of its flavonoids as possible.

Small onions have a higher flavonoid content.

The cooking methods in order of flavonoid destructiveness are frying, sautéing, boiling, steaming, microwaving, baking, and roasting on an open flame.

So, do pick your recipe with an eye on exploiting the onion's rich store of phytochemicals.

## Garlic

Garlic is onion's celebrated cousin, with all its magic molecules, and then some. It has been promoted top dog in the nutraceutical business. Its impressive pong gives it such cachet that the belief that it is medicinal is near universal. People pop 'garlic pearls' and garlic decoctions and pills, convinced that it is the only way to combat atherosclerosis and heart disease.

Is there any truth to such claims?

There is certain evidence that garlic has a therapeutic effect on fat metabolism through its actions on the liver, thereby reducing the deposition of fat in the walls of blood vessels. But, its actions on platelets is uncertain. Platelets clump on the sites of injury in the blood vessel wall where fat deposition (plaque) has set up a strong inflammation. This leads to the formation of a clot (thrombus), which cuts off blood to the area of supply, which then, in the absence of oxygen, undergoes a destructive injury (infarct). Infarcts can be life threatening when they involve the brain (stroke) or heart muscle (heart attacks). Garlic is believed to prevent that.

I have used the word 'believed' advisedly.

Although garlic does inhibit platelet aggregation in the laboratory, there is very little to suggest it does the same within the body. When large amounts of garlic are eaten, bleeding episodes may occur. And most importantly, garlic may precipitate the platelet disorder associated with COVID-19.

Yes, certainly, enjoy the flavour of garlic. But for heaven's sake don't swallow it as a pill, especially in this time of siege.

## Potatoes

Potatoes are as Indian as chilli. Usually, anybody who disputes our claim to *aloo* is in big trouble. But *aloo* isn't Indian. All you need to prove this is the Marathi term for our heart's delight: *batata*. That's a direct transfer from the Portuguese word, which the Iberians got out of Columbus when he massacred the Taíno people of Haiti. The Taíno called sweet potato, batata.

The Peruvians, master horticulturists and the original cultivators, called the potato, *pau*.

But that's all in the past.

India, like the rest of the world, fattens on this fruit of genocide.

The average Indian adult eats 16–18 kg of potatoes/year.

Despite its ubiquity and popularity, or perhaps because of it, the potato is blamed for its 'fattening' properties. It is spoken about with scorn as 'only starch'. While we shudder at the humble *aloo ki sabzi* as the very incarnation of diabetes, no such terrors assail us over mounds of French fries.

Potatoes are not fattening, but what we put them through certainly is.

A potato is mostly water.

This is what makes a steamed potato so delightful in texture. Baking produces a drier, more fragmented fluff. Indian cuisine usually steams or boils the potato, when it doesn't take the deep fried route.

Potato contains phytochemicals aplenty: phenolics, flavonoids, polyamines, and carotenoids.

How does cooking affect them?

Potato phenolics and flavonoids are concentrated in the peel, which we generally discard. But good portions of these phytochemicals are in the flesh too. And the good news is that these phytochemicals largely survive the assaults of cooking.

Why, then, do we criminalize the potato?

Potato starch is extremely and quickly digestible. This has earned it the bad reputation of being a very high glycaemic food. Cooking the potato in the commonest way of Indian cuisine, by boiling or steaming, can change this.

Resistant starches are those that reach the large intestine undigested and are fermented there by the microbiome to give rise to the extremely beneficial SCFAs, which stabilize metabolism.

Cooking the potato and then refrigerating it changes a large proportion of its starch to the resistant variety. Cooking it further will not reverse the change.

Glycoalkaloids are toxic compounds the potato plant produces to defend itself against predators. Though most of these are concentrated in stems and leaves, they pop up occasionally in the tubers as well. They appear as green patches, and are located just beneath the skin. They may also develop if potatoes are stored in bright light. These alkaloids, *solanine* and *chaconine,* can cause symptoms that vary from nausea and vomiting to severe illness. However, they are restricted to the green patches, and, after cutting those away, the rest of the potato is quite safe to cook.

# Fruits

What's the difference between a fruit and a vegetable?

Sweetness! Also, juiciness, tartness, and the unbeatable deliciousness contained in the word *ripe*.

Many unripe fruits are cooked as vegetables.

So, the real difference is neither colour, nor texture, nor taste, but, ripeness.

Ripeness converts a vegetable into an instant food. All you have to do is bite and get that welcome rush of sugar, electrolytes, and, above all, water that dismisses exhaustion.

A fruit, any fruit, is nature's elixir.

It is tonic, nutraceutical, rejuvenanant, aphrodisiac – all in one delectable mouthful.

A fruit is something you anticipate, whether on the bough or in the bazaar. That period of waiting is the fruit's too. It is gathering energy to perfect its purpose.

Is it any wonder then, that it is the world's emblem of plenitude, generosity, and utter selflessness?

Its only purpose is to be eaten. And for that, it must ripen.

What is the change we recognize as ripeness?

Colour? Aroma? Consistency?

All of these, plus an ineffable change in heft that promises sweetness.

The entire plant is hard at work to alchemize ripeness. But the simplest plant hormone among them is the one that transforms: *ethylene.*

There are two sorts of fruits: those that ripen on the bough, and climacteric fruits, those that continue ripening after harvest. Bananas, tomatoes, and apples are climacteric fruits. Citrus fruits and grapes are not.

Fruits that ripen on the plant, generally don't need a surge of ethylene to turn soft and sweet.

Plants produce their own ethylene from the amino-acid methionine. Ethylene has effects on non-climacteric fruits as well, even if it doesn't help in ripening them. It causes a change in colour in citrus fruit by degrading chlorophyll into orange, and in grapes and cherries by increased anthocyanin production to deepen hues of red and violet.

Other chemicals work their magic too. Strawberries have high levels of the hormone auxin, produced by immature seeds. This blocks ripening. When the seeds mature, auxin production falls, and the strawberry begins to ripen.

In grapes, *abscisic acid* is the trigger for ripening.

Climacteric fruits ripen after harvesting in response to ethylene in their environment.

As a fruit ripens, its texture changes. Cell walls soften and their components undergo chemical changes under the influence of enzymes.

Fruits that are rich in starch, like banana, grow sweeter as starch is broken down into free sugars.

Citrus fruits become softer as they lose turgor pressure.

To pick a ripe melon, I don't touch, I inhale. I breathe in the delicious scent of sweet and juicy tenderness: volatile esters that ethylene has liberated. The starting materials for these scents are fatty acids and branched amino acids. Ethylene acts on them to release esters, alcohols, aldehydes, ketones, and terpenes which we recognize as the scent of ripe fruit. If ethylene is prevented from acting, these aromas are dampened.

Ripening can be artificially controlled, but not always safely. The commercial implications of ripening are tremendous. The presence of even a single ripe banana can push a truckload into squashy liquefaction by journey's end, and render the entire consignment worthless.

Plant scientists have come up with chemicals that block ethylene receptors and retard ripening. This explains why fruit is often disappointingly short on aroma.

Artificial ripening of fruits is old as history.

Slip a couple of not-yet-there bananas with a squishy one into a paper bag. Those firm bananas will soften in a few hours. By tomorrow, they will be squishy. Ripe bananas exhale ethylene and trigger the ripening process in green fruit. Traditionally, bananas are treated in covered pits with smoke from a smoldering fire: the acetylene and ethylene in the smoke do the trick.

Commercial ripening often resorts to chemicals other than ethylene. Acetylene, produced by the hydrolysis of calcium carbide is the most common and also the most hazardous. Ethephon, another ripening agent, is equally dangerous.

It is horrific to think that the fruit we buy may have been ripened by these dangerous chemicals, then polished and waxed to make them appear attractive.

Wash fruits in running water for at least five minutes before you peel them – that's your best guarantee for safety.

'Dry fruit' is India's label for luxury. The fruit could be any juicy drupe, but we know the familiars: dates, apricots, twenty different kinds of grapes from the humble *kishmish* to the magnificent *sultana,* figs, and our new acquisitions – cranberries, blueberries, loganberries. Oh, lest I forget, the term includes nuts as well. Almonds, walnuts, pistachios, *chilghozas**, cashews, cucumber seeds, we love them all.

'Dry fruit' is a metaphor for worth. Homes display their collections ostentatiously in the areas where they receive their guests.

Come Diwali, dry fruit is carefully metered in gift hampers to convey an exact value of the recipient's worth.

Dry fruit *mithai* – mysteriously 'sugar free' – is at a premium. Even chocolates wear that label.

The magical thinking behind this is rather retro: 'natural remedy, rejuvenant from remote and inaccessible source'. Nothing is remote or inaccessible any longer. As for those remedies and rejuvenants, yes or no, they are lost in the concentrated sugar that's left behind when the fruit dries out.

And nuts? They're wonderful too – they are solid drops of oil.

Dried fruit and nuts are survival foods. If we consume them when we are already well fed, it is greed, not indulgence. Eating them by the fistful means obesity, diabetes, and heart disease. Eating a few every day is still excess.

---

*Pine nuts.

How do we maximize the valuable nutrients in vegetables and fruits?

1. Cooking makes vegetables more digestible, but can destroy vitamins and leach out minerals. Brief cooking time prevents much of this loss. Very high temperatures are not only destructive, they also lead to inadequate cooking in the centre of the food. So, cut vegetables small, preserve cooking water, steam before sautéing.
2. Cooking different vegetables together has the compensatory benefit of nutrients from several sources.
3. Cooking vegetables with *dals* or milk gets rid of many anti-nutrients like tannins, and retains many nutrients.
4. The addition of acids and alkalis can alter the texture and integrity of the vegetable. Alkali makes vegetables mushy. If you must use one, use milk, not soda, which leaches out salts and minerals.
5. Colour can be preserved by brief cooking, whether steaming, blanching, or sautéing. Covering the cooking vessel will turn bright green vegetables olive green.
6. Cooking vegetables to retain colour, texture, taste, and nutritive value demands attention.
7. If you must boil vegetables, do so in salted water and retain the water. Use it, if necessary, in another dish.
8. Blanching is a much better alternative. Here, the volume of water should be large, the stay in water no more than a minute or two before the vegetables are transferred to a bowl of ice water, or refrigerated to arrest the cooking process. Blanching does not cook the vegetable completely. It reduces the cooking time in assembling the dish.

# Part Four

## Proem

Time now to test out these truths. The rest of this book puts into action all you've read so far. It will be an uncomfortable read because it will challenge things you've been doing skillfully and successfully for years. After all, you have been a home cook for most of your adult life, you nourished and nurtured, planned and fed, did it all in a twinkling, day in and day out. Frankly, what's the point of even reading further?

*So, thanks for the information, good to know, and I really don't have time –*

Believe me, I understand.

Any other time, I would take the hint.

But this pandemic has made a pachyderm of me. I am armoured against every sort of rejection by sheer necessity.

We are in a mess, and there is no point yammering on about it. We just have to fix it.

That's what the rest of this book is about: fixing this mess we are mired in.

And we must begin by acknowledging this truth: If home food has made us overweight, obese, diabetic, dyslipidemic, and just plain sick, there is something about home food that needs fixing.

Many of the things that need changing are sacred, enshrined in habit or prejudice.

Here are ten of the most common protests I have encountered. You are welcome to add to this list:

1. You can't possibly *cook* fruit!
2. You can't add fruit to a lunchtime salad!
3. You can't eat porridge at teatime – that's *breakfast*!

4. You can't make *parathas* in so little oil or *ghee.*
5. You can't make *upma* in next to no oil.
6. You can't eat potatoes at breakfast – that's indulgent, fattening, and just the wrong thing to do.
7. You can't make anything tasty and crisp without oil.
8. You can't cook vegetables right unless they're coated well with oil and turmeric.
9. You can't cook vegetables with *dal.*
10. You can never add milk to vegetables, nor can you mix vegetables.

I can only answer by providing solutions. If you try them, you will find they work.

Time and energy are precious, and this book is meant to reduce your kitchen time.

I have provided the shortcuts and hacks that have saved me time and again.

This is not a recipe book, so I am constrained by space to include just the few that might seem unfamiliar to you.

You have honoured me by inviting me into your kitchen, and I haven't arrived empty handed.

Take the afternoon off. We have chatted long enough. I'll wash up, while you get started ...

# Le Menu

A menu is for restaurants, surely! Who ever heard of one in the kitchen?

The word itself is a sham, and not even remotely appetizing. It is grammar, not gastronomy. It means *summary* or *résumé.* Techies who seem to love culinary epithets, for once, picked right.

*Menu* became a restaurant basic because of its ambiguity. It could be read as a polite take-it-or-leave-it warning to customers. Conversely, it could create an aura of expectation, even mystery, especially if partially (and ignorantly) Frenched.

The home cook, cheated of this intelligent cop-out, must prove herself on the plate, meal after meal after meal after meal after meal after meal after meal, and so on to the $n^{th}$ decimal of $\pi$.

The rushed home cook – and which of us isn't – has it even rougher.

Breakfast is the worst.

One eye on the clock, I yank open the fridge, and what do

I find? Last week's vegetables in a shriveled huddle. The egg tray's sightless stare. Not a fruit in sight.

I grab the milk, slam the fridge door. Reach for that cardboard carton, shake out some puzzle pieces, slosh in just enough milk to magic them into wood pulp. Using a long spoon to force-feed myself, I swallow.

On the way out, I rescue a lone banana bletting on the counter, and trash it at first smear.

My Monday morning, that.

Yours, too?

A menu can change all that magically. You don't have to write it out, though that does help, sometimes. A menu is a very pleasant mental exercise you can do while falling asleep.

Maybe we've been writing menus all our lives, supremely unconscious that it rates a special word. We could junk the word and call it *planning a meal.* But the phrase is joyless, it becomes a *process.* It lacks swish. My stomach turns inside out at the thought of food that is planned or processed. Where's the joy in it?

*Menu* factors in the missing element: appetite.

*Menu* extends way beyond the kitchen.

Try shopping with a menu. It is quick, adventurous, and way more economical.

A successful menu ticks all these boxes:

1. Quick and easy to cook, with minimal fuss and mess.
2. Scientifically nutritious in content.
3. Alluring and seductive to the senses.
4. Simply delectable!
5. Satisfying, but light on the stomach.
6. And, most importantly, it will not pile up the kitchen sink.

## Designing a Menu

You can't enjoy a fabulous dinner for breakfast, or lunch for a teatime snack – well, not every day. We expect different sorts of delight through the day, and we design the menu around these expectations.

| | | |
|---|---|---|
| Breakfast | : | Quick, easy to eat, light. |
| Lunch | : | Aromatic. A variety of tastes and textures. Satisfying but not stupefying. |
| Teatime (the rule breaker) | : | Something you fancy, something to revive the spirit and leave you comfortable for a few more hours of work. |
| Dinner | : | Relaxing. A sit-down meal. Familiar food, eaten leisurely. With maybe a dessert to be enjoyed later. |

To the kitchen, then!

## Breakfast

### Check Out Food Groups

**Carbohydrates**: All cereals. Potatoes, bananas. And, of course, bread!
**Protein**: Milk, curds, cheese. Eggs. Pulses and *dals*.
**Added Fat**: Oil. Butter. Oil seeds. Nuts.

Eggs and dairy foods in the proteins group are rich in fat too, so it is smart to cut out added fat – or keep it to the bare necessity.

### Get Picky

**Carbohydrates**
Cereals?

Rice? Wheat? Millets? Which should you pick?

All cereals pack the same amount of energy – but some of them release it slowly.

Many traditional Indian breakfasts exploit this by using whole grains and by employing cooking methods that render them delicious and digestible: as porridge, flat breads, or ferments that are steamed. Originally meant to sustain long physically exhausting mornings, the principle still works perfectly for today's sedentary worker.

*No-cook cereal?*

Try beaten rice (flattened rice or rice flakes, *chuda, poha, aval*).

Grab a fistful, soak to soften, drain, add a dice of fresh fruit, and splash in some milk. Flavours unfurl with every mouthful. The tongue explores textures. Milk tastes creamier and sweeter as fruits release their nectar. Delicious, down to the last drop.

Still want to reach for that cardboard box?

Cooking time practically zero, enough variety for a treasury of textures and flavours, served sweet, savoury, or unspoilt, *and* a winner in taste and nutrition. What's not to like?

*Breakfast in a bowl?*

Porridge, that rural staple, has a rightful place in the modern urban breakfast, usually as oats. Wheat (as *lapsi* or *daliya*), or a combination of millets make a quick-cook porridge that is delicious with milk, buttermilk, fresh fruit or vegetables.

*Crisp, not squishy?*

Bread is unbeatable as a breakfast staple – *if* it is not made from bleached flour.

Here are some very familiar cereal dishes:

*Roti* or *paratha* (plain or stuffed)

*Daliya*, as porridge

*Poha*, with milk, or as a savoury
Vermicelli, with milk, or as a savoury
*Idli, dhokla*
*Dosai* or *uthappam*
Sandwiches or toast
*Upma*, from *rava, poha* or *vermicelli*

All of these probably already feature on your breakfast menu, along with:

*Accompaniments*: Sauces, chutneys, spreads, spiced powders, butter, *ghee*.

*Tempering*: Oil, oil seeds, red chilli.

You've spotted the two drawbacks, haven't you?

Oil and chilli irritate the twitchy early morning stomach, even when they don't leave you singed with heartburn or embarrassed by burps.

The coconut in chutney and oil in the tempering can give you a false sense of satiety. You'll be too full to move on to the next important part of your breakfast – protein.

*Other Breakfast Carbohydrates:*

Don't disdain potatoes! They can form a delicious base for breakfasts, especially for kids. Potatoes are excellent 'protein carriers'.

And that banana lying torpid and spotty like an exhausted jaguar? Two minutes will transform it into haute cuisine.

Fresh fruit is great for breakfast – but just as an add-on. It works better as a mid-morning snack.

**Proteins**

The gold standard for protein is egg.

There are a zillion ways of cooking eggs.

*Do include at least one whole egg in your breakfast menu.*

Eggs don't really need toast or bread. They lend themselves beautifully to the cereal dishes on your list, either as accompaniments or as part of the dish. They are excellent transporters of fruit and vegetables with practically no effort.

Eggs are the home cook's opportunity to start the day with applause. Too early in the day for creativity? Check out the 'Recipes' section.

So you won't be persuaded into eggs?

No worries. Let's work out rough, very rough, equivalents:

One egg = 200 ml of milk (or curd made from that amount of milk) or one unit of sliced processed cheese.

Vegetable proteins like pulses cannot be consumed in quantities to deliver all the protein you need to start the day with, but they work beautifully as add-ons. A sweet made with any of the cooked pulses is a great side dish.

**Added Fats**

100 ml of milk (standard 3% fat) – has already provided half your fat requirement at breakfast. An egg (4 gm fat) tops it.

But you still need some fat – oil or *ghee* – to get the breakfast together, right?

Check out 'Quick Cuts and Cooking Hacks' on how to cut back and still retain premium taste and texture.

## Setting the Table

Here are some sample menus. If you find any of the items or suggestions unfamiliar – or if you want to go wild – check out

'Recipes'. Oh, and we do have a special menu for breakfast haters.

1. Porridge with milk and fruit, egg, toast
2. *Idli/dosai/uthappam*+chutney, egg, either served separately or as part of the dish, a cup of milk
3. Porridge, quick fruit muffins
4. *Aloo paratha*, egg, cup of milk
5. Baked *upma*, cup of milk
6. The too-rushed-for-breakfast breakfast smoothie: milk, egg, fruit and chocolate make a heavenly smoothie. Check out the recipe on pg. 305.

Breakfasts without eggs:

1. *Roti* roll with *tawa* kabab and 1/2 a slice of cheese, porridge with milk and fruit
2. *Paratha* with *dahi chaat*
3. *Idli/dosai/uthappam* with chutney, sweet pulses, a cup of milk
4. The too-rushed-for-breakfast breakfast: Breakfast of Champions Smoothie: check this one out, it is delicious.

What about that magic list? The one full of 'immunity-boosters' that promises brains, beauty, and, of course, immortality?

Is this your list?

- *Nuts*: Almonds, walnuts, and nuts you've never heard of before. (Cashews, coconut and peanuts are outcastes in health stores, but are just as nutty as those aristocrats.)
- *Seeds*: Flax, sunflower, chia, and counting...

- *Seed and Nut pastes and powders*: Tahini, hazelnut paste and almond powder for choice
- *Dried fruit*: Dates of varying provenance, twenty or more grape varieties, apricots, cranberries, and a rainbow collection of crystallized fruit.

All these exotics are either sugar concentrates or fat concentrates, and the worst things you can break your fast on. I mentioned them only to get them out of the way.

*Avoid!*

# Lunch

Lunch is the home cook's heartbeat. It dictates the pulse of the day. It is the very essence of 'home food', and it will be defended to death against the merest particle of change. And guess what? No matter where you're from, your 'home lunch' is nutritionally sound. As usual, the trouble lies in shortcuts and add-ons.

Our expectations of delight are very high for this meal. It is a sensorial orgy – we crave everything: aroma, taste, texture, variety.

So how do we match delight and nutrition for the perfect lunch?

## The Home Lunch

The home lunch is pretty much the same all over India:

- Rice or *roti* of wheat or millet
- *Dal* or pulse preparation
- Vegetables with gravy
- 'Dry' vegetable dishes
- Curds or buttermilk

'Everything is *dal* and rice!' sneered a young guest after a hearty lunch.

I've never forgotten the chef's response. 'I've been doing *dal* and rice for sixty years and it still tastes different every day.'

How amazing is that?

*Dal*-and-rice is generic. You can do just about anything with that combination and our great traditional dishes vary from basic rustic to the very acme of sophistication.

Each local speciality has a distinctive *masala* or tempering that enhances the flavour, a different cooking method to vary texture.

Really though, *dal* and rice need no additives at all. A jot of *ghee*, a grain of salt, and the meld is sheer heaven. Add a dish of vegetables and a dollop of curds, and it is a perfect meal, delicious and satisfying.

The same goes for *roti*. The perfect *phulka* is a poem in itself. It can turn even an unimaginative meal into a feast.

With all these advantages, what makes the home lunch go so terribly wrong to push the nation into obesity and diabetes?

The truth is not as easy to swallow as that delicious lunch.

It is the oil and *masala* fixation (Include *ghee* and *vanaspati* in that).

This makes the vegetarian lunch low on vegetables, low on protein, and practically soaked in fat.

That's very simple to fix, even without altering our home lunch or going through extra labour and expense.

Why not try an experiment? Pick your usual familiar recipes for:

- vegetable with gravy
- *dal*/pulse preparation
- 'dry' vegetable

STEP 1: Oil

Measure the amount of oil used in every step of each dish.

A few days later, repeat the same menu, cutting those measured amounts of oil by half.

STEP 2: Flavour

The following week, repeat the same menu, using the reduced oil amounts from STEP 1, with this additional change:

Cut back *by half* the spices you use at each step, beginning with turmeric. If the dish demands a freshly ground *masala* paste with a base of coconut, cut down the coconut to 1/3rd.

The sour element, be it tamarind, curd, kokum, or lemon juice, balances the heat, so when you cut back on the pepper, chilli, ginger, you must cut back on this element too.

Experienced home cooks will have no problems – others can easily taste their way into perfect balance.

STEP 3: Salt

Implementing all the changes from the earlier experiments, now check the salt. Cut back by 1/3rd or more, using your judgment.

STEP 4: Aroma and Taste

Does your cooking make passersby pause and revel in the aroma floating out of your kitchen window?

After STEP 2, you should have discovered that aroma doesn't depend on the quantity of *masala*, but on how it's deployed.

Look at what this experiment accomplished:

By cutting back oil, you not only made the dish healthier, but you also discovered it is tastier. This is because excess oil coats the taste buds, so we need more of everything to experience taste and flavour.

The cutback in spices and salt results in deeper flavours and a richer dish as the ingredients assert themselves.

## Ingredients

Now that you've changed those dishes to make them more nourishing, you're ready to choose ingredients and cooking methods.

### Vegetables

Choose vegetables from all four groups:

*Roots and tubers*
*Green vegetables*
*Red and yellow vegetables*
*Gourds*

The cooking method, of course, depends on the dish you're preparing. Vegetables taste delicious when cooked together. To some home cooks, this appears to go against the grain, literally. Others flinch at the very thought of cooking vegetables with *dal.*

'We just don't *do* it this way'?

Perhaps you should. After all, you've agreed to make your home lunch more nutritious, and that does call for a few changes!

### *Dals* and Pulses

As the protein backbone of the vegetarian lunch, *dals* and pulses deserve a lot of attention in the way they're cooked.

You've read the principles already, let's apply them to the menu:

1. It is a good idea to have two different sorts of *dals,* or one *dal* + one pulse, as they lend themselves to different textures. So, they can build two contrasting dishes on the menu.
2. Digestibility is the keyword here, so make certain the *dals* and pulses have been prepped well.
3. Retain the cooking water in the dish. If it is to be a dry dish, transfer the water to a cooking gravy.
4. If you're making a *dahi chaat* using pulses, add them to the bowl only at the table, or you'll find your soft, cooked beans have turned stiff and hard after a dousing in curd.
5. The cooking water of *dals* and pulses can be used to cook rice. It gives a deep flavour to *pulao* and *biryani.*

**Taste and Aroma**

The menu should have aromas and flavours that appeal to everyone at the table.

Every family has a few dissenters to common kitchen smells – *hing,* garlic, ginger.

Respect that.

Just skip that particular ingredient. There's so much else to choose from. If you can't make a particular dish without it, skip the dish.

No, that was not a diversion – *a meal should never become an area of conflict.*

The brain registers both taste and aroma as the single sensation of 'taste'. Remember how tasteless food seems when you have a heavy cold?

**Condiments**

The usual fallback to a dull meal is the pickle bottle. Our formidable array of pickles, chutneys, spiced powders, and other spectacular relishes can galvanize the most phlegmatic lunch into fiery oratory.

Let's push them off the table right away. They're not going to improve the menu.

If that hurts, how about table pickles that offer some nutritional punch? They last for three to four days in the fridge, but are so delicious, the bowl's licked clean long before that.

Some home cooks (guilty!) take months to recover from the innocent query: 'Do you have any pickle?' We regard it as a personal failure. A good lunch needs no condiments.

One way to avoid them is the traditional pattern of matching a fiery dish with a bland accompaniment and vice versa. This traditional pairing is not only delicious, it often covers nutritional deficits.

Another trick is to include a dish that contains all possible tastes. This is the intelligence behind a *chaat*. A fruit *chaat*, with or without *dahi*, is an excellent addition, and one that includes cooked pulses, is even better.

One ingredient that makes a terrific condiment is fresh fruit. Yes, you read that right.

Fruit – fresh, braised, or roasted – is a wonderful presence at lunch.

It can be used as a topping – to add a sparkle of humour to a deep and ferocious gravy, or a tart and sweet tingle to a sauté. It has a very definite presence in salads.

Do I hear you protest that fruit is dessert?

Served as a dessert – which means a fair quantity – it can

often make you bloat. So use fruits at the table in the dishes on the menu.

**Salads**

Salads are tricky. Raw vegetables are not always digestible and may cause bloating. Besides, a salad is not about raw vegetables. It is about juice.

The usual cucumber, carrot, tomato, onion display is a line-up, not a salad. There is no conversation, no dalliance, no rapier exchange of wit. The vegetables just stand shoulder to shoulder till they shrivel up and die. Drenching them in vinegar and olive oil works fine elsewhere, but not for a population fighting as hard as we are, to get fit.

We need a salad that retains its sparkle, all tickle and giggle, and delivers its nutritional promise.

Again, it is a great idea to use fruits in the salad.

Do we absolutely need a salad?

A burning question, really.

If you've learned the trick of cooking vegetables right, every sauté will be tender and delicious, and, in that case, you can skip the salad.

If not, do rustle up a bowl of freshness.

But do note: you can't lunch off a salad.

It is just a condiment.

What about those 'healthy' salads?

Raw sprouts, soaked wheat or quinoa, half the rainforest canopy still on the branch, a fistful of nuts, all oozing tahini and olive oil?

It has no place in the vegetarian lunch where protein is at a premium.

Salads should be fresh and juicy and sparkle on the tongue with little pops of every delight you crave: the *Navarasa* (p. 311) is a case in point but go on, invent your own!

**Crisps**

Crisp foods have an allure that seduces the most reluctant eater. *Pappad, appalam,* and various types of *farsaan* are items of universal desire. They are all deep fried. Unless you are an expert at this technique, this will soak up a lot of oil. In one fell swoop, it will exhaust a whole week's ration of oil.

Yes, *pappads* can be microwaved, but the *pappad* contains enough oil as is.

Once a month is fine.

And while waiting for that happy day, why not hone your deep frying skills?

Till then, why deprive yourself of the pleasure of something crisp? There's a whole range of dishes you can crisp on the tawa. I'm sure you have plenty in your treasury – but there's always room for more.

**Dairy**

Milk and curd are important sources of protein, and it is intelligent to include them in the vegetarian lunch menu.

*No, plant milks don't work as substitutes.*

Present them either as is, or as a dish, choosing from the million ways in the vegetarian repertoire.

Do remember: dairy is also rich in fat, so do not include both dairy and fried dishes.

### The Revised Lunch Menu

*Roti*/rice
Vegetable with gravy
'Dry vegetable': tender sauté or crisp roast
*Dal*/pulse
*Raita* or *chaat* with/fruit/pulse or salad
Curd or buttermilk

Despite all the changes you've made, the home lunch menu doesn't read so very different from your usual one, does it?

But your changes have achieved three important goals:

- Reduced the fat content to a safe amount.
- Raised the protein content
- Increased the availability of micronutrients from fruits and vegetables, which is just a complicated way of saying they taste juicier and better.

Tired of the daily lunch? Strike out, bold and brave, with meal-in-a-bowl combinations. We have a spectacular variety of these all over the country, and they all taste different, though your mental label for all of them may be 'khichdi'. Traditionally, they are served with curd or a *raita* or *pachadi*.

Take my advice and lose that label: use the local name, discover new flavours and textures. The internet is full of recipes, and you can try them out after you have read 'How to Read a Recipe' (p. 291).

# Teatime

Teatime – ah!

A little of what we fancy.

We aren't exactly hungry, but could do with a nibble. And that hot drink.

Today, for most of us, teatime augurs at least two hours of work ahead. But it is also a pause that anticipates pleasure: conversation, togetherness, consolation, hope.

And we home cooks have to deliver all that in the teatime snack.

Snack! If there's a more popular word in our country, do enlighten me. *Nashta* in the north, *tiffin* in the south, this in-between meal is gorged with delight in offices and college canteens. Street vendors are mobbed at five o'clock. Commuters get their fix on the platform before the mad scramble to board the train home.

But all that is Outside food.

What's on at home?

Since we are all working from home now, let us discount

that outside snack altogether.

Oh, you're right, you're right.

One can still call for an outside snack, guaranteed to arrive still sizzling.

India's inexhaustible repertoire of snacks, north or south, east or west, is usually savoury and fat and carbohydrate rich. They aren't snacks. They are actual meals. Even if they are innocent of fat and sugar, their sidekicks – chutney, sauces, toppings of crunch – are fat and sugar concentrates.

The more you think about it, it is these sidekicks we crave at teatime.

Alright, you only have a cup of tea. One biscuit. Maybe two. That's it.

My inner clock is messed up at teatime.

Lunch is still mid-digestion. Since it was such a clever lunch, a slow release of energy has kept me ticking all afternoon. Insulin in top form gives a faint edge of expectation – not appetite exactly, no, my stomach is still full. It is just a sudden curiosity. If, at this moment, a curl of aroma should float up from the onion *pakodas* frying on the street, I could get suddenly ravenous.

And then, if I got hold of those *pakodas*, a plateful might disappear before I've noticed. I might also raid my stash of sauces or whip up a lip-smacking date and tamarind chutney. And after that, a cup of strong syrupy tea to set me straight.

No, I don't do this every day, of course not.

Maybe once a month? Twice?

You can see how my brain has worked this swindle. The

hunger factor has been completely overridden by the pleasure circuit, which means, also, that my 'Enough!' setting is nearly non-operational. I could pig out till I am sick.

So, dear fellow home cook, this is our hour of challenge. We can't be deaf to the clamour for pleasure. But we need not be bullied by it. We must respond with intelligence.

Not difficult at all, if we read the brain's compulsion correctly.

It isn't asking for onion *pakodas*. It is asking for – joy.

Why not indulge it?

Enlarge the canvas of pleasure. Acknowledge other senses besides taste in the meal you put together.

The teatime menu should be pretty.

It shouldn't be a standup, nor 'at my elbow, thanks, I'll grab it' kind of meal.

It should be eaten in company.

Live alone?

Phone a friend, pick up a book, chat up the crow on your windowsill. Sing. Doodle. Dance.

Communication and self-expression are the deepest among human pleasures.

So, even if you have just five minutes, let those be intense.

Don't eat off the nearest parking spot. Find a pretty plate, a cozy chair, a mantelpiece for the cup, a patch of sky with a passing cloud, a sparrow on a branch. That, a cup of tea, and some fruit, would be paradise enow. It might work for you and me. But not for those we cook for. So, our teatime menu should have these:

1. Taste

2. Texture
3. Delight
4. Low energy

*Taste*: Intense tastes are called for! Sweet or *chatpata*.

*Texture*: Crisp wins every time.

*Delight*: Make your teatime snack aromatic and visually appealing.

*Low energy*: Aye, there's the rub. But if the top three are satisfactory, a little goes a long way – *if*... you also provide a slow release 'filler'.

There is a trick dish that traditionally provides everything teatime – *chaat*. The word itself tells you it is finger-licking good. The slow release 'filler' comes from the handful of cooked pulses and potato. Texture comes from puffed rice or a sprinkle of homemade *chivda*. No. *Sookha bhel* or diet *bhel* – with its generous whack of *sev* – will not work. Add a medley of fruit and vegetable slivers to the crunch of onion. Toss in your favourite *masala*, dot with chutney, scatter some gems, rubies for choice, by cracking a pomegranate.

*Chaat* isn't everyone's cup of tea, pardon the mixed metaphor. Oh, you want something hot? Try out some of the recipes at the back of the book.

Here is my teatime menu from yesterday. But then, everybody was so *very* hungry:

Vermicelli *upma*: low fat, quick cooking, slow-release filler.

Coffee and banana frappé: delicious, intense, swift energy provider.

Today, when everybody is more laidback:

*Daliya* or millet porridge with fruit: slow energy release, high on taste. Fruit gives enough instant energy and sweetness. Teatime porridge is thinner than what you serve at breakfast.

It should be one tablespoon of the raw cereal per person, measured out before cooking. It can be made extra delicious by adding fruit as it is cooking.

It takes about 100 ml milk per person.

Homemade *chivda* is at hand, but after that delicious porridge, I know the *dabba* won't be opened.

Tea or coffee, if still desired.

Vital question here: *How* hungry are you?

### *Very?*

One basic good carbohydrate dish, small portion, accompanying sauce/chutney home-made (see 'Quick Cuts and Recipes').

Choose one from these:

- Vermicelli or *poha upma* (using 1 tsp oil if making for three)
- *Roti* roll with *channa* and fillings, roasted on tawa.
- *Chaat* with pulses and vegetables
- Porridge with fruit
- Two *idli*/one *dosai* or *uthappam*

### *Just mildly hungry?*

Cup of tea or coffee with fruit or a cup of milk.

Can you skip a teatime snack?

Certainly!

But then you must have an early dinner. Or, after a pleasant walk, eat some fruit.

# Dinner

Dinner should relax you.

We canny home cooks meet this bill by providing comfort food.

Keep it light, low on fat and spice.

*Dals* are better than pulses, to avoid abdominal discomfort.

Ideally, dinner should be early, at least two hours before bed time.

Home cooks know it is difficult to draw up a menu for dinner – one never knows.

Will the leftovers from lunch be sufficient?

They may be. With something to perk up interest as a side?

But the dinner menu really depends on what kind of day it has been, on everybody's state of mind, and what's on TV.

Most people eat dinner watching TV. No conversation, true, but often families bond deeply over TV serials.

That's one way of solving personal crises. But it also means we often don't notice what we eat. We just pile everything on the plate and keep eating till the commercial break, when we quickly reload.

The result is often distressing.

'Acidity.'

'Just can't fall asleep.'

The reason is obvious.

Overeating.

Overeating at dinner turns Home food into Outside food.

We burp. We bloat. We wake up in the middle of the night. We don't want breakfast next morning.

So, keep it light.

How light?

'I just have a glass of milk and a banana.'

That is 150 calories from 200 ml milk and 125 calories from a decent banana.

6 gm proteins, 6 gm fat, 35 gm carbohydrates.

Not bad.

Milk and banana are both high energy foods. Milk's high energy comes from fat, banana's from carbohydrate.

Quick come, quick go. You will wake up hungry in the middle of the night.

But had you made that a cup of milk (100 ml) or *dahi*, a *roti* and *sabzi*, it will ensure a slower buildup of energy, and a more sustained one. You'll sleep soundly until dawn.

One word of caution: When the family, moved by the home cook's toils, decides to order dinner – protest!

If you must, ever, have to order in, make it lunch, never dinner.

## *Amuse Bouche* for Dreams

An *amuse bouche* is an exquisite morsel, a gastronomic tease at the beginning of a meal.

But how about an amuse bouche for dreams?

NOT your five *badam* and fig and dates, please!

Why NOT?

You know already – you don't need that extra jab of fat or that intense overload of sugar. You've eaten enough for the day.

Let's find something to help you fall asleep, and get rid of the aches and pains that one invariably feels at the end of a long day.

Is there such a magical potion?

You bet there is.

It is so good, it used to be given to marathon runners – even though they weren't called that. They were given a bowl of the stuff, steered to a mat, and left alone till dawn – when they were off running towards the next stop at sundown and the next bowl of –

You guessed it.

*Chocolate.*

Cocoa and milk with a bit of banana spritzed in will give you a relaxed night's sleep.

Why not try it?

# Chocolate, Coffee, and Tea

What are your pleasures?

Chocolate heads my list. Yours too?

Why do we love it so? There is a lot of hooey about how pleasure circuits buzz into overdrive when you nibble chocolate. It is way beyond pleasure, the hype goes, it is orgasmic. Dark nirvana. Ten little deaths to the bar.

Oh, for god's sake!

In advertising, everything is about sex. Must we fall for that again?

We may not cook with chocolate very often – I hope you don't at all – but we eat it all the time, both as chocolate and as flavour.

The consumption of chocolate by children is definitely toxic. It is the childhood word for 'more' and the adult word for 'decadence'. The differentiation is mere sophistry. Adult chocolate is dark, often bitter. Simply saying *dark chocolate* produces a frisson. Eating it may not, though.

What are we celebrating, in our enjoyment of chocolate?

Aroma?

Yes!

Taste?

Chocolate has a flat uninteresting bitterness. No grace notes relieve its plangent twang.

Texture?

That's the same as any fatty food. It smears the tongue.

What then? What are we celebrating?

Are our thrills purely those of brainwashed consumers?

In which case, here's the sell:

*Chocolate is an aphrodisiac.* Chocolate is exclusive, almost secretively select in its clientele. It is sourced from plantations so remote and pristine, it takes a year of interplanetary travel to get here. And then the crafting of chocolate – oh, no we are not talking manufacture – this is hand crafted chocolate, and these mysteries we cannot, even to you, reveal.

Monogrammed, foil wrapped, boxed and beribboned, chocolate nestles among flowers, among vials of perfume, among scattered lingerie.

Is that all we are swallowing when we eat chocolate?

Judging from its effects on the body, apparently not.

The immediate effect of eating chocolate is an increase in blood flow to the brain. This produces an operatic progression of events.

Opioids are released, and provide a high, that's mildly, very mildly, disinhibiting.

Taste and aroma perception grow keener.

Mental fatigue is replaced by distractibility – which means you can shut that file and watch a movie.

Most importantly, all these effects crystallize into one supreme command: MORE!

Chocolate demands more chocolate.

Make no mistake, chocolate is a drug.

A drug with a strong addictive potential.

Should children be eating so much of it?

Should we?

This needs more clarity. Couldn't these effects of chocolate be related merely to the hefty amount of fat and sugar chocolate contains?

What? There are no fats in dark chocolate?

The cocoa bean is ground into a paste called cocoa liquor, which contains non-fat cocoa solids and cocoa butter.

Cocoa powder is cocoa solids minus some of the cocoa butter.

Dark chocolate is cocoa liquor plus more cocoa butter and sugar.

White chocolate is cocoa butter only and sugar.

Milk chocolate is cocoa plus butter plus milk solids plus sugar.

How does chocolate work without fat or sugar?

Now, it is no longer chocolate, but cocoa powder, dry and bitter. It contains, among other things, those magic molecules, polyphenols.

Cocoa reduces fat deposition in the liver and in arteries. It raises HDL and lowers LDL. These effects are attributed to cocoa's ability to increase the expression of genes related to fat metabolism. Cocoa, by itself, can reduce or prevent obesity.

Cocoa also stops platelet aggregation and lowers blood pressure. This strong cardio-protective effect is achieved by its relaxing action on the muscle in blood vessels by the release of nitrous oxide.

Predictably, cocoa affects the microbiome, and encourages the growth of bacteria that modulate inflammation.

All good stuff, right?

Cocoa is, yes.

But when consumed as chocolate, the hype is mainly justified by the tons of fat and sugar that go into it.

Childhood obesity is a killer disease, and much of it is caused by chocolate.

So why not use chocolate as the Aztecs did? As a drug that revives.

Nibble it, don't gorge on it.

One square, not the whole bar, please!

## Coffee and Tea

Would you believe these pleasures can actually work towards health and longevity?

They do, with the usual caveat. Their magic depends on how you use them. Coffee and tea are bursting with antioxidants.

Coffee : 200–550 mg antioxidants/cup.

Tea : 150–400 mg antioxidants/cup.

Nonetheless, it is naïve to expect them to perform the advertized miracle of rejuvenation. Not visibly, anyway.

The invisible scenario is interesting. And, considering the national consumption of tea and coffee, worth a closer look.

- Coffee consumption: 1,210 thousand 60 kg bags across India in 2020.
- (Global consumption in 2020: 162,841 thousand 60 kg bags.)

Our tea consumption is gargantuan: One BILLION kg in 2020–21.

These figures tell us that, while coffee has a niche market, tea is swilled by everyone, everywhere. That is misleading. Coffee is popular in the southern states and tea in the north. Geography dictates taste. Both beverages are drunk in offices almost obsessively.

A cup of tea contains almost as much caffeine as a cup of coffee. That should state the obvious: coffee isn't only about caffeine.

A 120 ml cup of brewed black coffee can contain anything between 100–200 mg of caffeine, the compound most commonly identified with coffee, principally due to its effects on the brain: alertness, wakefulness, irritability.

About 400 mg of caffeine can leave you with twitchiness and insomnia.

Also, the response to caffeine is not uniform. You could find yourself regretting a 6 p.m. cup of coffee as you stare at the dark at 2 a.m., while it seems to have had no effect on your snoring partner.

It is smart to check on your own tolerance for coffee, and decide when to have your last cup of the day.

But are these effects really the result of caffeine on the brain?

Yes, caffeine blocks the action of adenosine. Daylight results in adenosine buildup in the brain. This is a strong signal for sleep. Adenosine receptors inhibit brain activity, and we doze off. The chemical formula of caffeine is 1,3,7-trimethylxanthine. It mimics the chemical structure of adenosine and competes with adenosine for binding to brain cells. Once caffeine has docked in, there is no dampening of brain activity, so the overtired brain no longer feels 'sleep pressure'.

This goes further. Every clock in the body – there is one in each cell – is set by the Supra-Chiasmatic Nucleus (SCN) in the brain. This super-clock is set by light. When we perceive light, the SCN telegraphs the pineal gland to stop producing the 'sleep chemical' melatonin. At dusk, it sends the opposite message and the pineal gland secretes melatonin and makes us fall asleep.

Melatonin production depends on an enzyme that begins to act a few hours after dark. Surprisingly, in teenagers, this may be considerably slower, so their sleep cycle is often timed to a later setting.

As the young are coffee and tea consumers, this understanding can save them and us a lot of grief. Drinking tea or coffee late in the day can push back melatonin production to a later hour. But when they're woken up early, melatonin levels stay high well into the morning, making them sleepy in class. So, if you find yourself beleaguering your teenager with 'Why can't you wake up on time?' – stop.

Coffee hang outs should be limited to daytime for teenagers. Brewed coffee has about 100–200 mg of caffeine as opposed to instant coffee which delivers half as much.

Caffeine apart, coffee has some 600 compounds that are considered bioactive. There is evidence that coffee polyphenols, especially chlorogenic acids and trigonelline have the most beneficial actions imaginable on fat metabolism. There are some tall claims about coffee: it staves off diabetes, lowers blood pressure, prevents platelet clumping, and also guarantees better health. However, what we do know for certain is that coffee brews contain enough phenols to produce recognizable antioxidant effects.

Coffee brew is rich in niacin, vitamin B3, enough to supply our daily requirement.

As opposed to its original reputation as a nervy, hypertensive, cardiac stimulant, coffee, today, is regarded as cardio-protective, beneficial to the liver, and very likely protective against diabetes.

Cautions still apply: coffee can interfere with sleep, irritate your stomach, and leave you feeling twitchy and hungover.

Tea has much better press than coffee, simply because of its populist stance. This takeover is barely a century old, considering tea has only been drunk on the subcontinent since the Britishers took to cultivating it after 1840. Tea drinking was practically imposed on the population in the early years of the twentieth century when Brooke Bond began its expansion. Today, tea is an 'Indian tradition', just as ancient as many other habits with that label.

Tea is not brewed but boiled in India. The delicate and sophisticated flavour of tea has few takers here. It is more popularly swamped with a *masala* of spices that impart a rich, even ostentatious, bouquet. With generous amounts of milk and sugar, boiled down almost to a syrup, tea keeps the nation on its feet.

The tea at home isn't very different. It is the day's indulgence, the cup that connects, the brokerage of tolerance and trade. It is a social gaffe to refuse a cup of tea.

It is also *de trop* to call it tea or serve it in a cup. We have been having *chai-biskoot* since Vedic times – or so we are expected to believe.

The research on tea does not add up to observable fact. Its rich polyphenols, flavonoids and catechins are sworn to protect against diabetes. That has no meaning in a nation that swills 1 billion kg of tea and is still mortally sick with diabetes.

Possibly, the virtues of tea are all lost in the way we prepare it.

Green tea is drunk by the gallon in the hope of instant rejuvenation. It differs from the usual black tea in that the leaf is not fermented. Thanks to new-age hype, it is largely consumed without milk or sugar.

The polyphenols in green tea are catechins, especially epigallocatechin gallate, which has been lauded as a miracle compound. Catechins get oxidized, when the tea leaf is fermented, into theaflavins, which give black tea its wonderful spectrum of ruby hues, and also its incomparable fragrance.

Black tea contains thearubigins, theaflavins, flavonols and catechins – no different, really, from green tea, just a tad more oxidized.

A word of caution here.

Green tea may not be as innocuous as it is hyped to be. The upper limit of safe consumption has been recorded as an incredible twenty-four cups a day! I am quoting that just to illustrate how fallacious a statement like that can be.

The method employed to extract flavours decides the concentration of chemicals in the product. This is a delicate and complicated pharmacological process, and it is employed with a great deal of science in Ayurveda and Unani medicine. Cold water steeping, steeping in hot water, boiling – they all liberate different phytochemicals into the infusion.

This is what makes the domestic 'home remedy' so dangerous. This is also true of the wide variety of herbal teas, so magically accepted as safe because they are 'natural'.

'Natural remedies' all contain unnatural toxins. Please, dear home cook, don't tamper with them!

To give you one example: green tea so trustingly drunk as a tea bag infusion is fine. But when it is used as an extract, as it is sold in any number of patented 'nutraceuticals', it has been known to cause fatal liver failure.

So why not go back to drinking tea, black or green, in the manner the Chinese people have drunk it for millennia?

As a gentle infusion, fragrant and uncorrupted, as lovely as its Latin name, *Camellia sinensis*, the Rose of China.

# Part Five

# Home Remedies

## *When Good for You* **Is** *Bad for You*

This threatens to be the shortest chapter in this book. One word could say it all: DON'T!

I don't like bans, and will state my reasons, and leave you to make your choice.

There is one reason that overwhelms all others, and pushes every objection off the board. And that is the magic of the familiar.

When illness threatens, the evolutionary response is to seek out familiar comforts. Your own bed, that soft near-ragged T-shirt, a familiar touch. The only thing you can bear to taste is your own particular comfort food, and that too no more than a spoonful. The world is your enemy. Reason has backed off.

Time now for magic, faith, belief.

'Just drink this.'

The voice is flat. This is command, not request.

This is the fíat that will put an end to that evolutionary tantrum, because –

Because it is the voice of the magician, the All Knowing One, the keeper of the flame, so far back in time, it is above gender and probably a dinosaur.

And that glass contains what has held up humanity since then.

It is the Elixir of Life, the one and only universal panacea.

It looks, smells, and tastes bloody awful.

You drain it to the last drop.

Then you turn your face to the wall and black out for the next five hours.

When you wake up, the fever is gone, and you are back in the land of the living.

Miracle? Thaumaturgy?

Undeniably, the home remedy has worked.

What was it?

*Kanda kadha?*

*Jeera kashayam?*

*Haldi doodh?*

It could have been any of these. Or your family's closely guarded secret, the one that rescued your great-grand-uncle from the perils of typhoid/cholera/smallpox/bubonic plague back in 1896.

Whatever it was, it worked.

There is a lot of science in your body's response to that miracle remedy.

Trust overcame your restless battle against the exhaustion of fever. It put you to sleep as it invariably does. And sleep allowed your body to counter the illness in the ways it does so secretly and so well.

Home remedies do have the advantage of making you

shut up and rest when nothing else will. They are beyond argument in that attribute. But their contents have nothing to do with curing you.

All Indian home remedies have their roots in traditional systems of medicine: Ayurveda, Unani, Siddha. These sciences are spectacular in their understanding of how fruits, vegetables, and minerals act on the body. Their textbooks are still followed unchanged by *vaidyas* and *hakims*. They contain specific directions for sourcing, preparation and indications for use. None of these is followed in the 'home remedy', which is the hand-me-down of memory or hearsay, and unadvised by any kind of science.

Now for those familiar kitchen ingredients that make up home remedies.

If they are really useless, why were they in use for centuries?

Hold on, I didn't say they were useless. They are useless *only* when employed as home remedies.

The kitchen should not double as a pharmacy.

'Why not?' you demand. 'Everybody says these things are good for us, and they boost immunity.'

Sure. These days everything boosts immunity, even cooking oil. I'd like to take you up on that phrase 'good for us' and its frequent opposite 'bad for us'.

Most 'good for you' stuff works in the kitchen as seasoning and spice. It makes food tastier and more digestible in quantities judged right for the dish. If any of these aromatics overwhelm, the dish becomes inedible.

When used as home remedies, these same ingredients are pushed into excess. In this form or dosage, they act in one of these ways:

1. They are intolerable, and may induce nausea and vomiting
2. They have no effect whatsoever
3. They cause actual harm

The last one is of great interest to me.

Encountering even one instance of harm is enough to declare these home remedies dangerous.

'Good for you' is often based on good science. Most 'home remedy' dependables have interesting pharmacological actions, which is to say they could be the source of drugs that cure or relieve diseases. That is how they have been used by *vaidyas* and *hakims*. The home cook, though, is not qualified to dose herself, or her family, with dangerous drugs on the basis of imagined benefits.

Here are some of the dangerous potentials of 'home remedies' based on four common kitchen ingredients:

| | | |
|---|---|---|
| Garlic | : | platelet dysfunction and bleeding |
| Turmeric | : | severe liver damage |
| Ginger | : | stomach irritation, diarrhea |
| Cumin (*jeera*) | : | liver failure, bleeding, sudden fall of blood sugar |

They can, in addition, interact with common medications, which you may be taking if you are diabetic or have high blood pressure or heart disease.

We use them all the time, you say, and have never heard of any of these disasters.

That is because the trace amounts of actives contained in these spices are too little to do anything beyond flavouring and enhancing the foods they are cooked with. In such small amounts, they cannot exert the pharmacological activities observable in a laboratory on a bunch of unfortunate rats.

These laboratory actions of garlic, ginger, turmeric, and cumin are spectacular enough to banish every ill from the face of the earth.

But that decoction or extract made in your kitchen is nothing but disaster waiting in a cup because it is uncalibrated and contains unknown amounts of active molecules, which can upset physiological processes – specifically, the process of inflammation.

This is especially true now, when our destiny is being dictated by a virus that disorders our immune process by causing inflammation.

I think we need to talk a little more about that, and relate events to the kitchen shelf, and I will.

A *nutraceutical* is just a home remedy in cute packaging. The same rules apply, so stay off them, please!

The word, in itself, is a sham. Nutrition turned pharmaceutical?

Why not, instead, just eat sensibly and enjoyably?

# Hazards

The kitchen can bristle with hazards. Some of our own creation. But common foods themselves may conceal hazards.

## Chilli

The Nobel Prize in Medicine, in 2021, was awarded to David Julius of the University of California, San Francisco, and Ardem Patapoutian of Scripps Research Institute in La Jolla, California, for their discovery of receptors for temperature and touch. These were based on a food so ubiquitous it is difficult to imagine Indian cuisine without it. And yet, it hasn't been with us very long. Like the tomato, the potato, the *sapota* and chocolate, it was a gift from the Aztecs and other Native American cultures annihilated by Europeans. As they rampaged round the globe, marauding European hordes distributed their plunder of horticultural skill among other cultures. After the Portuguese had massacred Goa (1510), they consoled us with chilli. From 1510 to 2021, chilli has had a brilliant global career, crowned by the Nobel

Prize. It is a suitable moment to reconsider this burning fruit of genocide.

The Nobel was awarded for an investigation centred on chilli's principal ingredient, *capsaicin,* which stings the tongue with unbearable heat. Today, the heat of chilli is culinary machismo. Chilli, fresh green, dried, red, powdered or ground down to its essence, spikes every dish like a snarl of barbed wire. Why does chilli, and specifically capsaicin, burn?

In 1997, Julius discovered a receptor for capsaicin. Soon, he found that this receptor could be activated by heat as well – so this was a receptor that transmitted the message 'burn' to the brain.

Patapoutian, working independently, discovered a receptor that messaged the 'delightfully cool' sensation of menthol to the brain. These discoveries led on to a deeper understanding of how we feel heat, cold, touch, pressure, and pain.

Chilli and its capsaicin inspired this tremendous surge of perception of the tactile world. And that's ironic because capsaicin does just the opposite: it numbs, after first sear. It stops cells from communicating, so pain signals are suppressed. You can no longer feel what's happening – the stimulus has to be much stronger to elicit a response.

In culinary terms, this translates as *MORE!*

When you use chilli you also must:

1. Use MORE oil to disseminate heat through the dish. Capsaicin is not water soluble. It takes fat to dissolve it enough to permeate the dish.
2. Use MORE salt, MORE spice, to make these flavours register on the numbed tongue and palate so liberally coated with capsaicin.

There are capsaicin receptors lower down in the throat, food pipe, stomach, and small intestine. All of them register capsaicin as PAIN.

Chilli's malice bites even deeper. The burn it produces leaves no external evidence of inflammation. You'd expect your mouth to look like a battlefield after you've chewed a chilli – ragged and bloody, what's left of it, through the smoke. Not at all. A faint flush, perhaps, but no more.

Chilli is the experience of injury and pain.

Why then, is it so pleasurable? Are we aficionados of algolagnia and masochism?

Perhaps so, judging from the tyrannies we endure. Perhaps not, judging from chemistry.

Capsaicin causes a brief release of endorphins, the pleasure chemicals, in the brain. Just enough to provide an instant high, and make us demand more.

Why did India embrace chilli so readily when we were so rich with pepper and ginger to perk up our cuisine?

There's an answer to that question that has been hiding in plain sight for centuries.

It is some kind of poetic justice too.

When Vasco da Gama and his successors plundered us, they were plundered in turn by scurvy, the killer deficiency of vitamin C that assailed sailors on long voyages. But scurvy is common among us landlubbers too – when we don't eat enough fresh vegetables and fruit.

Chilli is one of the richest sources of vitamin C, and it grows wild. In no time at all, our people found themselves feeling better for a bite of chilli with their gruel. It seemed to take away their aches and pains. It improved the appetite. It improved *life*.

From the perspective of this pandemic, how should we interpret chilli's story?

We eat a lot of it – and so, by now, does the rest of the planet – for it's 'feel good' factor. This 'high' makes it addictive. Its vitamin C certainly shores up metabolism.

The more chilli, the more fat, the more salt, the more everything.

The benumbed mouth and stomach also demand more food.

Chilli is the spice of excess.

Can't do without it?

Try a simple experiment: increase the amount of fruit you eat. Tomatoes and citrus, mango, kiwi, pomegranate. Do it for a week. You might soon surprise yourself wincing when you take a mouthful of your favourite fiery curry.

Cut back on oil. Now the injury caused by capsaicin will become more intense – and yes, you'll find yourself holding back on chilli.

Cut back on chilli and you'll start tasting food again, soothing a lifelong burn from the mouth all the way down to the exit.

And if it's heat you crave, why not give India's treasure a try?

Pepper contains piperine, an alkaloid that stings – but not as much as chilli. It has the added advantage of shaking loose and accelerating the phytochemicals in vegetables when cooked with them. Even in the trace amounts achieved through the kitchen use of pepper, piperine protects the respiratory system. In this time of COVID-19, then, why not reacquaint yourself with this historic spice?

## Soy

In December 2020, there were 7.8 million women living with breast cancer. It is the world's most prevalent cancer.

In the 1960s, the global production of soy was 20 to 30 million tonnes per year. Today it is 350 million tonnes.

Is there any connection between these two facts?

Soy is an ancient legume. Cultivation began in China around 10,000 BCE, and it has nourished the Far East ever since. It has lent itself to many imaginative and texturally varied cuisines. It contains more protein than any other legume, and also more fat. What's not to like?

Soy is also rich in phytoestrogens. While this may not impact a population that has historically thrived on soy, it is worth asking if it poses a risk to more recent consumers. The West imbibes soy as oil in almost all packaged foods – and so does down-the-food-chain India. We have also recently started cultivating soy. We now consume soy flour, soy oil, and soy milk, while tofu, pressed soybean curd, has a niche clientele.

Phytoestrogens are carcinogenic, especially in post-menopausal women.

I've given you the statistics. Go figure.

## Storage and Spoilage

All foods spoil, and we often don't find out till it is too late. That's because very few spoiled foods actually smell or taste 'off'.

Foods spoil for the same reason that we eat them –

they're packed with energy. So, bacteria and fungi feast on them too.

A huge amount of foods are lost to spoilage before they reach us. It is estimated that 30% of India's vegetable produce rots on its way to market. High temperature and humidity favour rot. Vegetables and fruits, which are acidic, are susceptible to rot by fungi. Alkaline fruits and vegetables are colonized by bacteria.

But except in the case of accidents or oversight, fruits and vegetables so afflicted seldom enter the kitchen.

We need to worry about spoilage of what's already in here.

Let's take a look at those bottles at the back of the shelf.

Jam. Pickle. Sauce.

Sniff – smells a bit medicinal, doesn't it? But these are preserves, surely! They're supposed to last for years. Get real. They don't. They'll soon be growing beards if you keep them. Yeasts grow well in high-sugar high-salt foods. And it's no surprise to find little patches of fuzz on the surface of a pickle.

You have a bottle of squash in the fridge? Aha. Home-made? Great.

But – fungus, eh?

Look, it isn't your fault. You haven't been 'unclean'. The bottle was not filthy. You took every precaution to be as meticulous as possible.

What then?

Ours is a humid country. Fungal spores are everywhere, so are bacteria and viruses. We live among them.

But why in the fridge?

Most organisms aren't deterred from growth at 10°C. They may grow slower, yes, but they grow.

What should you do?

Skim off the top?

Reheat?

No. Just throw it out unless you want a series of tummy troubles.

Stale bread grows mold easily because these fungi thrive without much moisture. And if one slice has mold, the rest of the loaf has thriving spores too and will be visibly moldy tomorrow. This can happen even if the loaf is refrigerated, as many molds flourish at low temperatures.

*Aspergillus* is a dangerous kind of mold that secretes mycotoxins, among which are *aflatoxins*. These often contaminate grain, especially rice. Washing rice before cooking gets rid of most of it, pressure cooking destroys it.

Aspergillus also infests peanuts very often, as the pale green smear in the heart of the nut. This sort of aflatoxin is specially harmful to the liver.

You might wonder how a cooked dish, which after all has been exposed to high temperatures, can go bad after being nuked for ten minutes on the stove. Many bacterial spores are heat resistant. So don't be surprised if the curry you left in the fridge overnight tastes 'off'.

The worry is you may not know – by odour, by appearance, even by taste – that it is 'off'. But a crippling diarrhea later in the day will make you wonder what caused it.

'Nothing, nothing, only home food' is what most alarmed patients recall when they seek advice. It is hard to convince them that yes, this can happen despite refrigeration.

Of course, the sensible solution is to eat freshly cooked food. But this is not always practical. *So, the safe and practical way is to freeze that extra portion.*

'Ropiness', or the appearance of strings, when you stir food is another sign of decay caused by bacteria. Throw the food out! And, after you have scoured the vessel, sterilize it in the pressure cooker for a couple of whistles.

Protein-containing foods – *dals* and pulses in the main – can quickly spoil, often within hours. They may form a slimy layer on the surface. They should never be left overnight in the main compartment of the refrigerator.

Eggs will last for a couple of weeks in the fridge, but are best eaten within the week.

Milk should not be kept for more than a day in the main compartment. Despite pasteurization – or rather, past it – contamination by common bacteria causes breakdown of milk proteins and fats even if the milk doesn't 'split'. Curdling or splitting is, of course, the most common change, and it is caused by actic acid bacteria.

Cooked food spoils quickly because its nutrients are freely available, so bacteria and fungi grow with glee. The safety rule is: *Never leave cooked food on the counter.* As it cools from hot to warm, it gets closer to the temperatures suitable for bacterial growth. Eat it now – or refrigerate up to 12 hours. If it has to wait past that, freeze.

Food poisoning is the dramatic term used for an illness that results from consuming ordinary food.

No poisoner has been at work here.

There is no malicious intent.

But the food is contaminated with bacterial spores that burgeon with heat and humidity to form colonies of bacteria that often secrete toxins. When this food is eaten, these toxins irritate the gastrointestinal lining to produce vomiting or diarrhea, sometimes both.

The results can be frighteningly severe. Usually, food poisoning is diagnosed, rather clumsily, from the answer to the question: How many people were affected?

Food poisoning is not always a group activity. It can occur in your own home, under the best of conditions.

Here are a few cautions:

1. Milk-based sweets (all milk-based – *khoya* – *mithai*, not just 'Bengali Sweets', please) – are notorious for this. So buy these only from a trusted outlet. The contamination usually occurs at the milk source.
2. Check dates on Tetra Paks and packaged foods. Avoid if the container appears deformed or bloated.
3. Wash, squeeze, and dry out your scrubber after each use. Scrubbers are germ traps!
4. Rice, kept overnight in the fridge, must be pressure cooked before it is used the next day.
5. Remember, spices are not preservatives, neither is oil.
6. If you feel sick and vomit a few hours after a meal, call your doctor.

# How to Read a Recipe

Every home has a tattered recipe book. Some, like mine, have a whole shelf of them. Written by chefs past, these are inheritance, not just reference books. Most of these chefs were people who fed us: mothers, aunts, grandmothers, even the rare uncle or two. And those who aren't biological family, have become that and more over the years of trust invested in them.

But we haven't been reaching for these guides much of late, have we? The internet is so completely devoted to all things culinary, one can easily find any recipe in the world.

If you have located that recipe, I suggest you take a break. Read the recipe, and think it through.

Take a simple everyday dish like *upma*. It is only *rava* (semolina), water, and vegetables.

Why would it even need a recipe? Nonetheless, read through it.

What are you looking for in the dish?

It should be easy and quick, have the typical flavour, and

the texture should be neither gummy nor sandy.

Does the recipe fix this?

Speed is of the essence if you are making it for breakfast, but you can achieve that easily by prepping the vegetables ahead of time.

The typical flavour is in the seasonings, so that's fine.

The texture is the sticking point. *Rava* + water = gum. How does the recipe prevent that?

Oil, of course!

How much oil does the recipe demand?

'Oh. Let me check...'

Had you thought of asking that question before my prompt? Terrific!

You'll find most recipes use 30 ml of oil for 100 gm of *rava*. That feeds two people.

*But that's the entire day's allowance of oil in one serving!*

Exactly.

Why did the recipe recommend so much oil when the cooking medium is water?

The usual answer is: to achieve that 'typical flavour' and to keep the *rava* from becoming gummy.

The flavour can be achieved with less oil, but is there any other way of preventing the *rava* from gumming up?

The moment you ask the right questions, you are halfway to the answers. And you asked those questions because you have already rejected a recipe that uses up the day's allowance of oil in a single helping at breakfast.

I selected *upma* as the first exercise because it really is a poser.

Take something simpler – *chhole*. Call it chickpeas in piquant sauce, or what you will. Pick six recipes off the net, one from every part of the subcontinent, because everybody cooks *channa* under different names. It is the gravy that makes all the difference.

Line up those recipes, and what do you find?

- Distinctly different flavours and taste
- Different oils

The more modest ones work on this ratio:

- 2 tablespoons of oil for every 100 gm of *channa*

What does the oil accomplish? The usual answer is:

- It brings out the flavour of the masala. Without it the flavour won't suffuse the entire dish.
- You need all that oil to brown the onions, otherwise they would char.

I disagree with these reasons, but I'll venture another:

- Oil/*ghee* is used as flavouring.

This is what gives distinction to the dish: *ghee* in a Punjabi *chhole,* mustard oil in *ghungni,* coconut oil in *kadala curry*.

All it takes to impart that flavour, believe you me, is just a drop as garnish on the cooked dish, which you should instantly cover. The flavour suffuses through the steaming hot dish to permeate every morsel.

This leaves the weighty question about the onions in the gravy.

The secret to delicious gravy is *body.* Unlike Western cuisine, Indian food does not demand a smooth mouthfeel. It can be chunky, or even granular, but it must be bursting with flavour and juice.

We wrote the book on flavour and juice, but when it comes to giving gravy a body, we fall back lamely on an onion-tomato meld that is brain-dead by the time the oil's done with it.

Most recipes use this proportion: 100 gm onion takes 30 gm oil.

*And cook till the oil separates* is a standard directive.

Yes, I know, you have always done it this way.

But that was before you read this book.

The secret to successfully caramelizing onions is not oil. It is being there and noticing what's happening in the pan.

Not convinced?

Take one large onion, chop it fine and try out the least amount of oil it takes to caramelize. No can do? Move on to the next chapter.

Now that you know how to read recipes, I urge you to read recipes you are never going to cook.

This is a fun exercise, but it also hones your skills in judging amounts, and understanding how ingredients work.

You might even be emboldened to try a few substitutions.

What if your teenager announces she's turned forever vegan?

Your partner is newly gluten-sensitive, your dad is diabetic, and you are plain deadbeat tired?

There is a solution. There always is.

So, as your teen might put it, just chill.

# Quick Cuts and Cooking Hacks

Here are a few ways of cutting down kitchen time and labour. On days when I have just fifteen minutes to fix lunch, eat and wash up, I fall back on them. I'm a very lazy person, so I can assure you they work!

Don't grudge yourself those golden ten minutes you spend at the window, steaming cup in hand. Making space for thought is always a good beginning. On the way to the window, you did peek in the fridge to check supplies.

You know what's there to work with, so plan now, in this oasis of peace, not with everything jostling on the counter, clamouring to be cooked. Once you've decided, you can stroll in whistling and deal with the next problem.

Waiting on the counter to guilt you are the pots and pans your mom (and perhaps hers too) used to cook for a family larger than yours.

A large vessel always means more of everything, and that happens before we quite realize it. Do switch to cookware commensurate with the portions your family needs. Refrigerating till it's eaten through only opens the door to waste and spoilage.

A *tawa*, a skillet, a pan are all you need, in addition to a pressure cooker. If you have an oven or toaster, that helps too.

Mechanize all you can: blender/mixer, a heavy duty one; a vegetable chopper is a boon.

Oh yes, measuring spoons, please! Down to a 1 ml one you can use for oil.

Most Indian kitchens have a masala *dabba* for the counter. Refilled every week from the mother jars on the shelf, it contains dinky little *katoris* for the spices and masalas you need for the day's cooking, each with its tiny spoon.

This is brilliant, and I hope you have one.

No?

It is worth the effort of making it. It will also give you an idea of the spices you favour the most – and how much.

I'm going to show you some of my quick cuts and cooking hacks. You may know them already, or know better. Why not act on them?

**Prepping:** 15 min

1. Prep for the entire menu. This puts the jobs ahead in perspective. The menu has informed you of the ingredients, cooking medium, and the cooking methods each dish requires. So set out ingredients, the vessels you'll be using and the fats – oil and *ghee*. Also, keep your measuring spoons at hand.
2. At the end of the prep phase, you should have on the counter several bowls:
   - Vegetables for each dish.
   - *Dals* washed and soaking
   - Pulses soaked overnight ready for pressure cooking or

- Pulses cooked ahead and frozen, thawing on the counter.

3. Also, smaller bowls that have any fresh *masalas* your menu demands. They could be chopped, ground, or ready frozen, set to thaw.
4. Any other ingredient that needs prepping, like kokum or tamarind, that needs soaking.

*Setting the pressure cooker:*

This heavy-duty vessel can take on several jobs besides cooking *dal*, rice, and pulses. Time it right to get perfect results.

When steaming vegetables for a sauté, the time depends on how tender the vegetables are and how fine they have been chopped. Here you need the vegetables to retain their crispness, colour, and structure as you will be cooking them further. Don't drown the vegetable in water. Sprinkle a few grains of sugar before you steam, to retain colour and texture.

When steaming vegetables to end point for adding them to a gravy, do add enough water to cover the vegetables, and use the cooking water in the gravy.

Don't add soda!

Potatoes are best steamed with their skins intact.

Many 'hard' vegetables can also be steamed in large chunks and chopped later. It makes life easier.

Foods with the same cooking time can be cooked at one go in the cooker. Make certain you have fitting containers.

**Assembly:** 15 min

*Mise en place*: This fancy culinary term translates as everything in place. But I will refine it further. It means everything in place on the counter and in your mind.

On the counter:

- All the prepped bowls organized with satellite bowls of *masala*/herbs.
- The *masala dabba* at the ready. It should also have one or two small *katoris* with *tadka* ingredients.
- The oil can or cup, with a pastry brush and a 1 ml spoon alongside.

Really, how long did that take?

If your menu includes *roti* or *paratha,* the dough should be ready rested.

If it includes a batter preparation, like *idli* or *dosai,* keep that ready too.

Now, get cracking!

You will find how much quicker things move.

## Oil

Try these ways to cut down the use of oil.

1. Use a dropper. One ml = 16 drops. A soft and fluffy *aloo paratha* takes 1 ml. An omelette takes 2 drops.
2. Rub your skillet with 2 drops of oil before you add 2 drops more for a *tadka.* Then, when you slide in the steamed vegetables, they won't stick to the pan.
3. Use a pastry brush to prime your *tawa.* Dip just the tips of the brush in oil, shake off the excess. The brush should not be dripping with oil. Now, paint your skillet or tawa with it. This method works brilliantly with *parathas* – brush, flip, brush, done!

4. Use your toaster – if you have a horizontal one – for all your roasts. It is also great for crisping.

**Vegetables & fruits**

1. Cooking makes vegetables more digestible, but can destroy vitamins and leach out minerals. Brief cooking time prevents much of this loss. Very high temperatures are not only destructive, they also lead to inadequate cooking in the centre of the food. So, cut vegetables small, preserve cooking water, steam before sautéing.
2. Cooking different vegetables together has the compensatory benefit of nutrients from several sources.
3. Cooking vegetables with dals or milk gets rid of many anti-nutrients like tannins, and retains many nutrients.
4. The addition of acids and alkalis can alter the texture and integrity of the vegetable. Alkali makes vegetables mushy. If you must use one, use milk, not soda, which leaches out salts and minerals.
5. Colour can be preserved by brief cooking, whether steaming, blanching or sautéing. Covering the cooking vessel will turn bright green vegetables olive green.
6. Cooking vegetables to retain colour, texture, taste, and nutritive value demands attention.
7. If you must boil vegetables, do so in salted water and retain the water. Use it, if necessary, in another dish.
8. Blanching is a much better alternative. Here the volume of water should be large, the stay in water no

more than a minute or two before the vegetables are transferred to a bowl of ice water, or refrigerated to arrest the cooking process. Blanching does not cook the vegetable completely. It reduces the cooking time in assembling the dish.

To sauté, you could try this instead of your usual method:

1. Two drops of oil to rub the skillet. Two more for tadka.
2. Add spices, then slide in steamed or blanched vegetables, and add seasoning. If you cannot cook without turmeric, a pinch will more than suffice.
3. Cover and uncover your skillet every half minute or so. This will let the vegetables cook to end point without loss of structure or change in colour. When cooking green vegetables like peas and French beans, don't cover at all. Keep sprinkling water and shaking the pan. Done in under two minutes. Never stir a sauté. Why torment those tender vegetables?
4. Fruit can be added to any sauté at the end. Try cabbage with apple.
5. If you want a spicy sauté, you could try finishing with one of the dal-spice powders in the next chapter. Sprinkle, toss, and cover for a few seconds. Toss again and serve.
6. For vegetables in gravy, try the tomato concentrate in 'Recipes'.

## Meal-in-a-Bowl

The saviour of the harried cook, the meal in a bowl can be:

1. Cooked quickly
2. Cooked and frozen
3. Assembled from basic cooked ingredients within minutes
4. Served with a *raita,* curd, a salad, or just on its own – it works as a hot dish
5. You can fix your own delicious meal-in-a-bowl with any spice or flavouring. The ideal proportion is: 3 parts vegetables: 2 parts rice or *daliya*: 1 or even 2 parts *dal* or pulses. (You will find the spice powders in the next chapter helpful.)
6. With a side of vegetables you can also try three basic techniques:
   - The *khichdi* way, in which the ingredients are cooked together.
   - Mixed rice: as in curd and rice.
   - Tossed rice: as in lemon rice or tamarind rice.

## The Fridge

Besides fruits, vegetables, eggs, and milk, do keep some basics handy.

- *Roti* dough
- *Idli* batter – extra can be frozen, it thaws well.

Store freshly ground *masala* powders in tightly capped jars in the fridge. This prevents oxidation of volatile oils and keeps the aroma intact for much longer.

The main compartment of your fridge must not store leftovers for beyond six hours. It is always sensible to freeze extra portions (after they've been cooled down on the counter.)

## The Freezer

Stocking your freezer with precooked ingredients is a trick that saves a lot of time.

1. Vegetables can be blanched and frozen for up to two weeks. To thaw, place overnight in the main compartment of the fridge, and on the counter about two hours before cooking.
2. Pulses can be cooked and frozen for up to two weeks. Freeze them with the water. They can be pressure cooked again after thawing, or simmered in an open pan.
3. All doughs and batters freeze well: that includes bread and *roti* dough, *idli/dosai* batter. *But you can't hurry the thawing process.* Overnight in the main compartment, then five to six hours on the counter, depending on the ambient temperature of your kitchen.
4. Butter and cheese can be frozen for another reason besides the obvious one of preventing rancidity. Frozen butter can be rubbed on a cold pan for an omelette, even on a mildly warming one. Cheese can be grated less messily, and less exuberantly – just enough to flavour, not enough to glut.
5. Cooked dishes can be frozen for up to ten days. Meal-in-a-bowl dishes freeze beautifully, and also intensify flavours.

6. It is always useful to have a modest stash of frozen meals – not just for unexpected guests, but more for yourself for days when cooking is the last thing on your mind. Freeze only delicious meals, please! It is always a cheery thought to have a treat on hand.
7. Do remember to freeze portions, or you'll be faced with a block you either have to hack your way through with an ice-pick or thaw entirely and then refreeze – never a good idea.

# Recipes

Here are the recipes mentioned in this book – just those you might be unfamiliar with. Let me know how they turn out!

## *Breakfast*

### Baked *Upma*

1. Uses eggs, but completely disguised.
2. This can be made three ways, depending on the texture you prefer.
3. Baked version tastes good straight from the fridge too, can be sliced and toasted on a tawa.
4. Of course this contains fat too – 8 gm from the egg yolks + 1 gm oil for *tadka*. (Compare with the standard 30 ml oil.)
5. This makes two generous servings.
6. Also can double as the main dish at lunch or dinner.

***Ingredients***

- 100 gm grated vegetables – or diced and steamed/

blanched. Carrot, cabbage, peas (whole), beans – whatever else you like, but always include onions.

- Vegetables chopped fine in a chopper don't need steaming or blanching.
- Herbs: chiffonade of coriander, ginger finely diced, curry leaves left whole.
- 6 tablespoons of *rava* (100 gm)
- 2 whole eggs
- Boiling water: 50 ml
- Salt for seasoning
- *Upma* seasoning: In 1 ml of *til* oil (or any bland unflavoured oil or *ghee*): 1/4 tsp mustard seeds. 1/2 tsp *urad dal* + *channa dal* together. Generous pinch of asafoetida powder.

***Method***

Preheat oven to 350°F.

1. Transfer *rava* to bowl 1.
   Pour boiling water on it, enough to moisten it completely.
   Leave undisturbed for ten minutes.
2. Whisk and season eggs thoroughly – this is the tricky step. You can also spritz them in the blender to save time.
3. Prepare the *tadka* in a ladle.
4. Add it to the cooled *rava* and mix well.
5. Add the egg and mix till well combined.
6. Add the vegetables and the herbs.

Give it all a good mix and transfer into baking dish.

Bake in moderate oven till the skewer comes out clean.

***Time***

Prep: ten minutes for *rava* to absorb water.

Baking time: 10 min

***Version 2:***

Steamed

This mixture can be steamed too – two whistles does it.

***Version 3:***

As a *rava uthappam*. Just put it on a *tawa*. You may need to add a little more water.

***Textures***

*Baked version:*

- Soft, close grained, succulent, sliceable.

*Steamed version:*

- Maintains structure. Little softer and moister, but not squishy and definitely not gummy!

*Uthappam:*

- This is *uthappam*, not *upma*.

**The Breakfast Hater's Breakfast (for two people)**

1. Steam an apple whole. Slide off the skin. Remove the core.
2. Use one tablespoon of breakfast powder of your preferred flavour, whisk in a little water till a smooth slurry is formed. Transfer to saucepan.
3. Break an egg, separate white and yellow.
4. Whisk yellow with 1 tsp sugar + 1/2 tsp instant coffee or cocoa powder.

5. Beat the white to a froth.
6. Cook the breakfast powder slurry in a saucepan after adding 1/4 cup water and whisking till it looks shiny.
7. Pour a teaspoon of this into the yellow, whisk briskly.
8. Add the yellow to the saucepan, turn down the heat. Add half a cup of milk.
9. Pour this hot liquid into the egg whites bowl, whisking vigorously.
10. Blend the steamed apple with half a cup of hot milk.
11. Add the cooked mixture. Blend and pour into two cups.
12. Top with grated chocolate or cinnamon or a dusting of instant coffee.

This can also be made without eggs:

- Cook the breakfast powder with milk as above.
- Blend the steamed apple with 1/2 tsp instant coffee + 1 tsp sugar or honey.
- Blend the two liquids and serve hot.

This can also be served chilled.

Breakfast haters will find it easy to tackle more breakfast after sipping on this.

**Quick Fruit Muffins**

***Ingredients***

1 egg
Half medium-sized apple/pear, cut up

Fresh ginger, if liked
1 tbsp *daliya*
1 inch segment of *doodhi*, grated
A little sugar

***Cookware***

For muffins: Silicon muffin cups. Or if you have aluminum ones, greased and floured
Or a one cup foil case.
2 bowls.
Whisk.

***Method***

1. Sprinkle a little sugar on the fruit, squeeze lemon juice, grate a little ginger, toss and set aside. A pinch of cinnamon can substitute for ginger.
2. In another bowl, pour a little boiling water over the *daliya*, enough to soak it.
3. Preheat oven.
4. Keep two silicon muffin cups ready, or grease and flour metal cups.
5. Separate the egg. Beat yolk, mix with the apple/pear chunks and cooled *daliya*, which would have absorbed water by now.
6. Grate *doodhi* into this mixture.
7. Whip egg white till frothy.
8. Fold whipped white into mixture with a gentle movement.
9. Top with apple crescents (use a mandolin to get wafer-thin slices), a few grains of sugar and ginger or cinnamon.

10. Take care not to overfill muffin cases.
11. Bake in the middle of the oven till the tester comes out clean. Takes about ten minutes.

On opening the oven, muffins will sink a little, but only a little!

For a savoury version of the same, use grated vegetables and your favourite seasoning.

**Breakfast Powders**

a. 1 cup oats + 1 cup *ragi* powder + 1 square of good grade, above 70% bitter chocolate
b. 1 cup oats + 1 cup *ragi* powder + 3 walnuts + 2 almonds + 3 *elaichi* + ginger powder 1 tsp + pinch of good grade saffron.

***Breakfast of Champions*** (no eggs) – Serves 2.

- 3 tbsp of cooked *thuvar dal* + 50 ml milk. Blend and set aside.
- 1 tbsp of powder B + 1 tsp of grated *gur* (jaggery). Make into a slurry and cook.
- When shiny, add the cup of blended *dal.*
- Add 50 ml more milk.
- Serve hot or chilled.

***Coffee or Chocolate Frappe*** (with eggs) – Serves 2.

- Blend together 1 small *elaichi* banana + 1 tsp of cocoa powder + 50 ml milk.
- Separate 1 egg, whisk yellow with 1 tsp instant coffee + 1 tsp sugar.

- Cook 1 tsp of breakfast powder A in 50 ml milk.
- Add a tsp of the hot mixture to the yellow, whisk, then transfer yellow into the saucepan on low heat.
- Whisk whites.
- Add hot mixture to the whites, continue whisking.
- Add this to the banana mixture and spritz once in the blender.
- Can be served warm or chilled. Do not reheat.

**Condiments**

These powders can be bottled, and are worth the trouble as they simplify life.

***Dal Powder***

- *Channa dal* + *Urad dal* equal quantities.
- Dry roast with asafoetida + sesame seeds 1 tsp
- Powder coarse with salt and a pinch of sugar.

***Curry Leaf Powder***

- Bowl of curry leaves + *urad dal* 2 tsp + pepper 1 tsp + *til* seeds 1 tsp + *zeera* 1 tsp
  1 tamarind segment (marble sized).
- Dry roast and powder fine.

***'Tops any Savoury' Powder***

- 2 tsp *thuvar dal* + 1 tbsp *dhaniya* + 1 tsp pepper + 1 tsp *methi* + 1 marble tamarind + 1 tsp asafoetida powder.
- Dry roast and powder coarsely.

***Panch Phoran***

- 1 tsp *zeera* + 2 tsp *saunf* + 1 tsp mustard seeds + 1 tsp *methi* + 1 tsp *kallonji.*
- Dry roast mildly and powder.

***Chinese Five Spices***

- 2 star anise + 2 sticks cinnamon + 2 tsp Sizchuan pepper (triphal) + 6 cloves.
- Dry roast mildly and powder.

**Tomato Concentrate**

- 1/2 kg tomato + 2 large onions. Steam. Blend with fresh ginger, few peppercorns, two tsp sugar, 1 tsp salt.
- Transfer to skillet, simmer down to a thickish paste.
- Pour into ice trays and freeze.
- Use this instead of the tomato base for gravies, adding seasonings to suit your taste. Quicker, avoids oil, you can use as many cubes as you want.

*Note:* Red chillis can be added, if you want, to any of the above powders. My advice is: avoid it. You can always add this later at the table, if you still wish to.

***Navarasa Salad***

Finely chop together:

- 1/2 small *karela*
- 1 inch of ginger
- 1 small tomato
- 1/2 small onion or 1 small bulb of spring onion
- Grated carrot
- Grated green mango

- 1 slice of apple
- 1 segment of orange
- 1 tsp of pomegranate arils
- A few coriander leaves

Every ingredient should be cut as fine and small as possible.

Empty into a bowl.

- Squeeze 1 whole lemon
- Sprinkle a few grains of sugar
- A pinch of salt
- Toss well, cover, and refrigerate.

Consume within 24 hours.

# Coda

# Streetscape, Kitchenscape, Inscape, Bookscape

Where do we go from here?

I'm headed back to my kitchen, to think over what I've learned from you.

All along during our conversation, I have been listening to you.

The end of a book is a starting point for a writer, and perhaps for the reader too. But before that, there is one more, rather exciting, experiment before us.

This book has dealt with three landscapes: the streetscape, the kitchenscape, and the inscape, the interior landscape of the mind.

This experiment involves merging these.

Our purpose has been to discover how to eat past pandemics. What does this merged bookscape show us?

Out on the street, the pandemic still rages. The demands of life are irrepressible and must be met. Fear and dread constrained us through 2020, but they can hold us back no longer. Soon, most of us will be vaccinated, and all of us are masked.

What does the vaccine do? How long will it protect?

What about variants? What will the rest of 2022 be like?

We worry.

We know the answers.

The vaccine primes the immune system into producing antibodies and killer cells that will fight the virus. It keeps us from falling seriously ill. But it may not keep us from getting infected. Immunity lasts 6–8 months, at best. We need booster shots after that. And again. And again. Not only to protect us against new variants, but to prompt immune memory.

And where does it reside, this memory of immunity?

Everywhere.

Today, we know that immune cells are in every tissue, and in the circulation. Immune cells are factories that turn out molecules that start off, terminate, and fine tune inflammation, which is the body's response to any intrusion.

Immunity requires a great deal of energy. Immunity siphons energy off from all functioning organs. The body often switches to a different metabolic state to conserve energy in order to mount the immune response.

COVID-19 demonstrated our vulnerability due to co-morbidities, which maintained a chronic state of inflammation and put us at a serious disadvantage. This prolonged suffering and increased mortality. The very deficits stare us in the face when it comes to immunity.

We know, by now, that the virus is everywhere, and disease is decided only by *our response to it.*

Will we be able to generate a controlled immune response that will dust off COVID-19 like the common cold? We are vaccinated, yes. But vaccination is merely a cue. The vaccinated body will recognize the virus and mount a response. *How effective will this response be?*

That depends on the integrity of the immune system. Host response is two-fold:

1. Resistance to counter the virus, and
2. Tolerance to limit tissue damage.

We know, from the first two years of the pandemic, that COVID-19 turns dangerous and life-threatening when uncontrolled inflammation causes widespread tissue damage. People with chronic inflammation – co-morbidities – suffer this complication because obesity and its complications – metabolic syndrome and diabetes – undo our ability to control inflammation.

Vaccines will work successfully only if we optimize metabolism by lowering insulin resistance and allow the successful transformation of food into energy.

That, and that alone, will enable us to survive this or any other imminent pandemic. Or indeed, any disease.

This is a large brief, but once achieved, it establishes a stable state. There are no medicines that can work this miracle for us. So, it is all up to us, and what we do in the kitchen.

For this, we need to merge that streetscape we just delineated with our own altered inscape.

We have considered the dangers of excess. We have understood how the brain's control mechanisms cave in to the seduction of high-fat, high-sugar foods. And, we have seen how these foods can increase insulin resistance to leave us tired and defenseless against infections. Awareness and acknowledgement have made us review our value system with regard to food. It is time to test that out.

What can be more pleasant than an afternoon of shopping when you don't intend to buy anything?

Stroll with me down the street, and make your choices for the coming week. It is going to be an exciting week at work, you will be having guests for dinner over the weekend, and there are two birthdays, one of them yours. This shopping trip will equip you for all that. Go on, I'll be waiting for you with something to revive you when you return.

When you were out, I slipped across to the market and stocked your fridge. We can put away your shopping later. You look overwhelmed – try this, while you tell me all about it.

I notice you didn't say, 'I never eat fruit at this time of day.'

Nor, 'Why so many different kinds? Orange, grapes, kiwi, papaya, pineapple.' Nor, 'What am I supposed to do with the rest of the fruit in the fridge?'

I also notice there aren't any tinsel packets showing in your shopping. Are they at the bottom?

No?

What, you didn't get any? No chips? No biscuits? Not even with a birthday round the corner? I trust you placed an order at the patisserie.

What's that you just said?

You weren't born eating cake but you might die eating one? Neat.

I wish I had thought that one up myself.

Some more fruit?

Alright, you get it. I'll get on with my work.

My, how pretty! I love the way the sun falls on the dish, turning the grapes into garnets.

The terracotta dish? It is only the lid of the *matka*? It is perfect for the fruit.

Let's put the shopping away – hello!

See what I mean?

Your inscape has changed.

Your shopping today was quite different from last week's. It tells me you are ready to change the kitchenscape.

I notice those large *handis* and *kadhais* are missing. Just a skillet, a tawa, a pan? Well, why not. The counter's pretty empty too. What happened to all those?

Oh, here we are.

Everything downsized. Small containers for spices, masalas. Small spoons. A 100 ml canister for oil.

Brava!

Where are those jars of nuts? Those bottles bright with crystallized fruit? Those cookie tins?

And my! That entire shelf of tonics, health pills, herbal teas ...

I remember you called it your Immunity Shelf earlier. All gone.

Right. I won't say another word. You can switch off that defiant glare.

I never realized you had such a big kitchen. But then, as you remark, neither did you.

And that's my bookscape as I envision it – a plan for the confident provision of energy for the household. From my kitchen to yours, from your thought to mine, a game plan for health.

That's what this pandemic could be, the turning point to rethink our food.

To divest it of prejudice and superstition, and recognize its universality; to recognize it as a unifying force, not a divisive one; to enquire into its science and embrace its truths, and not rely on magic or belief.

This is now. This is a pandemic. And you, dear home cook, are going to stop it with the next step you take in your kitchen.

# Vaxed and Cool!

The dictionary, we hear, has made vaccination officially cool. 'Vax' is now a word. I hope vax will stay, and replace the senseless 'vaccination'. We definitely need a new word, one without history, to mark this pandemic, which could spell the beginning of a new era of health awareness and self-care.

How cool is it, exactly, for a nation struggling with metabolic syndrome, to be vaxed?

Vaxed! That's such a relief.

Is it?

What happens within the body after vaccination, and curiosity apart, why should we know about it?

Think of vaccination as an expensive piece of silk you save up for. Finally, it is yours. Still, it has to be tailored to suit you.

Immunity is that perfectly designed and tailored garment you wear to dazzle the world. Long forgotten is the longing for that silk. Even the pleasure of handling it for the first time is a distant memory. You have dusted off worries over picking the right design. It is here, now, and it is just so perfectly you.

This invisible transition from silk to svelte sophistication is the magic vaccinations work within you.

By now, everyone talks about immunity glibly.

We dismiss antibodies as if they are loose change. Macrophages, T-cells, all that trivia, is so yesterday. 'Just keep your eye on those platelets, and it's cool,' we tell ourselves.

These are but words, and devoid of meaning.

What implications do they have for the home cook? Does the invisible process of designing immunity have anything to do with designing the everyday menu?

Immunity, as we know by now, has two components.

The first has to do with antibodies that 'neutralize' the antigen.

The second has to do with killer cells that vanquish the intruding germ in battle.

It is a two-way street.

The process of immunity alters energy pathways for speed and efficiency. And the energy balance of the body is itself influenced by immunity.

After a vaccination, your immunity proceeds in the following steps:

1. Macrophages grab the vaccinated antigen and fragment it. They then hold up these fragments on their surface.
2. T cells recognize these antigens.
3. They stimulate B cells to produce antibodies.

All these cells secrete chemicals called cytokines, which prompt antibody production. Ultimately, antibody production is individualistic, it depends on the person's cytokine profile.

After an injection delivers the vaccine, dendritic cells and macrophages in the muscle pick up the antigen and liberate type-1 interferon. This is a double signal to the T cells in local lymph nodes:

a. It introduces the antigen, the spike protein of SARS-CoV-2,
b. It sets off the process of inflammation.

So, not only has the innate immunity response of inflammation started off, but the 'learned' or adaptive immunity specific to this virus has also begun.

T cells differentiate into effector cells and memory cells.

Effector cells do the work of inflammation and destruction.

Memory cells stimulate B cells into making antibodies.

When inflammation is provoked by an antigen, macrophages, initially, use up a lot of glucose. As a result, there is a lot of lactic acid accumulation in tissues. These actions become amplified over the next 24 hours by a change in the metabolic pathway. Under the influence of this burst of high energy, inflammatory chemicals are secreted. At the same time, anti-inflammatory chemicals are produced in antagonism, using up as much energy.

Meanwhile, as 'immune imprinting' takes place, T cells organize a more specific immune response.

These cells use glucose as the primary fuel for their important actions, and what's more, they speed up the breakdown of glucose for energy. Protein synthesis also speeds up, as many of the chemicals of immunity must be manufactured at great speed.

We marvelled at the speed at which vaccines were produced during this pandemic, but the production of the immune chemicals within the body puts these huge factories to shame.

A special population of T cells – T-regulatory or T-reg cells – manage a very important facet of immunity: they maintain tolerance to 'self' proteins and prevent an auto-immune response. Unlike other T cells, they get their energy from fat metabolism.

T-reg cells in the adipose tissue are important to the insulin response. They encourage the secretion of a hormone from fat cells, which prevents excess fat from leaking into the circulation.

When excessive fat deposition occurs in obesity, the T-reg cells are replaced by other T cells which produce chemicals that set up inflammation. Tregs are then no longer available for the important role they have in immunity. They can no longer encourage insulin, which permits inflammation to proceed unchecked.

T-regs also need amino acids to be primed into activity. For fuel, T-reg cells rely on fatty acids: these are propionate, butyrate and acetate produced by the microbiome.

From this outline, two facts are evident:

1. Immunity demands a great deal of energy. And because the demand is so immediate, the body is forced to shift to quicker, but less efficient, metabolic pathways.
2. The cellular responses are coordinated by insulin activity and a functionally intact microbiome.

Also, the initial response is followed by a buildup of reactive oxygen species, which clear away the effector cells, leaving only the memory-imprinted cells as safeguards against future infections. The integrity of this depends upon enough energy being available throughout the process, despite the switches in metabolic pathways.

In obesity, T cells are recruited into adipose tissue, and there they assume pro-inflammatory profiles and increase insulin resistance.

We home cooks have our work cut out for us. To attain vaccine cool, we need to provide the right ambience for immunity:

- Cut out high-fat, high-sugar decadence to lower insulin resistance.
- Serve up plenty of resistant starches, fibre, and fruit to encourage the microbiome into liberating enough saturated fatty acids to power immune cells.
- Cook vegetables right to preserve as much of their phytochemicals as possible.
- Relish fruit.

And, since you are an expert at all that now, put your feet up, and enjoy that cup of tea.

# References

## Prelude

Tripathy, J.P., J.S. Thakur, G. Jeet, S. Chawla, S. Jain, and R. Prasad, 'Urban Rural Differences in Diet, Physical Activity and Obesity in India: Are We Witnessing the Great Indian Equalization? Results from a Cross-sectional STEPS Survey'. *BMC Public Health* 16: 816 (2016).

World Health Organization (WHO), 'Fact Sheet on Obesity and Overweight', 2021, available at: https://www.who.int/newsroom/fact-sheets/detail/obesity-and-overweight.

## Part One

Aoun, A., F. Darwish, and N. Hamod, 'The Influence of the Gut Microbiome on Obesity in Adults and the Role of Probiotics, Prebiotics, and Symbiotics for Weight Loss'. *Preventive Nutrition and Food Science* 25(2): 113–123 (2020).

Kamath, P., and K.A. Shenoy, 'Yellapragada Subba Row: The

Unsung Hero'. *Muller Journal of Medical Sciences and Research* 4: 130–132 (2013).

Maruyama, K., 'The Discovery of Adenosine Triphosphate and the Establishment of Its Structure'. *Journal of History of Biology* 24: 145–154 (1991).

Vecchio, I., C. Tornali, N.L. Bragazzi, and M. Martini, 'The Discovery of Insulin: An Important Milestone in the History of Medicine'. *Frontiers in Endocrinology* 9: 613 (2018).

## Part Two

Iqbal, J., and M.M. Hussain, 'Intestinal Lipid Absorption'. *American Journal of Physiology-Endocrinology and Metabolism* 296(6): E1183–94 (2009).

Jomard, A., and E. Osto, 'High Density Lipoproteins: Metabolism, Function, and Therapeutic Potential'. *Frontiers in Cardiovascular Medicine* 7: 39 (2020).

Luca, F., G.H. Perry, and A. Di Rienzo, 'Evolutionary Adaptations to Dietary Changes'. *Annual Review of Nutrition* 30: 291–314 (2010).

## Part Three

Ahmadzai, M.M., L. Seguella, and B.D. Gulbransen, 'Circuit-Specific Enteric Glia Regulate Intestinal Motor Neurocircuits'. *Proceedings of the National Academy of Sciences of the United States of America* 118(40): (2021).

Asif, M., 'Physico-Chemical Properties and Toxic Effect of Fruit-Ripening Agent Calcium Carbide'. *Annals of Tropical Medicine and Public Health* 5(3): 150–156 (2012).

Barrett, Jacqueline S., and Peter R. Gibson, 'Fermentable

Oligosaccharides, Disaccharides, Monosaccharides and Polyols (FODMAPs) and Nonallergic Food Intolerance: FODMAPs or Food Chemicals?' *Therapeutic Advances in Gastroenterology* 5(4): 261–268 (2012).

Bhardwaj, Swati, Santosh Jain Passi, Anoop Misra, Kamal K. Pant, Khalid Anwar, R.M. Pandey, and Vikas Kardam, 'Effect of Heating/Reheating of Fats/Oils as Used by Asian Indians, on Trans-fatty Acid Formation'. *Food Chemistry* 212: 663–670 (2016).

Bhutia, D.T., 'Protein Energy Malnutrition in India: The Plight of Our under Five Children'. *Journal of Family Medicine and Primary Care* 3(1): 63–67 (2014).

Caron, J., D. Domenger, P. Dhulster, R. Ravallec, and B. Cudennec, 'Protein Digestion-Derived Peptides and the Peripheral Regulation of Food Intake'. *Frontiers in Endocrinology* 8: 85 (2017).

Biscuit People, 'The Most Effective Online Solution for the Biscuit Industry'. Available at: https://www.biscuitpeople.com.

Chadt, A., and H. Al-Hasani, 'Glucose Transporters in Adipose Tissue, Liver, and Skeletal Muscle in Metabolic Health and Disease'. *Pflügers Archiv - European Journal of Physiology* 472(9): 1273–1298 (2020).

Chaurasia, R.N., A. Pathak, S. Singh, D. Joshi, and V.N. Mishra, 'Study of Knowledge, Attitude, and Practice in Participants with Regular Intake of Lathyrus, But No Spastic Paraparesis'. *Journal of Neurosciences in Rural Practice* 9(1): 11–13 (2018).

Chigwedere, Claire M., Daniel M. Njoroge, Ann M. Van Loey, and Marc E. Hendrickx, 'Understanding the Relations among the Storage, Soaking, and Cooking Behavior of Pulses: A Scientific Basis for Innovations in Sustainable Foods for the

Future', *Comprehensive Reviews in Food Science and Food Safety* 18(4): 1135–1165 (2019).

Cummings, J., and A. Stephen, 'Carbohydrate Terminology and Classification'. *European Journal of Clinical Nutrition* 61: S5–S18 (2007).

Dhembare, A.J., 'Bitter Truth about Fruit with Reference to Artificial Ripener'. *Archives of Applied Science Research* 5(5): 45–54 (2015).

Dhingra, Devinder, Mona Michael, Hradesh Rajput, and R.T. Patil, 'Dietary Fibre in Foods: A Review'. *Journal of Food Science and Technology* 49(3): 255–266 (2012).

DiMenna, F.J., and A.D. Arad, 'Exercise as "Precision Medicine" for Insulin Resistance and Its Progression to Type 2 Diabetes: A Research Review'. *BMC Sports Science, Medicine and Rehabilitation* 10: 21 (2018).

Dixit, S., and M. Das, 'Fatty Acid Composition Including Trans-fatty Acids in Edible Oils and Fats: Probable Intake in Indian Population'. *Journal of Food Science* 77(10): T188–99 (2012).

Elia, M., and J.H. Cummings, 'Physiological Aspects of Energy Metabolism and Gastrointestinal Effects of Carbohydrates'. *European Journal of Clinical Nutrition* 61 Suppl 1: S40–74 (2007).

Evans, P.L., S.L. McMillin, L.A. Weyrauch, C.A. Witczak, 'Regulation of Skeletal Muscle Glucose Transport and Glucose Metabolism by Exercise Training'. *Nutrients* 11(10): 2432 (2019).

Ghafoorunissa, G. 'Role of Trans-fatty Acids in Health and Challenges to Their Reduction in Indian Foods'. *Asia Pacific Journal of Clinical Nutrition* 17 Suppl 1: 212–215 (2008).

Goodman, B.E., 'Insights into Digestion and Absorption of Major Nutrients in Humans'. *Advances in Physiology Education* 34(2): 44–53 (2010).

Gulati, S., A. Misra, and M. Sharma, 'Dietary Fats and Oils in India'. *Current Diabetes Reviews* 13(5): 438–443 (2017).

Habeebrakuman, R., S.S. Kaki, P.D. Bethala Lakshmi Anu, S Maloo, B. Vellanki, and K. Mallampalli Sri Lakshmi, 'Influence of Flour Type on Physico-chemical Characteristics During Deep Frying'. *Journal of Food Science and Technology* 56(7): 3471–3480 (2019).

Hargreaves, M., and L.L. Spriet, 'Skeletal Muscle Energy Metabolism during Exercise'. *Nature Metabolism* 2(9): 817–828 (2020).

Hatting, M., C.D.J. Tavares, K. Sharabi, A.K. Rines, and P. Puigserver, 'Insulin Regulation of Gluconeogenesis'. *Annals of the New York Academy of Sciences* 1411(1): 21–35 (2018).

Henry, C.J., H.J. Lightowler, K. Newens, V. Sudha, G. Radhika, R.M. Sathya, and V. Mohan, 'Glycaemic Index of Common Foods Tested in the UK and India'. *British Journal of Nutrition* 99(4): 840–5 (2008).

Huffman, M.D., D. Prabhakaran, C. Osmond, C.H. Fall, N. Tandon, R. Lakshmy, S. Ramji, A. Khalil, T. Gera, P. Prabhakaran, S.K. Biswas, K.S. Reddy, S.K. Bhargava, and H.S. Sachdev, 'New Delhi Birth Cohort: Incidence of Cardiovascular Risk Factors in an Indian Urban Cohort Results from the New Delhi Birth Cohort'. *Journal of American College of Cardiology.* 57(17): 1765–1774 (2011).

Jomard, Anne, and Elena Osto, 'High Density Lipoproteins: Metabolism, Function, and Therapeutic Potential'. *Frontiers in Cardiovascular Medicine* 7(39) (2020).

Jukanti, A.K., P.M. Gaur, C.L. Gowda, and R.N. Chibbar, 'Nutritional Quality and Health Benefits of Chickpea (Cicer arietinum L.): A Review'. *British Journal of Nutrition* 108 Suppl 1: S11–26 (2012).

Khokhar, Santosh, and Richard K. Owusu, *Apenten.: Antinutritional Factors in Food Vegetables and Effects of Processing: The Role of Food, Agriculture, Forestry and Fisheries in Human Nutrition* (UK: Procter Department of Food Science, University of Leeds, 2004).

Krishnamoorthy, Y., S. Rajaa, S. Murali, T. Rehman, J. Sahoo, and S.S. Kar, 'Prevalence of Metabolic Syndrome among Adult Population in India: A Systematic Review and Meta-analysis'. *PLoS One* 15(10) (2020).

Kulkarni, B., and R.S. Mamidi 'Nutrition Rehabilitation of Children with Severe Acute Malnutrition: Revisiting Studies Undertaken by the National Institute of Nutrition'. *Indian Journal of Medical Research* 150(2): 139–152 (2019).

Kuzawa, C.W., and C. Blair, 'A Hypothesis Linking the Energy Demand of the Brain to Obesity Risk'. *Proceedings of the National Academy of Sciences of the United States of America.* 116(27): 13266–13275 (2019).

Molitor, Elena von, Katja Riedel, Michael Krohn, Mathias Hafner, Rüdiger Rudolf, and Tiziana Cesetti, 'Sweet Taste Is Complex: Signaling Cascades and Circuits Involved in Sweet Sensation'. *Frontiers in Human Neuroscience* (2021).

National Institution of Nutrition, *Dietary Guidelines for Indians – A Manual*, second edition (Hyderabad: National Institution of Nutrition, 2011).

Navale A.M., and A.N. Paranjape, 'Glucose Transporters: Physiological and Pathological Roles'. *Biophysical Reviews* 8(1): 5–9 (2016).

Nkhata, S.G., E. Ayua, E.H. Kamau, and J.B. Shingiro, 'Fermentation and Germination Improve Nutritional Value of Cereals and Legumes through Activation of Endogenous Enzymes'. *Food Science & Nutrition* 6(8): 2446–2458 (2018).

Pereira, Nádia, Maria Fernanda Naufel, Eliane Beraldi Ribeiro, Sergio Tu!k, and Helena Hachul, 'Influence of Dietary Sources of Melatonin on Sleep Quality: A Review' *Journal of Food Science* 85(1): 5–13 (2019).

Pokharia, Anil K., Jeewan Singh Kharakwal, and Alka Srivastava, 'Archaeobotanical Evidence of Millets in the Indian Subcontinent with Some Observations on Their Role in the Indus Civilization'. *Journal of Archaeological Science Journal* 42(1): 442–455 (2014).

Rao, B.N., 'Bioactive Phytochemicals in Indian Foods and Their Potential in Health Promotion and Disease Prevention'. *Asia Pacific Journal of Clinical Nutrition* 12(1): 9–22 (2003).

Rastall, R.A., F.J. Moreno, and O. Hernandez-Hernandez, 'Editorial: Dietary Carbohydrate Digestibility and Metabolic Effects in Human Health'. *Frontiers in Nutrition* 6: 164 (2019).

Reyniers, Stijn, Nand Ooms, and Jan A. Delcour, 'Transformations and Functional Role of Starch During Potato Crisp Making: A Review'. *Journal of Food Science* 85(12): 4118–4129 (2020).

Roland, Wibke, S.U., Laurice Pouvreau, Julianne Curran, Fred van de Velde, and Peter M.T. de Kok, 'Flavor Aspects of Pulse Ingredients'. *Cereal Chemistry* 94(1): 58–65 (2017).

Sawant, A., R. Mankeshwar, S. Shah, R. Raghavan, G. Dhongde, H. Raje, S. D'Souza, A. Subramanium, P. Dhairyawan, S. Todur, and T.F. Ashavaid, 'Prevalence of Metabolic Syndrome in Urban India'. *Cholesterol* (2011).

Saxena, V.B., and B.G. Prasad, 'An Epidemiological Study of Yaws in Madhya Pradesh – Social and Cultural Aspect'. *Indian Journal of Medical Research* 51: 784–804 (1963).

Schurich, Anna, and Sian M. Henson, 'The Many Unknowns Concerning the Bioenergetics of Exhaustion and Senescence During Chronic Viral Infection'. *Frontiers in Immunology* (2014).

Shewry, P.R., 'Do Ancient Types of Wheat Have Health Benefits Compared with Modern Bread Wheat?' *Journal of Cereal Science* 79: 469–476 (2018).

Shi, L., K. Mu, S.D. Arntfield, and M.T. Nickerson, 'Changes in Levels of Enzyme Inhibitors During Soaking and Cooking for Pulses Available in Canada'. *Journal of Food Science and Technology* 54(4): 1014–1022 (2017).

Siddiqui, W.M., and R.S. Dhua, 'Eating Artificially Ripened Fruits is Harmful'. *Current Science* 99(12): 1664–1667 (2010).

Singh, S.S., and S.L. Rao, 'Lessons from Neurolathyrism: A Disease of the Past & the Future of Lathyrus sativus (*Khesari Dal*)'. *Indian Journal of Medical Research* 138(1): 32–7 (2013).

Sreeniwas, Kumar A., and N. Sinha, 'Cardiovascular Disease in India: A 360 Degree Overview'. *Medical Journal Armed Forces India*. 76(1): 1–3 (2020).

Stringer, Danielle M., Peter Zahradka, and Carla G. Taylor, 'Glucose Transporters: Cellular Links to Hyperglycemia in Insulin Resistance and Diabetes'. *Nutrition Reviews* 73(3): 140–154 (2015).

Truswell, A.S., 'Glycaemic Index of Foods'. *European Journal of Clinical Nutrition* 46 Suppl 2: S91–101 (1992).

Van Drunen, R., and K. Eckel-Mahan, 'Circadian Rhythms of the Hypothalamus: From Function to Physiology'. *Clocks Sleep* 3(1): 189–226 (2021).

Vasan, S.K., B. Antonisamy, M. Gowri, H.Y. Selliah, F.S. Geethanjali, F.S. Jebasingh, T.V. Paul, N. Thomas, F. Karpe, M. Johnson, and C. Osmond. 'Prevalence, Incidence and Predictors of Cardiovascular Risk Factors: Longitudinal Data from Rural and Urban South India and Comparison with Global Data'. *BMJ Open Diabetes Research & Care*. 8(1) (2020).

Vasishtha, H., and R.P. Srivastava, 'Effect of Soaking and Cooking on Dietary Fibre Components of Different Type of Chickpea Genotypes'. *Journal of Food Science and Technology* 50(3): 579–584 (2013).

Wali, J.A., A.J. Milner, A.W.S. Luk, T.J. Pulpitel, T. Dodgson, H.J.W. Facey, D. Wahl, M.A. Kebede, A.M. Senior, M.A. Sullivan, A.E. Brandon, B. Yau, G.P. Lockwood, Y.C. Koay, R. Ribeiro, S.M. Solon-Biet, K.S. Bell-Anderson, J.F. O'Sullivan, L. Macia, J.M. Forbes, G.J. Cooney, V.C. Cogger, A. Holmes, D. Raubenheimer, D.G. Le Couteur, and S.J. Simpson, 'Impact of Dietary Carbohydrate Type and Protein-Carbohydrate Interaction on Metabolic Health'. *Nature Metabolism* 3(6): 810–828 (2021).

Wong, J.M., and D.J. Jenkins, 'Carbohydrate Digestibility and Metabolic Effects'. *The Journal of Nutrition* 137(11 Suppl): 2539S-2546S (2007).

Zucchi, R., G. Chiellini, T.S. Scanlan, and D.K. Grandy, 'Trace Amine-Associated Receptors and Their Ligands'. *British Journal of Pharmacology* 149(8): 967–978 (2006).

## Part Four

Banerjee, S.K., and S.K. Maulik, 'Effect of Garlic on Cardiovascular Disorders: A Review'. *Nutrition Journal* 1: 4 (2002).

'Coffee Consumption in India 2017–2021' Published by Statista Research Department, 4 April 2022, available at: https://www.statista.com/statistics/1227458/coffee-consumption-india/.

Ganeshan, K., J. Nikkanen, K. Man, Y.A. Leong, Y. Sogawa, J.A. Maschek, T. Van Ry, D.N. Chagwedera, J.E. Cox, and A.

Chawla, 'Energetic Trade-Offs and Hypometabolic States Promote Disease Tolerance'. *Cell* 177(2): 399–413 (2019).

Patel, S.S., S. Beer, D.L. Kearney, G. Phillips, and B.A. Carter, 'Green Tea Extract: A Potential Cause of Acute Liver Failure'. *World Journal of Gastroenterology* 19(31): 5174–7 (2013). doi: 10.3748/wjg.v19.i31.5174. PMID: 23964154; PMCID: PMC3746392.

Pereira, N., M.F. Naufel, E.B. Ribeiro, S. Tufik, and H. Hachul, 'Influence of Dietary Sources of Melatonin on Sleep Quality: A Review'. *Journal of Food Science.* 85(1): 5–13 (2020).

Preau, S., D. Vodovar, B. Jung, S. Lancel, L. Zafrani, A. Flatres, M. Oualha, G. Voiriot, Y. Jouan, J. Joffre, F. Huel, N. De Prost, S. Silva, E. Azabou, and P. Radermacher, 'Energetic Dysfunction in Sepsis: A Narrative Review'. *Annals of Intensive Care* 11(1): 104 (2021).

## Part Five

Calder, P.C., 'Nutrition and Immunity: Lessons for COVID-19'. *European Journal of Clinical Nutrition* 75: 1309–1318 (2021).

Frezza, Christian, and Claudio Mauro, 'Editorial: The Metabolic Challenges of Immune Cells in Health and Disease'. *Frontiers in Immunology* 6: 293 (2015).

Jagannath, A., N. Varga, R. Dallmann, G. Rando, P. Gosselin, F. Ebrahimjee, L. Taylor, D. Mosneagu, J. Stefaniak, S. Walsh, T. Palumaa, S. Di Pretoro, H. Sanghani, Z. Wakaf, G.C. Churchill, A. Galione, S.N. Peirson, D. Boison, S.A. Brown, R.G. Foster, S.R. Vasudevan, 'Adenosine Integrates Light and Sleep Signalling for the Regulation of Circadian Timing in Mice'. *Nature Communications* 12(1): 2113 (2021).

Kolb, H., M. Stumvoll, W. Kramer, K. Kempf, and S. Martin,

'Insulin Translates Unfavourable Lifestyle into Obesity'. *BMC Medicine* 16: 232 (2018).

Pinnell, Jeremy, Simon Turner, and Simon Howell, 'Cardiac Muscle Physiology'. *Continuing Education in Anaesthesia Critical Care & Pain* 7(3): 85–88 (2007).

X.W. Chen, E.S. Serag, K.B. Sneed, J. Liang, H. Chew, S.Y. Pan, and S.F. Zhou, 'Clinical Herbal Interactions with Conventional Drugs: From Molecules to Maladies'. *Current Medicinal Chemistry* 18(31): 4836–4850 (2011).

## Coda

Menting, J.G., J. Whittaker, M.B. Margetts, L.J. Whittaker, G.K. Kong, B.J. Smith, C.J. Watson, L. Záková, E. Kletvíková, J. Jiráček, S.J. Chan, D.F. Steiner, G.G. Dodson, A.M. Brzozowski, M.A. Weiss, C.W. Ward, and M.C. Lawrence, 'How Insulin Engages Its Primary Binding Site on the Insulin Receptor'. *Nature* 493(7431): 241–245 (2013).

Teijaro, J.R., and D.L. Farber, 'COVID-19 Vaccines: Modes of Immune Activation and Future Challenges'. *Nature Reviews Immunology*. 21(4): 195–197 (2021).

Vignali, D., L. Collison, and C. Workman, 'How Regulatory T Cells Work'. *Nature Reviews Immunology* 8: 523–532 (2008).